CHATSWORTH: A LANDSCAPE HISTORY

Chatsworth

A Landscape History

John Barnatt and Tom Williamson

WIND*gather*
PRESS

Chatsworth: A Landscape History

Copyright © The Peak District National Park Authority 2005

The Peak District National Park Authority has asserted its right under the Copyright, Designs and Patents Act 1988 to be identified as the copyright holder of this work.

The writing of this work has been in part funded by the Commissioned Archaeology Programme of English Heritage and is published under licence.

The Publishers also acknowledge the support of the Trustees of the Chatsworth Settlement in making publication possible.

Published by: Windgather Press Ltd, 29 Bishop Road, Bollington, Macclesfield, Cheshire SK10 5NX

Distributed by: Central Books Ltd, 99 Wallis Road, London E9 5LN

British Library Cataloguing-in-Publication Data
A catalogue record for this book is available from the British Library

ISBN 1-905119-01-1

Designed, typeset and originated by Carnegie Publishing Ltd, Chatsworth Road, Lancaster
Printed and bound by Cambridge University Press

Contents

List of Figures

Acknowledgements

....

This book would not have been possible without the enthusiastic support of the late 11th Duke of Devonshire; the Dowager Duchess of Devonshire; and the Trustees of the Chatsworth Settlement. They commissioned the surveys and research on which this book is based, and allowed unlimited access to estate land and archives. We also thank the Duke of Devonshire for permission to quote from the Devonshire Archives. The staff of the estate likewise provided a vast amount of help, support and information: our particular thanks go to Roger Wardle, Ian Else, Peter Day, Charles Noble, Tom Askey, Stuart Band, Andrew Peppitt, Simon Seligman, John Oliver, Diane Naylor and Sara Sweetland.

The archaeological survey work was carried out by John Barnatt in collaboration with Nicola Bannister, who was also responsible for surveying the parkland boundaries and woodlands. David Bannister recorded the standing buildings and John Roberts assisted with surveying of parts of the western parkland and New Piece Plantation. The documentary research was carried out by Tom Williamson, but the assessment of the current condition and significance of the designed landscape was the work of Elise Perciful and Steven Thomas, of Historic Landscape Management, who also provided many stimulating suggestions about the history of the landscape. The various discussions of the development of the parkland planting are based on a detailed tree survey carried out by James Carr, subsequently amended and recalibrated by Tom Williamson. Many other people have contributed ideas and information, including Mark Edmonds, John Popham, Jim Rieuwerts and Paul Smith.

The photographs and illustrations of maps, paintings and historic material are from the Chatsworth Photo Library at the Devonshire Collection, Chatsworth, and are reproduced by permission of the Chatsworth Settlement Trustees. Exceptions are Illustrations 9, 15, 20, 35, 37, 46, 50, 53, 54, 61, 62, 65, 72, 73, 76, 79, 80, 82, 83, 87, 91 and 94, which were taken by John Barnatt; 5, 6, 11, 21 and 71, from the Peak District National Park Authority photographic collection; and 30, 95, 96 and Front Cover, which were taken by Fran Halsall. The line drawings are by John Barnatt.

This publication is partly funded by English Heritage; they, and the Countryside Commission, also funded the initial surveys via The Trustees of the Chatsworth Settlement. Pete Wilson and Jonathan Last supervised the archaeological assessment for English Heritage, while Paul Walshe initiated the designed landscape survey for The Countryside Commission. Ken Smith of the Peak District National Park Authority was instrumental both in setting up the archaeological survey, and in the publication of this book. The National Park Authority kindly allowed John Barnatt work-time to complete the latter.

Last but not least, we would like to thank Richard Purslow, for publishing the book, and for his friendship and support throughout; and our families, for indulging our long obsession with the Chatsworth landscape.

CHAPTER ONE

Studying Chatsworth

A house and its landscape

Chatsworth is one of the most visited country houses in England: each year many thousands of visitors pay to enter the house and its grounds, while countless others enjoy the experience of walking through the adjacent park. In part Chatsworth's popularity is a consequence of its location, inside the Peak District National Park and within a few hours' drive of the great conurbations that surround it. But it is also a reflection of the sheer magnificence and beauty of its landscape, the consequence in large measure of successive transformations made by the Cavendish family, the estate's owners, over several centuries. The house – a relatively small late seventeenth- and early eighteenth-century building, as stately homes go, but with a great northern extension added in the nineteenth century – sits comfortably on the eastern side of its great park, overlooking the river Derwent to the west and backed by a steeply rising escarpment, clothed in woodland. It is approached by a drive which crosses the river on an elegant bridge, designed – like a number of other features in the park – by the noted architect James Paine: the view of the house from the bridge is unforgettable, and endlessly reproduced (Figure 1). The parkland extends not only to north and south of the house, but also to the west, the ground rising beyond the river to a ridge richly planted with woods and plantations. A vast area of gardens and pleasure grounds – some 55 acres (22 ha) in all – extends to the east and south of the house. These are largely of nineteenth-century date but include a number of much earlier features, most notably the great Cascade, completed in the early eighteenth century. This area includes elaborate rockworks, an extensive Arboretum, ornamental glasshouses, and the site of the Great Conservatory, created in the 1830s but demolished in the 1920s. Nineteenth-century, too, is the village of Edensor (pronounced 'Ensor'), which stands beside the north-western entrance of the park – a collection of estate buildings in a bizarre mixture of architectural styles. Great artists have worked at Chatsworth, the leading landscape and garden designers of their day: London and Wise, William Kent, Lancelot 'Capability' Brown, Joseph Paxton; all have left their mark. With its woods and vistas, ornamental buildings, gardens and waterworks, Chatsworth is indeed a magnificent place.

And unlike many great country houses Chatsworth is still a private residence, as well as a public spectacle. It remains, as it has since the sixteenth

century, the home of the Cavendish family – first the Earls and, since 1694, the Dukes of Devonshire. Both the Dowager Duchess and the late Duke, along with those responsible for running the estate, have always taken a keen interest in the historical importance of the place. As part of this interest, we were asked in the 1990s to prepare a comprehensive programme of archaeological and historical research into the park and gardens at Chatsworth.[1] This short volume presents the results of that research.

It is by no means the first book to be written about the history of Chatsworth. In 1949 Francis Thompson, then Chatsworth's librarian, produced a comprehensive account of the house and its grounds.[2] This he conceived as a supplement to the *Handbook of Chatsworth and Hardwick* which was written in 1844 and published in 1845 by the 6th Duke of Devonshire himself, to describe the numerous improvements which had been made under his direction.[3] Changes in the landscape have been dealt with, in passing, in the many books written about the Cavendish family, and about individual Earls and Dukes of Devonshire; and a number of articles, dealing with particular aspects of the historic landscape, have appeared in learned journals. Many of these we will refer to in the course of our enquiry. The Dowager Duchess herself has written extensive accounts of the house and its grounds, paying particular attention to the various changes which have occurred within living memory.[4] Why, the reader might ask, produce yet another book?

The main reason is that the recent research programme has, in innumerable ways, thrown new light on the history of this fascinating landscape, casting some doubt on previous suggestions and filling in important gaps in the story. This is partly because we have been able to use documentary material which was not available to some earlier writers, but also because we have used rather different kinds of evidence, and in particular that provided by the landscape itself: for our research involved a systematic survey of all archaeological earthworks and other structures within the park, and an examination of its trees. We are not garden historians, art historians, or architectural historians; nor are we experts in the history of horticulture. We are landscape archaeologists and landscape historians, and it is from these perspectives that we hope to shed new light on the history of this very special place.

The nature of designed landscapes

Great residences and extensive designed landscapes already existed in medieval times but it was only in the post-medieval period – that is, from the sixteenth century – that they began to make a major impact upon the rural environment we see today. They did not stand alone, as isolated incidents, but instead formed the core of much more extensive properties which historians usually describe as 'landed estates'. Great landowners like the Cavendishes often held far-flung lands, acquired through grant, purchase or the vicissitudes of marriage and inheritance. But they usually tried to build up their properties in such a way that their principal residence was surrounded by a large and continuous tract of land under their ownership; in this, Chatsworth is no exception. We may, for convenience, envisage great estates as a series of concentric circles. At the centre lay the mansion, grand and fashionable, a statement of the owner's wealth, taste and success. Around it lay gardens and a park, the latter of increasing importance as a setting for the house in the course of the eighteenth century (Figure 2). Beyond lay the estate land, mainly comprising tenanted farms, the rents from which were a major source of the owner's income, although in the case of Chatsworth the largest income came from industrial leases, especially of metalliferous and coal mines. As time passed, the influence of estate policies on the appearance of this wider estate land tended to increase, as leases replaced older forms of customary tenure, as enclosure removed areas of open common and as systematic purchase ensured the disappearance of small, intervening or intermixed properties. Throughout England much marginal land was reclaimed, reorganised, and 'improved' in the course of the eighteenth and nineteenth centuries through estate invest-ment. Woods and plantations were widely planted across the countryside, both for ornament and for profit – reversing the steady *loss* of tree cover which had continued across England in general, and the Peak District in particular, for centuries. And in the course of the nineteenth century, many farms and cottages were rebuilt, in whole or part, in ways which tended to demonstrate their status as the property of particular owners and estates.

In this book we will concentrate, not so much on the outer penumbra of estate land, but rather with the central 'core' of mansion, park and gardens at Chatsworth; our aim will be to unravel the complex ways in which this designed landscape has changed over the centuries. But we will not be concerned only with the landscapes of art and ornament. The making of a park or garden served to preserve, as well as to destroy, earlier landscapes. Previous features or structures – both from earlier phases of designed land-scape, or from the working countryside – were often given new uses and meanings, or simply survived, fossilised, as unnoticed relics of an earlier age. In spite of the vast amounts of money and effort which, as we shall see, were spent on the creation of Chatsworth Park in the eighteenth and nineteenth centuries, great tracts of the earlier countryside – in the form of earthworks and trees – were preserved in relict form within it. Features which have often been largely obliterated from similar locations by the successive 'improve-ments' carried out by landed estates, and by more general agricultural intensification in the course of the nineteenth and twentieth centuries, have thus been preserved by the very act of emparking. Studying Chatsworth Park, in other words, can tell us things about the history of the 'vernacular' countryside of the Peak District which we cannot learn as easily from the landscape existing *outside* the park.

Sources: *documents, maps and illustrations*

It will be useful at this stage to explain some of the sources which we can use to study the history and archaeology of the Chatsworth landscape – to say something about how we know what we know. Maps and illustrations are the first and perhaps most important form of evidence and we are fortunate indeed that Chatsworth was frequently drawn or painted in the course of the seventeenth, eighteenth and nineteenth centuries. Yet invaluable though they are, all illustrations need to be treated with caution. A painting is not like a photograph: artists will include, or exclude, anything which may make or detract from a pleasing composition, and where the work was commissioned by the Duke the temptation to flatter must have been immense. At the very least, no artist would make the house and grounds appear smaller, less fashionable, or less well maintained than they really were. In addition to all this, some drawings were made, not as representations of what was actually there, but as proposals for additions and improvements. The existence of such illustrations should not, of course, lead us to assume that the suggested alterations were necessarily carried out.

Maps are an even more important source of evidence and a large number were made of the estate, which have been carefully preserved in its archives. But maps should, if anything, be treated with even more caution than illustrations. We expect paintings and drawings to flatter, invent, and distort: maps, in contrast, have a seductively objective appearance, but can pose similar problems of interpretation. Some, moreover, contain demonstrable errors. George Barker's survey of 1773 for example – an otherwise invaluable source for the appearance of the park in the later eighteenth century – distorts the position and alignment of features to the north-east of the house, such as the First Duke's Greenhouse.[5] Similarly, while plans of the park made by the surveyor E. Campbell in 1857–58 show much that was certainly there, they also include some features that were proposed but never executed.[6] Careful checking and cross-checking of one map against another, and of maps against other sources of evidence, is always necessary if we are to gain a reliable picture of landscape development.

Maps and illustrations provide an important starting point but the details, and the detailed chronology, of a landscape's development are supplied by texts: letters; written descriptions; and estate accounts. Here again we are fortunate. The archives at Chatsworth House contain a vast quantity of documents, including very detailed estate accounts recording payments made for work carried out on the house and its grounds, and for items purchased for them. The organisation and layout of these accounts changed over time but their main purpose remained the same, from the sixteenth to the nineteenth century: to prevent the estate being defrauded by its administrators and to allow the Cavendishes to assess the state of their finances. These documents provide very basic, yet invaluable, information. The main difficulty lies in the fact that they are more detailed and complete for some periods than for others.

For example, in the middle decades of the eighteenth century, when the new park at Chatsworth was being created, the work carried out directly by the estate labourers – levelling ground, draining, planting, etc. – is described in some detail. But the bulk of the changes were carried out by a contractor, one Michael Millican, who simply received large sums of money: if he himself kept a record of how this was spent, it has not survived. There are other problems and challenges. Some arise from the nature of the terms used in accounts and letters for particular areas or features, which evidently changed over time; others from the vague or ambiguous nature of references to the activities of workmen or contractors. Often an event or structure is noted, but because of its familiarity to the writer, important details about its location and character are taken as read; we are left in the dark. Nevertheless, in spite of such problems, Chatsworth remains one of the best-documented designed landscapes in England, and letters and accounts provide a major source of information for our inquiry.

More colourful are the descriptions and accounts made by those who visited Chatsworth from the seventeenth century onwards. The house and its grounds feature in poems like those of Charles Cotton and Thomas Hobbes; in the descriptions of travellers like Celia Fiennes and Daniel Defoe; in guide books; and, in the nineteenth century, in innumerable articles written in the gardening press. Taken as a whole, these sources make Chatsworth one of the most written-about places in England and provide the icing, as it were, on the historical cake. They allow us a glimpse of how the landscape was actually experienced by contemporaries.

Archaeology

Although the history of the landscape is recorded in some detail in maps, illustrations and written texts, these sources do not tell us everything we want to know. Perhaps the most important evidence is contained within the landscape itself: the structures, trees and earthworks still surviving within the park and gardens at Chatsworth. Although much use is made in this volume of documentary sources, it is above all an exercise in *landscape archaeology*: it tries to explain the present appearance of the physical environment of Chatsworth and everything it contains, both natural and made, interpreting how people have inhabited this landscape and changed it through time. This approach may be less familiar to many readers than the use of written texts, maps and illustrations, and as it forms such an important part of this study it needs to be discussed in a little more detail.

Archaeology is the study of past people and landscapes using the physical remains that exist today. Although it is popularly thought that archaeologists are primarily concerned with discarded or lost artefacts, this is in fact only one small part of the evidence they employ. Similarly, people wrongly assume that excavation is the main activity of archaeologists; again the discipline does far more that this, often interpreting the broader landscape by observing and recording all that lies within it, most of which will never be excavated. The

whole of today's landscape contains a wealth of information; it can be likened
to a palimpsest in which layers of features reflect the ways in which people
have shaped the land over many millennia: these include villages and farmsteads, fields and their boundaries, routeways and industrial features; and in
places like Chatsworth, designed elements such as estate buildings, drives and
parkland trees. Archaeological features do not have to be abandoned and
ruined to be studied by archaeologists; when still in use they often incorporate
a greater wealth of surviving evidence that tells us much about their past
history. This said, the archaeologist is frequently faced with more difficult and
ambiguous challenges. These lie particularly in the study of earthworks, the

7

remains of features long since abandoned and often undocumented. These may date from prehistory to the present, and are often very insignificant landscape features, easily overlooked and problematic to interpret. Their exact form and position within the landscape, as well as damage by later activities or the superimposition of later features, can all give clues as to possible date and function. However, this type of interpretation is fraught with dangers if not put into a wider research context. For example, prehistoric settlement patterns cannot be fully comprehended from what survives above the ground; an understanding is necessary of other sites which have been destroyed, and the reasons for their destruction. Necessary, too, is an assessment as to why features have survived; perhaps, for example, they were built in stone or earth rather than solely in perishable materials such as timber. Similarly, at a local scale, missing elements of features need to be considered; for example, some low field boundary banks make little sense in a farming context until it is realised that they were once surmounted by hedges.

The archaeological survey of Chatsworth Park was carried out by one of the authors (JB) in 1996–97, as the first part of a larger project to record the whole of the estate around Chatsworth;[7] it included the detailed sketch plotting, after consultation of historic maps and aerial photographs, of all earthworks and other structures (see Figures 89–90, 92–93, 97–99). This was complemented by work undertaken by others on the buildings, field boundaries and woodlands,[8] and on the designed landscape.[9]

Archaeological recording taken in isolation tells only part of the story of the historic landscape. It is often only when landscape archaeology is combined with historical documentation that flesh can be put on the bones. Often the date of features can be tied down to an exact month or year and their relationships with other structures around them can therefore be unravelled. Similarly, names can be put to people and often their place in society can be investigated. In addition, the archaeological evidence acts as a cross-check to the historical: documents are rarely objective or inclusive but have inherent biases, governed by their author's pre-conceptions and place in society, and archaeology may give complementary or contradictory evidence which will assist in the overall analysis. Our knowledge and understanding of the past are increased exponentially when archaeological and historical approaches are combined, and it is hoped that this book provides a good example of the value of this multi-disciplinary approach.

Trees

Trees form the most important element of any large-scale designed landscape and Chatsworth Park contains specimens of widely varying ages, types and origins. In all, some 53 different varieties or species have been identified in the park, as individuals or within clumps, and still more can be found within the pleasure grounds. The most common tree by far is oak, of which there are over 1,900. Lime is the second most frequently-occurring tree, with around 350 examples, closely followed by beech, with 273. Alder, sycamore, horse chestnut, hawthorn, ash, walnut and crab apple are also relatively common. With the exception of alders, most of which were probably self-sown and grow on the damp ground beside the Derwent, the majority of these trees were deliberately planted, or at least intentionally preserved and encouraged. Some date back to the time before the present park was laid out, and were either features in the working countryside which it replaced, or else grew in the ancient deer park which, as we shall see, occupied the area to the north, south and east of the house. Others were planted at various times in the eighteenth and nineteenth centuries, as part of the successive designs which were laid out around the mansion (Figure 3).

With the exception of areas on the slopes north and south of the house, where there are many ancient deer park oaks, the oldest surviving trees in the park comprise old hedgerow trees which were retained when the hedges were removed in order to provide an instant sylvan scene in the new park. They were appropriated and reinterpreted, moving from functional features of the working countryside to objects valued primarily for their appearance. The majority are oaks, although examples of ash and sycamore also occur. Some were originally managed as *pollards* – cut on a recurrent cycle of 10–15 years at a height of about 2–3 m, in order to provide a regular crop of straight poles suitable for firewood, fencing, tools and a host of domestic uses. Some may also have been cut in late summer to provide winter fodder for livestock. They are usually easily recognised by their growth pattern: multiple stems branch out from a bulbous, damaged layer at the point where they were cut. In many cases, it is possible to see faint traces of the denuded hedge bank, the last vestiges of the hedge in which the tree once grew, and sometimes the trunk has an asymmetrical appearance when viewed from a slight distance, rising straighter from the ground on one side where it originally sent roots down into a ditch.

Most of the trees which were planted around Chatsworth as part of the successive phases of designed landscape date to the period after c. 1750. Few seem to relate to the formal avenues and other planting shown on various seventeenth and early eighteenth-century maps and illustrations. Deciduous trees, especially oak, lime, beech, horse chestnut and sycamore, predominate. The main difficulty in understanding the various phases of the designed landscape comes from the absence of a reliable method of dating trees – short of felling them and counting the rings! Two methods of dating by girth measurements are widely employed in landscape archaeology; one was developed by Alan Mitchell, and another by Ian Whyte.[10] The former is the simplest: it states that, in very rough terms, the age of a free-standing parkland tree – especially of an indigenous species like oak, ash, or beech – is equivalent to the number of inches of girth measured at waist height. In other words, a tree with a circumference of four metres ought to be around 160 years old. Whyte's method is more complex but more believable. It recognises that trees do not put on growth at a uniform rate throughout their life, that different species age in different ways, and that soil, aspect and other local environmental circumstances need to be taken into account. The method is slower and harder

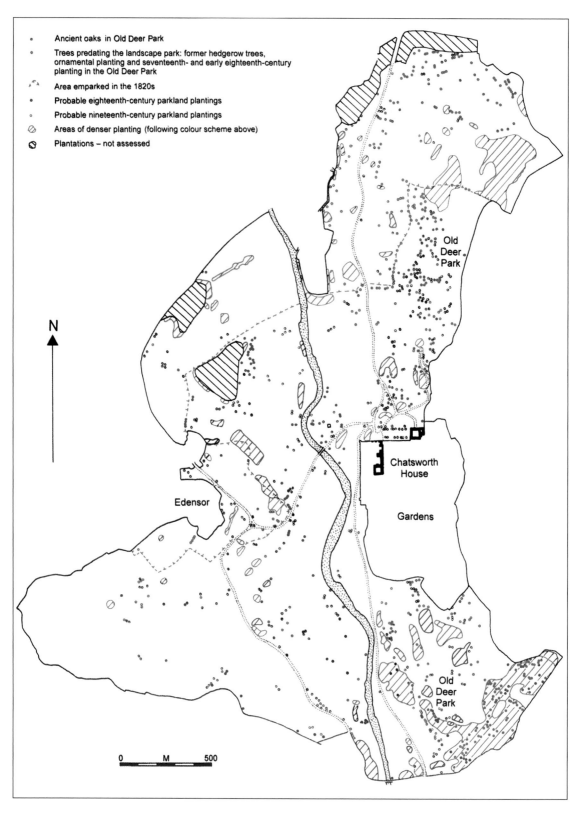

- Ancient oaks in Old Deer Park
- Trees predating the landscape park: former hedgerow trees, ornamental planting and seventeenth- and early eighteenth-century planting in the Old Deer Park
- Area emparked in the 1820s
- Probable eighteenth-century parkland plantings
- Probable nineteenth-century parkland plantings
- Areas of denser planting (following colour scheme above)
- Plantations – not assessed

N

Old Deer Park

Chatsworth House

Gardens

Edensor

Old Deer Park

0   M   500

to use than Mitchell's, and experience shows that it is not necessarily very much more accurate, but it does serve to emphasise that some trees will put on girth faster than others.

In Chatsworth Park, neither method seems to work very well. In particular, it is evident that some species of tree, especially the older oaks, put on girth rather more slowly than either method would suggest, and are considerably older than they appear. Specimens that were unquestionably in existence in the middle decades of the eighteenth century – for they are clearly associated with field boundaries removed when the park was created in the 1750s and 60s – look as much as a century younger. Conversely, many of the more ornamental parkland trees established in the later eighteenth and nineteenth centuries, especially lime and horse chestnut, appear to put on girth at a slightly *faster* rate than expected, and thus look *older* than they are. Quite why Chatsworth's trees, and especially its old oaks, should deviate from normal development in this way is not entirely clear. In part, the reasons may be environmental. In the sixteenth to late eighteenth centuries the Derwent valley had a number of water-powered lead smelters, including examples relatively near Chatsworth – around Rowsley to the south, and a little further away at Calver, and east of Baslow, to the north.[11] Levels of air pollution were presumably high, and this may have retarded the growth of trees established before the nineteenth century – that is, for the most part, the trees inherited from the pre-park land-scape. While the area had cupola furnaces for lead smelting from the mid eighteenth century onwards, the only one anywhere near Chatsworth was at Barbrook, east of Baslow, sited in the same tributary valley as one of the earlier smelters, but both in a situation where predominant westerly winds would take much of the airborne pollution eastwards rather than into the Derwent valley. Whatever the explanation, at Chatsworth, more than in many parks, estimating the age of trees from girth measurements is more an art than a science, and we can usually suggest only approximate dates for particular trees, extrapolating from the relatively few examples which can, with some confidence, be dated from cartographic or documentary sources, or by archaeological associations.

The contexts of landscape design

Mansions like Chatsworth, and the gardens and parks which surrounded them, were always in a state of change. They had to be, in order to express the continuing success, importance and sophistication of their owners. But, as we shall see, successive styles of design were not simply expressions of abstract aesthetics, a series of pretty pictures painted across the landscape using trees, plants, earth and stone. Consciously or unconsciously, they carried a range of philosophical and social meanings. Designed landscapes could be used to demonstrate political allegiances and beliefs, and reflected attitudes to society, science and nature. Some of these meanings were shared by all educated people. But the particular development of the Chatsworth landscape is

FIGURE 3.
Chatsworth Park: the pattern of tree planting. The trees are of varying dates and origins; some oaks are perhaps 600 years old, seeded well before the present landscape park was created. The diagram simplifies this rich complexity by omitting all trees planted since c. 1900. Dates are estimates only: in reality, at Chatsworth it is difficult to assess with any accuracy the age of a tree from its present size and appearance.

intimately tied to the individual attitudes and activities, political and otherwise, of its owners, and to those of the artists whose work they patronised.

Any great landscape is like a tapestry: particular individuals come and go, weave their distinctive threads and move on. Sometimes their time at Chatsworth might be fleeting, even if their impact on the landscape was profound: Capability Brown probably spent only a few days here. Sometimes that association was longer and more intimate, as with Joseph Paxton in the nineteenth century. Some of Chatsworth's creators, like these individuals, were and to some extent still are household names. But many were not: contractors and nurserymen whose names might be known only to local historians or specialists in garden history, or labourers who have not even left us their names. But whoever they were, the men and women who worked at Chatsworth generally had lives and careers which had stretched before and continued after they contributed their thread to the tapestry of the landscape. To understand the character of their contribution we will sometimes need to follow these threads, back and forward, in time and space, tracing the wider work of particular individuals and charting the influences on their style.

Their paymasters and patrons, too, were involved to very varying extents in the formation of the landscape, and had lives and careers which extended beyond Chatsworth itself. The Cavendish family have always had properties elsewhere in England, including London, and most of the Earls and Dukes of Devonshire were important political figures and therefore obliged to reside for much of the year in the capital – for politics, before the late nineteenth century, was the *raison d'être* of the landed rich, and profits from office could be a major source of their wealth. Politics might, in certain periods, be a spur to investment in the landscape, for great houses and their landscapes, and the wealth and taste they expressed, were an important tool in the political game. But, together with other attractions and interests, political involvement also led to prolonged absences, to a lack of interest in Chatsworth, and relative inactivity in the landscape. Some owners, such as the 5th Duke, did very little to Chatsworth, preferring to reside in London. Others, such as the 6th Duke, made the embellishment of the house and gardens the centre of their life.

Yet the character of the Chatsworth landscape does not arise simply from the particular mixture of individuals and personalities who have been involved with it over the centuries, or from the styles which were popular when its owners made the greatest changes. It is, above all, a consequence of the location of the house and its grounds: what eighteenth-century writers called the 'genius of the place'. The nature of the soils and topography were major determinants of the character of successive designs; so, too, was the particular form of the working countryside which the designed landscape sat within and in part replaced. Before we investigate the history of the Cavendishes, their mansion and its surroundings, we must first therefore look briefly at the natural and human landscape of the Peak District.

FIGURE 4.
The Peak District, showing principal rivers, landscape divisions and places. The Derwent valley is cut into soft shales between the limestone of the White Peak to the west, and the gritstone uplands of the East Moors to the east. Like similar valleys, it has long been a major focus of settlement. In contrast, much of the gritstone uplands comprise bleak moorland with only occasional farms. The large industrial conurbations of Manchester and Sheffield lie outside the Peak, to east and west, on the coal-rich peripheries of the region.

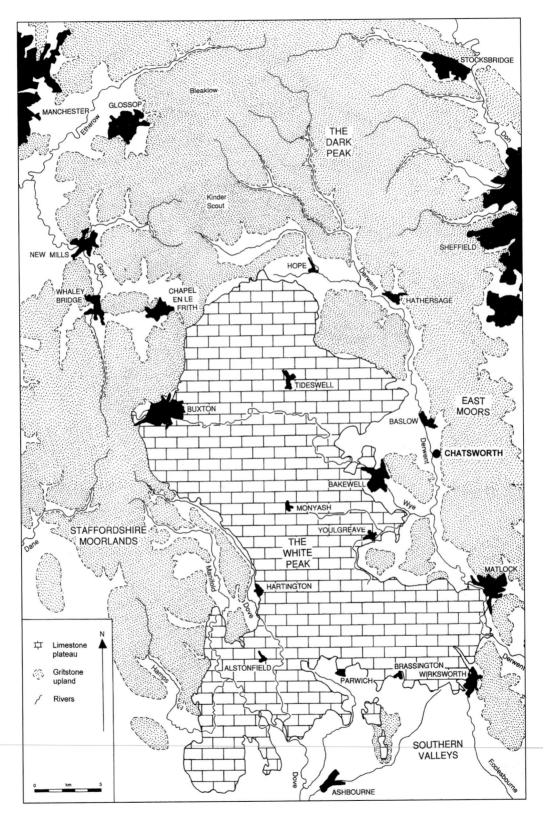

Chatsworth in its natural setting

Chatsworth House sits within the Derwent valley, the principal natural route into the Peak District uplands from the south. To the east the land rises steeply to the East Moors, mostly lying at over 250 m above sea level. These uplands are composed of coarse sandstones of Carboniferous age, known as Millstone Grit, which are particularly resistant to natural erosion and have provided a good source of stone for millstones, troughs, gateposts and buildings, while the interleaved softer shale beds contain thin beds of coal. They form an elevated tract of ground some 25 km long but only 4–5 km wide, with peaty podsolised soils which have been largely moorland since prehistoric times. There are only occasional scattered farmsteads, each in an island of walled fields, the stone here appearing dark because of centuries of atmospheric pollution. For centuries, most people merely passed through this inhospitable landscape, while a few tended sheep, quarried stone and delved for coal. Further north the bleak gritstone uplands around Kinderscout and Bleaklow comprise a vast expanse of moorland – traditionally of little use except for rough grazing and as source of peat for fuel. Here the only farmsteads are to be found in the remote, steep-sided valleys (Figure 4).

To the west of the Derwent valley there are more dissected gritstone and sandstone hills, some lying at a lower altitude than the East Moors. These are often divided into fields with shallow sandy soils of indifferent fertility, and have been farmed in various ways for several millennia. Still further to the west lies the Peak's central Carboniferous Limestone plateau, a large rolling expanse again mostly at over 250 m O.D., where there are many upland villages surrounded by fields bounded by mile upon mile of walls of near-white limestone, with scattered farms in the higher areas, particularly to the west. While the soils here are often thin, they are relatively fertile, which has made this a particularly favoured area for settlement since prehistory despite its altitude. Until a hundred years ago a dual economy was the norm in this area, with lead mining complementing income from farming.

The Derwent valley, and its tributary Wye valley to the west, both cut into thick beds of shales lying between the limestone and gritstone, and have always provided a sheltered environment, although in places, as at Chatsworth, farming has been inhibited by the narrowness of the valley bottom and the steep, stony, infertile character of the slopes above. Here there are often only scattered farms, some many centuries old: where the valleys are wider, in contrast, sizeable villages have grown up.

Chatsworth itself occupies a sheltered site to the east of the river. It lies snuggled at the base of a steep wooded slope which rises over 100 m to a scarp, with a broad upland shelf above; beyond this is a second scarp, at the top of which are the higher moorlands. Both scarps run virtually uninterrupted for over 2 km to north and south of Chatsworth, to where steep and narrow side valleys, at Baslow and Beeley, carry streams draining off the eastern moorlands. The main scarp is steep and in parts boulder-strewn. It has never been suitable for arable farming; woodland and grazing have probably dominated the scene here for millennia. Many similar slopes elsewhere along the Derwent valley lost their trees in the late medieval or early post-medieval period, in part as a consequence of the insatiable demands of the lead mines for timber; or else the woodland was brought into more intensive management, as coppice, in order to provide charcoal and kiln-dried wood for lead smelting. Stand Wood above Chatsworth, in contrast, survived in its *primitive* state because it lay within a deer park. The valley bottom below the slope, the area now occupied by house, gardens and landscape park, is relatively narrow, especially in contrast to the situation further north around Baslow, or on the western, Edensor side of the Derwent, where more extensive tracts of relatively level ground naturally provided a much greater area of productive farmland.

The wider context: the Peak District's landscape history

The house, gardens and park at Chatsworth stand out sharply from the surrounding landscape of hedged and drystone-walled fields and bleak upland moors. There are few parkland landscapes in the Peak District, especially in comparison to many lowland counties in Britain. The main exceptions are here in the Derwent and adjacent Wye valleys. There were medieval deer parks at Haddon Hall, Harthill and Snitterton, which have now disappeared, and nineteenth-century landscape parks – though none with the grandeur of Chatsworth – survive around Haddon, Hassop and Thornbridge Halls. For the most part, however, the landscape of the area around Chatsworth has been shaped by practical economic activities – by farming and by industry.

The Peak District's archaeology is exceptional, for as an upland region it has not suffered the ravages of modern arable farming experienced by England's lowlands, while at the same time it has much land lying at a sufficiently low altitude for it to have been extensively used by people in the past.[12] As much of the region has been traditionally used for pasture since medieval times, and as the abundant supplies of stone ensured that many structures were built of durable materials, there are many thousands of visible archaeological features. But the extent of archaeological survival must not be over-emphasised. While pastoral farming has dominated the region for over 700 years, until the twentieth century much land was ploughed at least occasionally, either to re-seed pastures or to grow crops for local use. Thus many earlier archaeological features have been removed or ploughed out, especially where they were only slight in the first place. For this reason, places like Chatsworth Park – large parts of which have remained unploughed for the last 250 years – are extremely important as an archaeological resource.

The gritstone East Moors, including the Chatsworth Estate moorlands above the house to the east, are of exceptional importance for their prehistoric remains – large swathes of land used only for rough grazing over the past two millennia are cluttered with now-abandoned farmsteads and fields, which were used from about 2000 BC to approximately the beginning of the Roman period. Many prehistoric clearance cairns and field boundary earthworks survive here, together with associated stone circles and round barrows, making for an extensive visible 'prehistoric landscape' only matched elsewhere in Britain in places like Dartmoor, the Cheviots and Perthshire. Elsewhere in the Peak District, in enclosed areas below the moorlands, only the more substantial or durable remains – such as scattered large prehistoric monuments and Romano-British settlements on rocky ground at the fringes of better agricultural land – tend to survive from pre-medieval times. Much of today's historic landscape on the limestone plateau and in the shale valleys has medieval origins, displayed in the distribution and layout of many villages, farms, fields, roads and old industrial sites, although subsequent radical changes over the last 500 years have added further layers to the complex palimpsest we have inherited.

The Peak District has been extensively inhabited by people for thousands of years.[13] In the earliest times, after the last Ice Age, gatherer-hunters roamed widely across the land, including the high northern gritstone uplands that have been little used in subsequent periods. It was they who began the deforestation of this area, which was undoubtedly once wooded, as ancient tree stumps can be commonly be found under the thick peat. The creation of clearings by burning encouraged animals such as deer to graze there, making them easier to hunt; but at this altitude the high rainfall ensured that the soils quickly deteriorated and the trees failed to regenerate. Later, across the lower parts of the gritstone moors, low levels of grazing by domesticated livestock prevented the re-establishment of woodland once it had been removed by prehistoric farmers. The East Moors, limestone plateau and shale valleys of the region have been farmed, often continuously, since about 4000 BC. The first farmers, in the Neolithic, may still have been relatively mobile, probably moving between upland summer pastures and winter bases in the valleys. The limestone plateau and eastern gritstone uplands were attractive to early farmers for, while there were still many trees, the forest cover was thinner and the land more easily grazed. These people built impressive monuments, mostly on the limestone plateau, such as chambered cairns and large henges. Here they congregated from time to time to carry out rituals, renew social ties and reinforce patterns of tenure.[14] Many of their monuments survive today, such as the massive Minninglow chambered barrow and the well-known Arbor Low henge with its collapsed stone circle and nearby long barrow. A large stone-banked enclosure, at Gardom's Edge just to the north of Chatsworth, is an exceptional site enclosing a gritstone scarp-top covered in boulders. This may well have been a seasonal meeting place, where many small groups of people living across the region came together for short periods to exchange goods, feast and take part in ceremonies.[15]

From around 2000 BC, in the late Neolithic and early Bronze Age, the pattern of farming began to change. People started to invest more time and effort in specific places, improving the land and practising sustainable mixed farming.[16] They lived in scattered farmsteads amongst the fields and built many small monuments such as stone circles and round barrows where rituals relating to family life, the seasons and the farmers' place in the natural and social world were performed.[17] In the first millennium BC the climate became cooler and wetter, placing pressure on some farms at altitude and also societies more generally. This is reflected in the construction of several hillforts, monuments which – like the Neolithic henges before them – functioned as communal meeting places and displays of group prestige, but now also stressed the martial prowess of those who built them. Eventually, after several generations of hanging on, many farms in places like the East Moors were abandoned at around the time the Romans arrived. From this time to the present, the focal areas for settlement have been the more favourable parts of the limestone plateau, and valleys such that of the Derwent, separated from the rest of the world on all sides except the south by high, but certainly not impassable, moorlands.

The Romans appear to have had little long-term impact on the region. They exploited the lead ores and built several forts with roads between them, but most people continued to live in dispersed farmsteads and hamlets, as they had done in the centuries before. The lives of the farming population of the Peak in the few centuries following the end of the Roman period are obscure to us, but we know that by the seventh century the people here were known as the *Pecsaetna* and the local elites buried some of their dead in round barrows. By the eighth century they had been absorbed into the kingdom of Mercia and later came under the political control of the Danelaw. By this time, farming and lead mining were the mainstays of the local economy.

In the early tenth century English lords again took control of the area and it is believed that around this time major changes in systems of social organisation and land management occurred.[18] In the more favourable parts of the Peak, people began to live in nucleated villages where farming was communally organised – like that at Edensor, near Chatsworth – where there were extensive areas of land which could be cultivated as arable.[19] Here, large open fields were laid out, divided into numerous strips: each farmer held a share of these in return for working parts of the fields for the lord of the manor. On the limestone plateau the former presence of these field is often still clear today, as small groups of strips were later fossilised by piecemeal enclosure, creating narrow walled closes with distinctive sinuous boundaries (Figure 5). However, in places like the Derwent valley, where later boundaries often took the form of hedges which subsequently grew out or have been moved, this pattern is now fragmentary; the former existence of open fields is often revealed only by surviving earthworks such as strip lynchets and ridge and furrow. Surrounding the open fields were extensive commons, often separating village fields from those of the neighbouring settlement. On the commons, the lords and the local people had rights to graze animals and take advantage of various other resources. In other parts of the Peak, in contrast, farming continued to be practised from dispersed farmsteads and hamlets. This was the norm to the west and north, but also in less favourable parts of the Derwent valley and on the gritstone shelves above. While many of these farmsteads were in secular ownership, a number of monastic 'granges' were created on land granted to abbeys and priories in the eleventh to thirteenth centuries. These again tended to be in the less agriculturally favourable areas, with a noticeable concentration on the higher areas of the limestone plateau.

The medieval feudal way of life started to break down in the fourteenth century with the ravages of climatic deterioration, the Black Death and civil strife. Many of the open fields, and the adjacent areas of some of the commons, were slowly enclosed into bounded fields as pastoral farming became more important in the local economy. Villages often contracted, while continuing to be populated by freeholders and tenants. But in a few instances

FIGURE 5.
Field patterns around Monyash, some 11 kilometres to the west of Chatsworth. The walled fields close to the village have sinuous shapes resulting from the gradual, piecemeal enclosure of open fields. In contrast, the land beyond, which survived as open common until it was enclosed by parliamentary act in 1776, has a rigidly rectilinear pattern of fields.

they were entirely and deliberately depopulated by manorial lords and their land turned over to grazing. Some lords chose to create deer parks; elsewhere, more efficient farming units were created by amalgamating farms. The survey of the Cavendish holdings in the Peak District, made by William Senior in the early seventeenth century, shows a number of dispersed farmsteads, some of which had previously been monastic holdings, set in the midst of large rectangular fields; however, it is unclear precisely when these were laid out.

The Peak District has traditionally been important for its industry, particularly lead and coalmining, stone quarrying and cloth manufacture. Most of these had medieval origins, but their scale of production increased in the sixteenth, seventeenth and eighteenth centuries. The lead industry was of particular significance and has left numerous traces in the landscape,[20] although about three-quarters of these important surface remains have been removed in the twentieth century as a consequence of agricultural 'improvement' or for the valuable minerals, such as fluorspar, which the waste hillocks contain. During the seventeenth and eighteenth centuries, lead mining became a large-scale industry and this generated wealth for much of the local population. Prior to the seventeenth century only churches and some manorial halls had been built in stone. However, many manor houses and the more substantial farm houses were re-built in stone in the seventeenth century and, by the end of the eighteenth, all buildings in the region, however humble, were of stone as well.

In the fields beyond the settlements, an even more radical transformation of the countryside's appearance took place. In the eighteenth century the progress of enclosure accelerated, often with the use of parliamentary enclosure acts; by the middle of the nineteenth century all the remaining parts of the open fields had gone, together with many of the commons. They were replaced by a landscape of neat rectangular fields, defined by many thousands of miles of drystone walling. This process was most marked on the limestone plateau, where virtually all of the extensive swathes of heath and rough grassland were removed and replaced by improved pastures, often with the aid of extensive application of lime from local field kilns. The highly rectilinear character of the new landscapes, with ruler-straight walls, reflects the fact that they were carefully planned on maps and professionally surveyed, as part of parliamentary awards or private enclosure agreements, or as properties were reorganised by estate administrators. Such changes took place throughout the country and were associated with the final disappearance of cooperative systems of agriculture, the adoption of new farming methods, and the increasing consolidation of land ownership in the hands of large estates.

Increasing levels of post-medieval economic activity are reflected in other ways in the landscape. Many of today's main roads were originally built in the eighteenth and early nineteenth centuries as toll roads, called turnpikes, in order to facilitate the long-distance movement of raw materials, farm produce and commercially produced goods. But most of the smaller country lanes have medieval origins, and traces of many other pre-eighteenth-century cross-country routes, particularly across the moorlands, survive as disused hollow-ways. Much traffic crossed the region from east to west, carrying a range of goods including salt from Cheshire, lead and millstones exported from the Peak, and imports from industrialised centres, such as the Potteries and Manchester to the west, and Sheffield and Chesterfield to the east.

In the nineteenth century the Peak's traditional industries started to decline. Economically viable reserves of coal and metal ores were becoming worked out; few of the coal mines seem to have operated after the early nineteenth century, while the lead mining industry had all but collapsed by the end of the century. New textile mills were built mostly in areas fringing the Peak, for example around Glossop, which were nearer their markets in the growing industrial cities. Thus, by 1850, the Peak had become once more an area dominated by farming, and the texture of the present landscape was fully established.

Away from the practical matters of farming and industry, perceptions of the remaining 'wild' moorlands of the Peak landscapes, which had been frowned upon by early visitors to Chatsworth, were shifting. Artists such as Turner and later followers of the Romantic movement changed fashionable attitudes to wild places, bringing to them a new, aesthetic, appreciation. However, it was a more down-to-earth factor that ensured the survival of the remaining areas of open moorland in places like the East Moors. Here the Dukes of Devonshire and Rutland transformed what had previously been common land into extensive private grouse moors, as the sport of shooting became increasingly fashionable in the course of the nineteenth century.

Society and economy in the Peak District continued to change through the twentieth century. Some of these developments are obvious, such as the all-pervading presence of the car and the crowds of visitors. Others, such as the loss of village shops and workshops, often pass unnoticed, except by locals. The dynamics of village life have changed radically with the influx of new residents who do not work locally, and of visitors who stay for short periods in holiday cottages and in bed and breakfast accommodation. Such social changes, considered by some to be a mixed blessing even though they can reinvigorate the local economy, have if anything slowed the process of landscape change. Incomers want to retain the rural idyll which they have bought into, while visitors mostly come here to appreciate what they see as an unchanging 'traditional' landscape. Few realise that just 250 years ago the whole appearance of the area was radically different, with hardly a field wall in sight over vast tracts of the limestone plateau, and with much of the landscape highly industrialised; that 500 years ago villages were built in wood and surrounded by open fields; or that 5,000 years ago even the heather moorlands that appear so 'natural' were being cleared of trees by local farmers. The local landscape, for all its 'natural' beauty, is an artefact: if we were to allow it to return to a state of nature, the scenic countryside for which the Peak District is so famous would very soon be entirely engulfed and hidden by trees.

Making sense of Chatsworth

Some readers may be unfamiliar with Chatsworth's complex and intricate landscape and the chapters that follow will make more sense if they first briefly consider Figure 6, which shows the main area of the gardens from the air; Figure 7, which shows how the areas of park and garden changed over time; and Figures 89–90, 92–93 and 97–99, which show the locations of the principal extant features. Moreover, the history of the park and garden is long and complex, and before we begin our account it might be helpful to sum up, baldly and briefly, its principal phases. Though the landscape around Chatsworth has been inhabited since prehistory, our main story begins in the 1550s with the construction of a grand Elizabethan house by William Cavendish and his wife, Elizabeth ('Bess') of Hardwick, complete with elaborate formal gardens featuring terraces and an extensive complex of ponds. At this time there was no park to the west of the river Derwent, but only fields and farms, together with a sheepwalk on the 'commons' above and a large rabbit warren near the river. However, a substantial deer park lay to the east of the hall, along and above the steep Millstone Grit escarpment. Various alterations were made to this landscape in the course of the seventeenth century, but it was only after the accession of the 4th Earl, later the 1st Duke, in 1684, that the old house and its grounds were completely transformed. The mansion was largely rebuilt in fashionable 'Baroque' mode, and massive new gardens were created around it, among the finest in England, replete with parterres, terraces, and elaborate waterworks. This vast and complex designed landscape went through several stages of development, one of which is illustrated in the famous engraving made by Kip and Knyff in 1699, and survived until around 1730. There were then further changes, which may have been associated with the famous designer William Kent, although they are less clearly documented in the surviving records. The rigid geometry of the old gardens was steadily simplified, many of the terraces smoothed and levelled, and the first attempts made to beautify the landscape on the western side of the river.

More radical changes occurred from the late 1750s. Most of the remaining geometric elements around the house were swept away, although some of the principal water features remained. A new 'landscape park' was created, which embraced a vast tract of land on either side of the river, complete with extensive plantations above, new stables, two stone bridges and an ornamental mill. The buildings were designed by James Paine but the overall landscape was undoubtedly the work of Lancelot 'Capability' Brown, the most noted landscape designer in eighteenth-century England.

Brown's landscape survived with only minor alterations until the accession of the 6th Duke in 1811. There then followed a phase of intense activity which continued into the 1840s. The park was expanded to the north and north-west; a new network of roads and drives was constructed; the village of Edensor was partially removed and its remaining section rebuilt as a 'model' settlement; and, above all, the gardens and pleasure grounds in the vicinity of the house were transformed yet again, this time under the direction of Joseph Paxton. The waterworks were improved, an extensive Arboretum planted, rockworks created, and the Great Conservatory – for several years the largest glass building in the world – was erected. It is this last phase which has, arguably, made the greatest mark on the Chatsworth landscape we see today, although important contributions have also been made by earlier periods.

FIGURE 6.

Chatsworth from the air, looking north-east. The house is surrounded by formal gardens which incorporate features created over a long period of time, from the seventeenth to the twentieth century. Behind, to the east, the wooded slopes of Stand Wood rise to a gritstone shelf: this was the area occupied by the old deer park, created in the late middle ages. In contrast, the land near the river only became parkland in the middle decades of the eighteenth century.

© PEAK DISTRICT NATIONAL PARK AUTHORITY

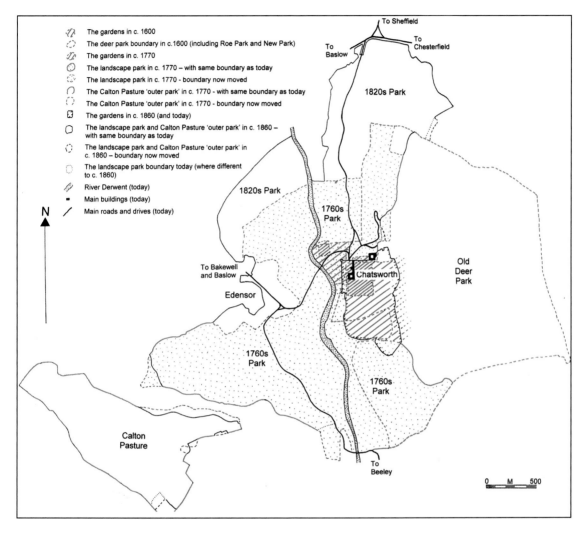

The gardens in c. 1600
The deer park boundary in c.1600 (including Roe Park and New Park)
The gardens in c. 1770
The landscape park in c. 1770 – with same boundary as today
The landscape park in c. 1770 - boundary now moved
The Calton Pasture 'outer park' in c. 1770 - with same boundary as today
The Calton Pasture 'outer park' in c. 1770 - boundary now moved
The gardens in c. 1860 (and today)
The landscape park and Calton Pasture 'outer park' in c. 1860 – with same boundary as today
The landscape park and Calton Pasture 'outer park' in c. 1860 – boundary now moved
The landscape park boundary today (where different to c. 1860)
River Derwent (today)
Main buildings (today)
Main roads and drives (today)

N

To Sheffield
To Chesterfield
To Baslow

1820s Park

1820s Park

1760s Park

To Bakewell and Baslow

Old Deer Park

Chatsworth

Edensor

1760s Park

1760s Park

Calton Pasture

To Beeley

0   M   500

FIGURE 7.
This map shows the changing areas occupied by the gardens, old deer park and later landscape park at Chatsworth over the centuries.

These are the broad outlines of the story. But, as we shall see, the real fascination lies in the details. Chatsworth holds a central place in the history of English landscape design. Indeed, that history could largely be written from the great works carried out at this one place. In the chapters that follow we will use all the rich evidence of documents and archaeology to reveal how this vital landscape, in all its rich complexity, came into being.

CHAPTER TWO

The Early History of the Chatsworth Landscape

Chatsworth BC ('Before Cavendish')

It is commonly said by workers on the Chatsworth Estate that the letters BC refer not to 'Before Christ', but to 'Before Cavendish'. The Cavendish family have certainly made a dramatic difference to the landscape since they came to Chatsworth in 1549; to describe the area before and after they purchased the estate is to adopt much more than a division of convenience. But the landscape visible today has, nevertheless, a much longer history.

Because of the intensity of subsequent land use, little surface evidence remains of the many generations who lived within and farmed the Derwent valley around Chatsworth in prehistory. However, the area has been extensively used by people for several millennia. Surviving as evidence of this use are several prehistoric round barrows, dating to the late Neolithic or early Bronze Age (c. 2500–1500 BC), both within the Park to the west of the river and on Calton Pasture above (Figure 8). Research in the Peak District as a whole strongly suggests that they were often built in areas that were favourable to agriculture, close to where people lived and farmed.[1] Barrows were foci for ritual activities: they were the burial places of selected representatives of local farming families, and they served to articulate relationships between the world of the spirits and the ancestors, and that of the living. The act of burying selected ancestors in prominent mounds served to legitimise a family's claim to the land which they overlooked, or in which they were located (Figure 9).

There are no recorded antiquarian excavations for the two or three barrows within the park, although such activity may still have taken place. Of the barrows on Calton Pasture, of which up to eight survive, three were investigated by Thomas Bateman, one of Britain's best known nineteenth-century antiquarians, who lived at nearby Lomberdale Hall in Middleton by Youlgreave. They were all dug in a single day, 2 May 1850.[2] In one he found a disturbed stone 'cist' with remains of a human cremation and sherds of a Food Vessel. This stone box may be the same as that which had already been dug by Major Rooke in the late eighteenth century, when an 'urn' was found full of 'ashes' between two flat stones.[3] The other two barrows had also been opened prior to Bateman's excavations and he found nothing except a disturbed skeleton within one of them.

Our knowledge of the Chatsworth area during the Roman and early medieval periods is very limited. It is probable that there were a number of farmsteads surrounded by fields on more favourable areas of ground but it is unlikely there were ever any Roman military roads, forts or villas in the vicinity. It is only in late Anglo-Saxon times, in the eleventh century, that the picture becomes any clearer. The first documentary references to local settlements are contained in Domesday Book. There are two relevant entries, phrased in Domesday's typically terse style, describing the situation in both 1086 and 1066:[4]

Land of the King

In Langley and Chatsworth, Leofnoth and Ketel had 10 bovates of land in the geld [taxable land]. Land for 10 oxen. This belongs to Edensor. William Peverel has charge for the King.

There 5 villeins [villagers] and 2 bordars [smallholders] have two ploughs [ploughteams] and meadow 1 acre, woodland pasture 1 league long and 1 wide; and a little underwood [scrubland].

Before 1066 worth 20s; now 16s.

Land of Henry de Ferrers

In Edensor, Leofnoth and Ketel had 2 carucates of land [each] as two manors.
Henry now 4 carucates to the geld [taxable land] and as many ploughs [ploughteams] for ploughing.
There are 10 villans [villagers] and 7 bordars [smallholders] with 6 ploughs [ploughteams] and 1 acre of meadow.

Formerly worth 40s, now 20s.

Edensor was evidently a relatively large village with significant amounts of arable land. On the other side of the river, Chatsworth and the now lost Langley had much less arable, instead having large quantities of woodland pasture, and were perhaps only hamlets; before the Norman Conquest they had been no more than berewicks (subsidiary settlements) of Edensor. Chatsworth probably occupied approximately the same site as today's house, or lay a little to the south-west; the site of Langley lay within the present Chatsworth township, almost certainly somewhere to the north of the house. A survey of Chatsworth made in 1617 by William Senior (a surveyor from Kingston-upon-Hull who began a comprehensive survey of the Devonshire estates in 1609) shows a small field named 'Langley' immediately to the east of the present walled kitchen gardens in the north-eastern part of the park (Figure 10).[5]

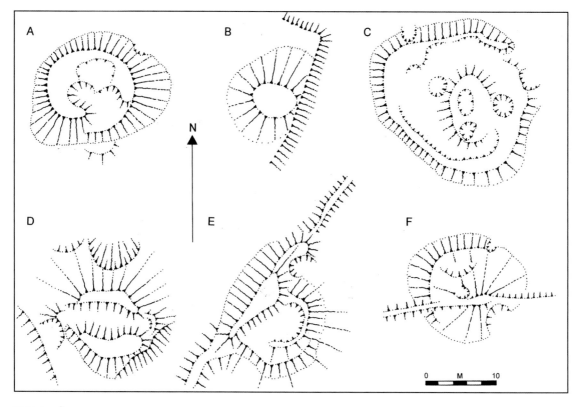

FIGURE 8.

The Park contains two or three round barrows (A-C), while on Calton Pasture to the south-west there are a further four definite and three possible examples, three of which are illustrated here (D-F). These burial mounds, dating from the late Neolithic or early Bronze Age, some four thousand years ago, are the oldest known archaeological features at Chatsworth (A: Figure 93 number 1, B: Figure 93 number 2, C: Figure 93 number 3, D: Figure 99 – south-easternmost barrow, E: Figure 99 – southern barrow crossed by a field boundary earthwork of seventeenth- or early eighteenth-century date, F: Figure 99 – south-westernmost barrow crossed by a bank of probable Romano-British or medieval date).

FIGURE 9.

Remains of a round barrow, on the rising ground to the west of the river Derwent. These burial mounds served to affirm claims to land by farming communities living here in the valley.

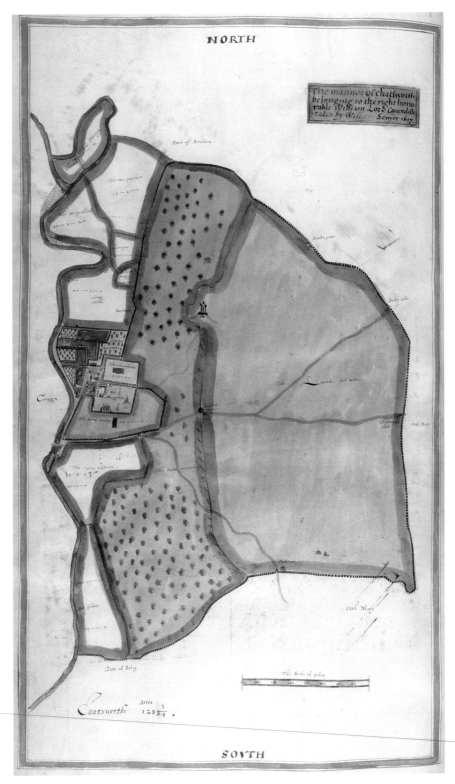

FIGURE 10.
William Senior's map
of Chatsworth was
made in 1617 as part of
a comprehensive survey
of all the Cavendish
family's far-flung
estates. It shows the
great house, built by
Elizabeth of Hardwick
and her husbands,
surrounded by
extensive gardens. A
deer park extends along
the escarpment to
north and south, and
up onto the gritstone
shelf to the east. The
map is one of our most
important sources of
evidence for the early
history of the
Chatsworth landscape.

In the Middle Ages large areas of what is now Chatsworth Park were occupied by 'open fields' – that is, areas in which the holdings of several farmers lay together as unenclosed, intermingled strips, which were mainly cultivated as arable but which were also grazed in common when not under crops. These particular fields were farmed from the village of Edensor, the hamlet at Chatsworth and probably other lost settlements nearby. The park contains particularly extensive and important archaeological traces of these fields, in the form of the low earthworks which archaeologists call 'strip lynchets' and 'ridge and furrow'; these were preserved by the creation of the landscape park around 1760 and thus escaped the ravages of more recent farming (Cover and Figure 11). With climatic deterioration and the demographic decline due to famines and the Black Death in the mid fourteenth century, livestock farming became more important and the open fields started to be enclosed, although the process was a very gradual one: small areas of open strips north of Edensor village still existed in 1617 when planned by William Senior.[6]

Domesday Book deals only with administrative or manorial units and other farms and hamlets may well have existed, scattered across the townships of Edensor and Chatsworth, which it passes over in silence. Some are certainly named in later medieval documents.[7] Besley, located somewhere to the east of the river and now long-abandoned, was first mentioned in 1296; and a monastic grange located somewhere within Chatsworth township is mentioned in a document of 1355, although which abbey or priory it belonged to is unknown.[8] On the other side of the river, the present hamlet of Calton Lees to the south of Edensor was first referred to in 1205 as 'Lees'.[9] A place called 'Calton' is recorded as early as 1192 but this may have been a separate settlement, its site perhaps marked by the earthworks of a deserted farmstead or hamlet which have been identified high on Calton Pasture (Figure 12). The site comprised an irregular arrangement of between three and five buildings, not necessarily all in use at any one time but presumably representing a mixture of dwellings and outbuildings which were, together with yards or garden plots, ranged along either side of a lane.

As we saw in the previous chapter, villages like Edensor, large planned feudal settlements surrounded by extensive open fields, began to appear in the Peak District from the early tenth century. When they were first laid out, each tenant was allocated a small strip of land, called a toft, upon which their farmstead or croft was placed. While buildings have generally migrated around these plots over the centuries the original property boundaries themselves have often been retained. Thus, something of Edensor's original medieval plan can be seen on Senior's survey of 1617 (Figure 13),[10] drawn before radical reorganisation of the village by the estate in the 1820s–30s. The majority of buildings lay along a long village street, part of the road leading from the old Chatsworth Bridge towards Bakewell. The medieval church lay part-way along the southern side of the street. This was rebuilt in the nineteenth century but there is still a medieval cross base in the churchyard. Nearby there was a crossroads, with a road running at an angle south-westwards before turning, outside the village, towards Calton. The road northwards from the crossroads ran towards Baslow. The houses north-east of the cross-roads, and possibly others elsewhere, appear from the map to have stood within medieval toft boundaries. If so, the medieval village must have had a relatively complex plan, perhaps the result of enlargement and modification in the course of the Middle Ages: many of the planned medieval villages in the Peak District have only a single street with tofts on one or both sides.

The earthwork remains of Edensor's medieval fields still survive within the park (Figure 14), and also in enclosed farmland to the north and west. It has been suggested that the village had only one large open field,[11] but this may well be an erroneous assumption, the product of incomplete later documentation. By the time Senior made his survey in 1617 large areas of Edensor's open fields had been subsumed within the warren belonging to Chatsworth House (see below), or had been enclosed piecemeal and converted to pasture. Only disconnected fragments remained, apparently still farmed in a traditional way; one parcel was known as '*The Arable Feeld*'. In fact, the extent and complexity of the surviving earthworks suggests there were probably several medieval open fields, perhaps three or four in number. High within the park to the southwest of Edensor the character of the medieval earthworks, with small parcels of strips overlying others at different orientations, suggests that here the land was used only intermittently for cultivation, forming an 'outfield' which was used when necessity demanded. By 1617, and probably from the late medieval period, this area had ceased to be used for arable and had become part of a large open 'sheepwalk' belonging to the lord of the manor. On the lower ground, in contrast, the land would have been farmed more regularly and intensively, not only in the medieval but into the post-medieval period: the surviving earthworks here represent nearly a thousand years of modification and re-organisation. While there are medieval elements, some of the visible cultivation strips no doubt reflect details of the farming regime as it existed in the eighteenth century, when ridge and furrow ploughing was still taking place, but within enclosed fields.

While the village of Edensor had large open fields, medieval farming at Chatsworth itself and at other smaller settlements in the vicinity was organised in a different way and had older origins. Emphasis was probably placed on livestock, with grazing both in enclosed meadows near the river and in the wood pastures on the steep slopes above. However, the earthwork evidence shows that areas of open-field land also existed: there are clusters of strip lynchets and broad ridge and furrow that cover much smaller areas than those over the river at Edensor (Figure 14). They were presumably cultivated by the small farming communities at Chatsworth, Langley and Besley, as well as by the lost grange at Chatsworth. We should note, however, that not far away on the East Moors, at Lawrence Field above Hathersage, a large oval enclosure, divided into a series of cleared strips and surrounded on all sides by extensive moorland, was associated with only a single farmstead, consisting of one longhouse and an outbuilding.[12] This illustrates that archaeological evidence for

FIGURE II.

Large areas of Chatsworth Park are covered by broad but low earthworks known as 'ridge and furrow', the remains of medieval cultivation within open fields. These examples stand out with particular clarity in the snow. © PEAK DISTRICT NATIONAL PARK AUTHORITY.

cultivation in strips does not necessarily mean that the land in question was being farmed communally as intermixed parcels.

In contrast, the areas of broad ridge and furrow lying further north, in Baslow parish, relate to the extensive open fields farmed from this important medieval village. To the west of the Derwent, high on Calton Pasture, in an area probably occupied by wastes and commons in the later medieval period, there are two further small areas of cultivation strips which, if indeed they are of medieval (rather than Romano-British) date, may be associated with the small medieval settlement of Calton.

In the medieval period, and in many cases up until the late eighteenth or early nineteenth century, wastes and commons in the Peak District were an important resource, used by the occupants of the townships for grazing and as a source of vital materials: building stone, peat and underwood (brushwood) for fuel, and bracken and heather for animal bedding and thatch. They would also have provided food such as bilberries and fungi. Mineral rights and wild game were usually reserved for the lord of the manor, although the former were sometimes leased to others. Wastes and commons existed above Edensor

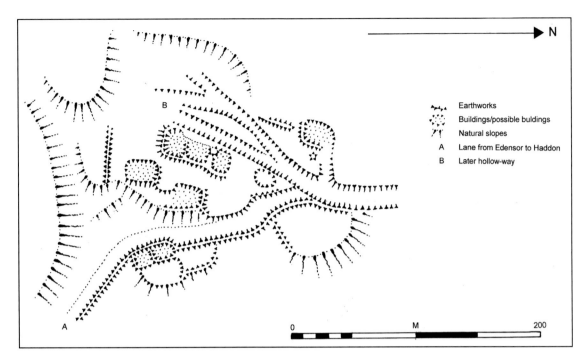

Earthworks

Buildings/possible buildings

Natural slopes

A Lane from Edensor to Haddon

B Later hollow-way

0 M 200

FIGURE 12.
The earthworks of a
probable deserted
medieval settlement
preserved high on
Calton Pasture. The
site, which comprised a
mixture of dwellings
and outbuildings
ranged along either side
of a lane, may represent
the settlement called
'Calton' referred to in a
document of 1192.

and Calton on the areas now known as Calton Pasture and Lees Moor, and above Chatsworth within the area which was later to become the deer park. Precisely how common grazing was organised locally is unclear, but each family would have had the right to pasture an agreed number of animals. Where commons were extensive they were often shared between the farmers of more than one community. This may have been the case within Chatsworth parish, and across the river at Edensor and Calton.

The original medieval boundaries of Chatsworth, and of the lost settlements of Langley, Besley and Chatsworth Grange, are unknown, as is the extent of their commons. By the early seventeenth century the eastern boundary of Chatsworth township was conterminous with that of the deer park attached to Chatsworth House, but this shared line may not have been of any great antiquity: there are signs that it was the result of a reorganisation which occurred just over a hundred years earlier. An earthwork in the wood above Park Gate Farm may mark an earlier line of the pale or the township boundary (Figure 19). If so, the park had been extended to the east by the time that Senior's survey was made in 1617,[13] and the medieval common land of Chatsworth may also have originally been restricted to the main shelf, rather than encroaching on the upper moors above, the major part of which is now in Baslow township. This boundary change is probably that referred to in the Baslow Court Rolls for 1504, when Phillip and George Leche were accused of having 'dimminished the moor called Basselow moor and now called Chattesworth moor, being part of Basselow moor'.[14] This was clearly a long-standing dispute, for Phillip Leche had appeared before the court in 1488 for impounding livestock on 'Basselow moor between Dawkyn waste and

Reddebonk' as he claimed the right to the land here.[15] Such disputes often occurred when the exploitation of common moorland was shared between neighbouring townships whose boundaries were ill-defined.

When Senior's map was surveyed the only dwelling at Chatsworth was the house itself – although then, as now, this would have accommodated a large extended 'household'. Langley and Besley had been abandoned by this time, although precisely when this occurred remains unclear. The documentary evidence shows that Langley was certainly still in existence in 1431, while the last known record of Besley is in 1355. A receipt roll of tithes paid for Chatsworth township to the Dean and Chapter of Lichfield survives for 1339. At this date seven men paid tithe on corn while two others only paid for hay, although there were further residents who held land here; there was also a water mill. In contrast, the records of lay subsidies paid to the Crown in the years 1448 to 1449 lists Chatsworth as 'devastated and laid waste', although the manor house certainly existed at this time.[16] The first certain reference to a manorial hall comes in 1441 and it has been suggested that the deer park was first created around this time.[17] While this seems plausible, the possibility cannot be discounted that it came into existence closer to the time that Sir William Cavendish and his wife Elizabeth Hardwick bought the manors of Chatsworth and Edensor in 1549. They purchased them following the death of Thomas Agard, who had acquired the estate in 1547 from Francis Leche.[18] Chatsworth had been in the hands of the Leche family for many years; it appears Sir John Leche had been granted the estate by Edward III in about 1330 [19] (although an earlier authority suggested that this acquisition did not take place until the 1430s–40s).[20] It seems likely that it was the Leches who depopulated Chatsworth and created the hunting park, as well as building the hall that was still standing when the Cavendishes began to erect their grand new house in the 1550s.

The old hall and outbuildings probably stood near to the site of the present house. Adjacent were the enclosures later known as the Old Orchard and Roe Park, while on higher ground there was a large deer park and by the river a number of meadows for stock. Like other great houses of the period Chatsworth was not only a high-status residence but also a 'home farm' that managed cattle and sheep as well as deer. It was a landscape entirely dominated by its lords; there were no commons, and presumably no freeholders, within the township. On the other side of the river, it is likely that the large rabbit warren shown by Senior had been created sometime between the fourteenth and sixteenth centuries, in what had formerly been one of Edensor's open fields. Warrens are often associated with important houses, with the rabbits both consumed by the household and sold as a 'cash crop'. Similarly, by this time the former commons of Edensor and Calton appear to have been managed as a private sheepwalk. Although there were still freehold properties within the township, Senior's inventory of 1617 gives no indication that common rights had been retained on the open ground above the closes surrounding the village.[21]

By the time that Chatsworth and Edensor were first mapped, by Senior in 1617,[22] the landscape had changed in a number of important ways. On the eastern side of the river, all the land in the valley below the deer park to both north and south of the house was now divided into enclosed fields, mainly of relatively large size. Most have left few earthwork traces, probably because of radical changes to the field pattern which occurred here in the later seventeenth or early eighteenth centuries. On the other side of the Derwent there were closes around Edensor, which also followed the riverbank southwards, while large areas of the former open fields now lay within an extensive demesne sheepwalk, or within the large rabbit warren to the north of the village.

Perhaps the most striking survivals in the modern landscape from the pre-Cavendish era are the fine old oaks growing in the present-day park to the north and south of Chatsworth House (Figure 15). These venerable trees once lay within the lower parts of the deer park and many have stood since late medieval times. Some of the steep slopes here must presumably have formed part of the woodland pasture noted in Domesday Book but none of the surviving trees are this old; some in the area to the south of the house are clearly growing on top of medieval strip-cultivation terraces. There is a persistent tale that the oaks are a relic of Sherwood Forest – this is not true. The story seems to have originated in the notion, now long disproved, that much of England was covered in forest in the medieval period, with swathes of trees running continuously from county to county. In reality, pollen analysis shows there have been few trees on the extensive moorlands to the east of Chatsworth since late prehistoric times, while the Derwent valley was never part of the formal medieval hunting forest of Sherwood, which lay some 30 km away to the east in Nottinghamshire.

The Cavendish family

The Cavendishes originated in Suffolk as a family of yeoman farmers. Their rise to prominence was due in the first instance to the success of John Cavendish, who became chief justice of the Kings Bench under Edward III; they were one of many noble families in England who owed their initial success to a clever lawyer. The money made by Sir John was ploughed back into building up a small landed estate around Cavendish, the Suffolk textile town from which the family took its name. Sir John was involved in the rigorous enforcement of the unpopular Statute of Labourers – an act which attempted to limit wage rates – and, together with the Prior of Bury St Edmunds, was beheaded by an angry mob during the Peasants' Revolt of 1381.[23] The family continued to reside on their Suffolk estates, however, pursuing an uneventful life until the next major improvement in their fortunes came under Henry VIII. This was a time when, after a period of civil war and internal instability, the Tudor dynasty were building their power and expanding the machinery of a centralised state; competent administrators were able to make fortunes in government business. George Cavendish became chief

NORTH

Part of Bakewell

Part of Pidley

Part of Baslow

Calton 824 acres

Cunigre

Part of Haddon

Edensore

Part of Chatsworthe

Lees

Calton more 208

Lees

Tenementes ——————— 208¼
Calton Moore ————————— 292
John Lees ffre grounde ——— 39¼

Terall 539½

Edensore

The Demesnes as Calton, the Cunigre &c ——— 1311¼
Tenementes & Cottages ——————— 310
Freehoulds ——————— 41

Terall 1602¼

The some of both ——— 2201¾

Part of Belsie

SOUTH

FIGURE 13.
William Senior's map of Edensor and Calton Lees, surveyed in 1617, shows land to the east of the river Derwent, which now mostly lies within the eighteenth-century park. By this time, large areas of the open fields had been subsumed within an extensive rabbit warren (named Cunigre) and a large sheep walk, both belonging to Chatsworth House, or had been enclosed piecemeal. Only disconnected fragments remained, one explicitly described as '*The Arable Feeld*'.

FIGURE 14.
Medieval earthworks in Chatsworth Park and Calton Pasture. Much of the area is carpeted with ridge and furrow and other features of medieval date. Edensor (and the village of Baslow to the north) had large open fields, those attached to the lesser settlements were generally much smaller.

secretary to Cardinal Wolsey (and wrote a Life of his master) while his brother William, who was born in 1505, became Treasurer of the Chamber and principal assistant to Thomas Cromwell. In this role he was actively involved in the Dissolution of the Monasteries and, like many others, received some of the resultant spoils, in the shape of scattered properties in south-east England. Following the death of King Henry, William continued as Treasurer of the Chamber under his successor, Edward VI.[24]

Two successive marriages brought him no children, but his third was more successful in this respect. Elizabeth, daughter of John Hardwick of Hardwick in Derbyshire, was several years younger than William but was already a widow and a great heiress. In a move which set the stage for much that was to follow, she persuaded William to sell his property in the south-east of England and concentrate his possessions in her part of the world, in Derbyshire and Nottinghamshire. This he did, his acquisitions including Welbeck Abbey and its associated estate, and Chatsworth itself, which, together with lands in Edensor, was purchased for £600 in December 1549.[25]

William was a bureaucrat, not a conviction politician, and like others in the government administration he kept his post even when the radical Protestant Edward died and was replaced by the staunchly Catholic Mary. William himself died in 1557, but not before he and his wife had begun the construction of their new house at Chatsworth. The house was completed by the widowed Elizabeth – more commonly known today as 'Bess' – who also constructed an innovative new house (which still survives, largely unaltered) at nearby Hardwick, as well as a number of others. Her passion for building was funded not only by the wealth inherited from William Cavendish, but also by that derived from a third marriage – to Sir William St Loe – and subsequent widowhood. Her fourth marriage, in 1568, was her most ambitious of all – to George Talbot, the 6th Earl of Shrewsbury. Elizabeth I was now on the throne, and it was she who sanctioned one of the most extraordinary pieces of arranged matrimony of the period, for on the day that 'Bess of Hardwick' married the Earl, her son Henry married his daughter Lady Grace Talbot, while her third daughter Mary married Shrewsbury's son, later the 7th Earl.

Elizabeth and Shrewsbury lived for much of the time at Chatsworth but their marriage was not a happy one: they rowed bitterly. The Earl was given the task of guarding Mary Queen of Scots after she fled from Scotland to England following the death of Darnley and the revolt of the Scots lords. She was kept at Chatsworth on a number of occasions in the 1570s and early 1580s, and has cast a long, romantic shadow over the landscape, as we shall see. Elizabeth also outlived Shrewsbury, who died in 1590, continuing to run Chatsworth until her death in her late eighties in 1608.

The building of Chatsworth House

The Cavendishes' mansion was built on a new site, probably to the south of the old manor house. Construction seems to have begun in the early 1550s, but it is

FIGURE 15.

The ancient oaks in the parkland to the north and south of the house once grew within the Tudor deer park. They represent one of the most important collections of veteran trees in England: some may be more than six centuries old.

possible that the 'platt' originally prepared for Bess and Sir William was altered and amended in grander style after the latter's death, as the fortunes of his widow blossomed yet further after her marriage to Shrewsbury in 1568.[26] The Chatsworth accounts are missing for the years between 1560 and 1576, by which time the interior decoration of the house was nearing completion. The house seems to have been finally finished around 1580. We have a good idea of its appearance and layout from a number of sources.[27] Its main entrance front – which faced westwards, towards the Derwent – is shown in a needlework view now preserved at Hardwick Hall and in an oil painting, an eighteenth-century copy (probably by the artist Richard Wilson) of a seventeenth-century original (perhaps by the Dutch artist Jan Siberechts) (Figure 16). In addition, a glimpse is provided by Kip and Knyff's aerial view of 1699: the eye is drawn to the recently reconstructed South Front: the older structure peeps at us obliquely, hardly noticeable (Figure 22). This West Front had four towers, each five storeys high; one at each corner and two in the centre, forming a gatehouse, above the arch of which, in typical Tudor fashion, the arms of Bess and her husband were proudly displayed. There was an outer western courtyard with a central circular lodge and two corner turrets. To the north there were stables and other outbuildings. The house covered more or less the same area of ground as the present house, excepting the long, northern extension built in the nineteenth century; and, like the present house, it was built around a central courtyard. But from the outside this would have been invisible and the solid mass, and height, of the building was its most striking aspect. In the words of Charles Cotton, who wrote a poem called 'Wonders of the Peake' in the 1670s in praise of Chatsworth:

> The noble front of the whole edefice
> In a surprising height is seen to rise.[28]

The building was, more or less, the same height as the present house, which is itself – at around 74 feet to the top of the balustrade – rather tall for a late seventeenth-century building. This is due to the fact that it represents, in large part, a remodelling rather than a wholesale rebuilding of the Elizabethan house, although this is nowhere very evident in the present appearance of the building. Indeed, much of the house's internal layout is a consequence of this fact. Unlike any other late seventeenth- or eighteenth-century mansion

FIGURE 17.

This strange, squat stone edifice to the north-west of the House, 'restored' in the 1820s, has long been known as Queen Mary's Bower. Mary Queen of Scots was certainly held at Chatsworth in the 1560s and 70s but there is no truth in the legend that the 'Bower' was built for her. It originally stood in the centre of a complex of ornamental ponds and orchards, and was probably used as a banqueting house. © THE DEVONSHIRE COLLECTION, CHATSWORTH. REPRODUCED BY PERMISSION OF THE CHATSWORTH SETTLEMENT TRUSTEES.

Chatsworth thus has its state rooms on the second floor, reached by a staircase from one end of the hall, because this was the way the Elizabethan house had been arranged. In fact, having the main reception rooms on the second floor was not normal practice even in the Elizabethan period, but Bess seems to have had a penchant for such an arrangement, which also appears at two of her other houses, at Worksop and Hardwick.[29]

All the illustrations agree in showing that in many ways the house was an old-fashioned building, certainly by comparison with Bess's other great building project, Hardwick, which was begun in the mid 1580s. This, with its unusual Greek cross plan, immense windows, and triple-pile structure (i.e., it was a house three rooms deep), was new and innovative; in a number of ways it looked forward to the houses of the following century. Chatsworth, in contrast, with its central courtyard, gatehouse, turrets and battlements, harked back to the houses of the early Tudor period, and ultimately to the mansions of the later Middle Ages. It was not a castle, but its design echoed the chivalrous architecture of medieval times. Perhaps William, a man whose wealth and status had been but recently acquired, consciously sought to display the symbols of an ancient aristocracy, rather than choosing to build a more innovative house, which might display or reveal his *parvenu* status.

The Elizabethan gardens

As well as providing evidence of the wider Chatsworth landscape, Senior's somewhat schematic map of 1617 also provides the earliest surviving depiction of the area in the immediate vicinity of the house (Figures 10, 19).[30] The most striking feature of the landscape was an arrangement of seven large rectangular ponds which occupied the flood plain of the river Derwent to the north-west of the house. Some writers have suggested that these were intended to drain this level area 'and prevent it from becoming a swamp from the Derwent's repeated floods'.[31] However, the archaeological evidence makes it clear that the local inhabitants had no difficulty in cultivating this area; traces of ridge and furrow, indicating former arable fields, extend right up to the edge of the river. By analogy with numerous other late medieval and sixteenth-century sites, the ponds probably had two main functions.

The first was a practical one: to provide fish for the household. Freshwater fish were an important part of the English diet in medieval and early post-medieval times, and extensive complexes of fish ponds (in effect, fish farms) were a normal feature of high-status residences. Different-sized ponds were used to stock fish of different sizes and ages and – to a lesser extent – different species, although carp was the principal one. Charles Cotton's poem *Wonders of the Peake* describes the ponds beside the entrance front:

> Over this *Pond*, opposite to the Gate,
> A *Bridge*, of a queint structure, strength and state,

40

Invites you to pass over it, where dry
You trample may on shoals of wanton *Fry*,
With which those breeding waters do abound,
And better *Carps* are no where to be found.[32]

The second purpose of the ponds, however, was aesthetic. Areas of water, especially associated with buildings, had a strong appeal in this period. The view of a mansion rising from a sheet of still water was generally considered attractive, and even in medieval times castles had often (as at Bodiam in Sussex) been surrounded by sheets of water, too shallow to have been 'moats' with any serious defensive purpose.[33] The two attributes – fish-production and aesthetics – were often combined, and fishponds thus doubled as water gardens. Cotton, again, captures the impression the great ponds at Chatsworth made as visitors approached the house:

The outward *Gate* stands neat enough, to look
Her *Oval* Front in the objected *Brook*;
But that she has better reflexion
From a large *Mirror* nearer of her own.
For a fair *Lake*, from wash of *Floods* unmixt.
Before it lies, as Area spread betwixt.[34]

The aesthetic function of the ponds is clear from Senior's map, which shows that the most southerly pond was spanned by a three-arched bridge and contained a central feature, probably a fountain. The map also shows a number of buildings in this area, presumably of an ornamental character. Two, which stood on opposite banks of the largest and most northerly pond, have disappeared without trace: but a third survives, although much altered and rebuilt in the nineteenth century. This is the structure now known as Queen Mary's Bower (Figure 17). Tradition, current since the eighteenth century, holds that this building was constructed in the 1570s when Mary Queen of Scots was held at Chatsworth, in order to provide a raised exercise ground for the captive queen (her presence at Chatsworth is recorded in 1570, 1573, 1577, 1578, and 1581).[35] There is no hard evidence to support this tradition, and while it is perfectly possible that the structure was used by the exiled queen there seems little doubt that the Bower was originally built as a garden feature. It may have served as a fishing lodge, a viewing platform, or perhaps as a 'banqueting house'. A 'banquet' was an elaborate final course to a meal: guests would retire from the hall or great chamber where the main meal had been served, and repair to some special room or structure, placed on the roof of the house or more usually, as here, within the park or gardens. In a manner which can be paralleled at a number of other contemporary or near-contemporary sites, the Bower would have provided dramatic views back towards the mansion, the great bulk of which would have been reflected in the intervening sheets of water. The construction of the 'Bower' is not clearly referred to in the surviving accounts, unless it is the 'taris on the fishpond wall' mentioned

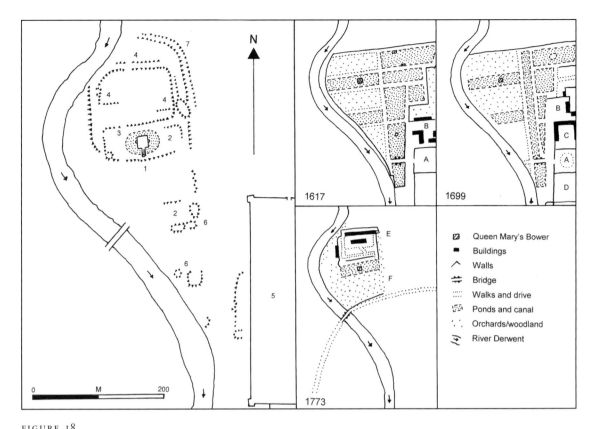

FIGURE 18.
The low earthworks in the parkland around Queen Mary's Bower represent the remains of an Elizabethan garden, subsequently modified in the eighteenth century and finally swept away in the 1820s. Comparison of the earthwork plan with maps from 1617 and 1773, and Kip and Knyff's engraving of 1699, show that the remains include features of a variety of dates (1: Queen Mary's Bower; 2: sixteenth-century ponds (sites); 3: sixteenth-century walks; 4: eighteenth-century garden earthwork details and enlargement to the north; 5: nineteenth-century garden terrace; 6: higher earthworks protected by mature trees; 7: late eighteenth- or nineteenth-century drain; A: the House forecourt; B: outbuildings; C: stables; D: formal garden; E: hothouses; F: The Rookery).

in 1581.[36] Its original form is uncertain. It was massively restored in the early nineteenth century (a drawing made in 1773 shows it in a very ruinous condition)[37] but always appears to have taken the form of a great raised stone platform, surmounted by a low balustrade and approached by wide stone steps. Later maps and drawings suggest that it stood within one of the ponds, which surrounded it like a moat, an arrangement not entirely apparent in Senior's schematic plan. The stairs, with their great arch, thus served as a kind of bridge.

The area around the Bower has been changed in many ways since the sixteenth century with, in particular, major alterations in the mid eighteenth century, when the ponds further to the east were swept away. But a number of low earthworks survive here which appear to be the remains of early garden features, perhaps in part contemporary with the building itself. The basic

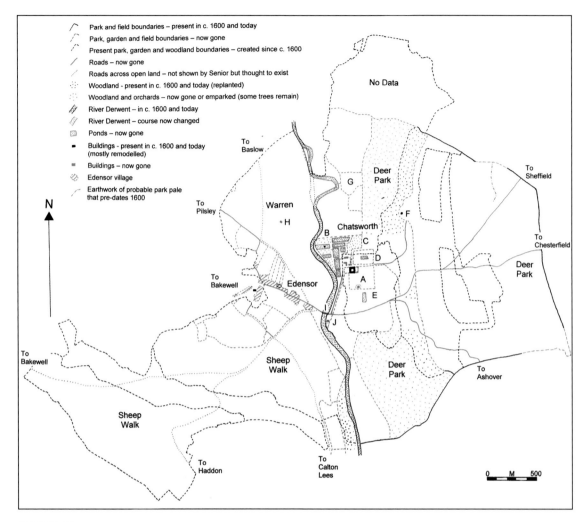

FIGURE 19.

The area covered by the gardens and park in 1617 as illustrated by Senior, compared with the disposition of features in the modern landscape (A: formal gardens, B: formal ponds and orchards, C: The Roe Park, D: The Old Orchard, E: The New Park, F: The Stand, G: Langley meadow, H: the warrener's lodge, I: Chatsworth Bridge, J: Chatsworth Mill).

layout of the two western ponds and the three orchards, as shown on Senior's map of 1617, can still be made out amongst the earthworks (Figure 18). Looked at closely, raised walkways along the edges of these compartments are obvious, but these may well be later features, for the gardens here continued to be maintained and modified into the early nineteenth century (pp. 116–17 and 161–4).

The 1617 map shows that immediately to north and south of the Bower there were small ornamental orchards in the area described in the accounts as the 'New Orchard', which was completed in the 1580s. Beyond the ponds to the east – that is, in the area to the north of the house – lay the 'Old Orchard', which had presumably ceased to be used as such by the early seventeenth century as Senior's map shows it bare of trees. A central pond shown on the map, and the area's proximity to the house, both proclaim its aesthetic function: it doubtless contained seats and 'arbours', and Senior shows some kind of garden building beside the pond, presumably the two-storey stone tower which appears here in the copy of the seventeenth-century painting attributed to Siebrechts. The main gardens, however, lay to the south – that is, they occupied the area to the south and east of the house. As early as 1560 a letter written by Bess of Hardwick refers to the 'letell garden weche ys by the newe howse', and describes her intention to 'sowe yt with all kind of earbes and flowres, and some pece of it with malos'.[38] Senior's map seems to show, immediately to the east of the house, a terrace with two small garden buildings or banqueting houses at each end – probably the two 'turrets' which are mentioned in an inventory of 1601. It also shows what is probably a fountain, as well as two obelisks and a feature, close to the south wall, which may be the 'turret in the mount'. This latter feature was presumably a garden building on a viewing mound or prospect mount, and is again mentioned in the inventory of 1601.[39] To judge from contemporary gardens of similar status, there would also have been 'knots' – that is, complex, interlaced patterns of boxwork – along with covered arbours and gravel walks, as well as areas of lawn (there were payments for 'mowing in the Garden and New Orchard' in 1577).[40]

Senior's depiction of a fountain in this area is corroborated elsewhere. Several sources indicate that there were waterworks at Chatsworth by the early seventeenth century, exploiting, as those of later generations were to do, the hydraulic possibilities provided by an abundant supply of water on the moors above the house, and the precipitous descent to the gardens below. Thomas Hobbes' poem *De Mirabilibus Pecci* of c. 1628 refers to:

> The Water that from native cliffs had source
> Once free and unconfin'd, throughout its course
> By its own Country metal is led on
> Captive to Rocks of Artificial stone.
> There buried deep, its streams it doubly throws
> Into two circling Channels as it goes
> Through thousand crannies, which by art it does
> Then girds the Rock with many a hollow vain,
> Frighting all under with surprising rain,
> Thence turning it a marble font does store,
> Until its lofty brims can hold no more.[41]

The deer park and warren

As already noted, Senior's map[42] shows that an extensive area to the east of the hall formed a large deer park (Figures 10, 19). Parks were the indispensable status symbol of the age, used in part for recreational hunting but also to produce venison for consumption by the household: parks were deer farms,

44

and venison the elite food par excellence, reserved for the rich, bestowed as a mark of particular favour.[43] Because the name 'Old Park' is now used to describe the densely-treed area to the *south* of the house and gardens, it is sometimes assumed that in the sixteenth and seventeenth centuries the deer park was limited to this area, or else to the escarpment, running northwards to the Stand and beyond. While the park did include the largely wooded slopes of Stand Wood both to the north and south of the house, it mostly lay on the level shelf above the Millstone Grit escarpment, and encroached into a vast expanse of moorland to either side and on even higher land to the east. This upper area is described on the map as *The Laundes*, perhaps to distinguish its more open aspect from the area of the park running along the escarpment, which had extensive tree cover. Most parks were more densely wooded than that at Chatsworth, and the word *laund* (which has given us the modern word 'lawn') was used to denote open glades within them.

Much of the boundary of the park can still be traced on the ground today, in the form of a prominent drystone wall. Most, if not all, of the wall has been rebuilt at various times since Senior's map was surveyed (the estate accounts are full of references to its repair). The oldest surviving section is probably the eastern part of the southern boundary, towards the top of the escarpment. This is built of large orthostatic stones and boulders, gathered from the surface, roughly squared and laid in courses. It is between 1.5 and 2 m high – to deter deer from jumping over it – and is surmounted by poorly-shaped coping stones.

The lower, more sheltered parts of the park, along and immediately below the escarpment, were more like a conventional deer park in appearance, in that they comprised areas of wood pasture in which wood and timber were produced but livestock – in this case, principally deer – were also grazed. Most of this land is now occupied by much later woodland, but part survives as the area now called the Deer Park, to the south of the house and gardens, as well as in the area to the north, although here in more fragmented form. Most of the ancient oak trees were once pollarded; only a minority seem to have been left to grow uncut, as timber trees. Some of these have only relatively small side branches indicating they were regularly shredded – that is, stripped to provide fodder for the deer. These pollarded and unpollarded oaks are the most ancient trees in Chatsworth Park: precisely *how* ancient is difficult to say because regular pollarding tends to reduce the rate at which trees put on girth. In other words, old though these trees appear, they are probably older still (Figure 20).

Shortly after the Cavendishes acquired the estate, for a brief time at least, the park was also used for industrial purposes. In 1571 the Earl imported eleven workmen from the Mendips in Somerset to build and operate a new and experimental type of lead smelter known as an ore hearth footblast.[44] This was presumably located high in the park, well out of view of the house, and was used until 1573–4 when a new water-powered smelter was built elsewhere on the estate. During this short time it produced about 60 tons of lead and to do this a significant amount of timber from the park must have been felled for

FIGURE 20.
One of the ancient
oaks growing within
the parkland to the
north of the house.

use as fuel. As we shall see, this was not the only industrial episode during the life of the deer park.

Senior's map shows that smaller deer enclosures, called the 'Newe Park' and the 'Roe Park', existed below the main area of parkland, in the immediate vicinity of the gardens, to north and south respectively. These may have been more ornamental in character than the wider parkland, areas in which the family and guests could take exercise beneath the trees. They would also have provided a pleasing view from the house, particularly necessary as the main area of parkland, on the exposed ground above the escarpment, would have been quite out of sight. Many large houses in the late Middle Ages and in Tudor times had such areas close to the mansion, often referred to as 'little parks'. Aesthetic pleasures were not confined to the area close to the house, however. The fact that, in the early seventeenth century, the deer park occupied not only the sloping ground of the escarpment but also an extensive tract of rough ground above it explains the location of the Stand, the tall sixteenth-century tower which still exists on the crest of the slope, clearly visible from the house and gardens (Figure 21). This was probably erected in the 1570s and is clearly shown on Senior's map. Its name implies that it was used as a

'standing', a vantage point from which the movements of the deer could be observed, and from which non-participants could enjoy, vicariously, the thrill of the chase. A tall tower, with four circular angle turrets carrying domed caps and mullion and transom windows, the Stand was described by one visitor in 1662 as a 'neat rotundo or Summer house' which was located 'upon a peake at the top of the Hill ... which seems as if it hangs over the other [the mansion] a quarter of a mile high in the Aire'.[45]

In spite of its name the Stand probably had a range of uses. Like the Bower and other buildings scattered around the grounds it may have functioned in part as a banqueting house and general place of resort. Indeed, it is perhaps best interpreted as one of a family of Elizabethan buildings described as 'lodges' – large, elaborate structures located at a distance from the mansion, used to escape from the rigid formality of contemporary social gatherings: as a setting for less formal parties, for solitary contemplation, or for love affairs. The Stand's position, carefully sited on the crest of the escarpment at the only point where a prominent spur projects westwards, would have allowed not only views along the west-facing slope and out across the level rough ground above, but also a panorama over the Derwent valley below. Such a prospect would have appealed to contemporaries. They clearly relished the strong visual contrast between the wild, uncultivated upland, and the more settled scenes in the valley below. Some sense of this is conveyed by Charles Cotton:

Chatsworth:
A Landscape
History

> To view from hence the glittering *Pile* above
> (Which must at once Wonder create and Love)
> Environ'd round with *Natures* Shames,
> and Ills, Black Heaths, wild Rocks, bleak Craggs, and naked Hills
> And the whole *Prospect* so inform, and rude?
> Who is it, but must presently conclude
> That this is *Paradise*, which seated stands
> In midst of *Desarts*, and of barren *Sands*
> So a bright *Diamond* would look, if set
> In a vile *socket* of ignoble *jet*.[46]

The view would have included, at this time, not only the ponds, orchards and gardens around the hall and the tree-scattered slopes of the escarpment, but also the fields around the village of Edensor on the western side of the Derwent. However, not all the ground to the west of the river was occupied by farmland. As already noted, a very extensive area to the north-east of the village, running down to the river and in clear view of the house, is shown on Senior's map of Edensor as a '*Cunigre*', a rabbit warren.[47] Rabbits had been introduced into England by the Normans and were for a long period semi-domesticated animals, kept in special enclosures.[48] They were valued both for their meat and for their fur. On some warrens special mounds were built, called 'buries' by contemporaries but 'pillow mounds' by modern archaeologists. These were usually less than a metre in height, rectangular or oval in shape, and usually surrounded by a ditch. They provided shelter for the animals, especially when a warren was first established, but also served to create constricted areas of burrows which would be easy and convenient to net.[49] Within the area marked as a warren by Senior, eight low, oval mounds still survive within the parkland turf, each c. 10–15 m long and about half this in width. Most are fairly indistinct, and rather lower than most earthworks of this type: they also now lack the usual encircling ditches. But they are clearly pillow mounds, and their current condition is perhaps the consequence of the ploughing of the warren which, as we shall see, accompanied its destruction in the middle of the eighteenth century.

The sixteenth and seventeenth centuries were an age in which superior resources of production were proudly, boastfully displayed around great mansions. Water mill, orchards, barns and farmyards lay in close proximity to Chatsworth House in a way that eighteenth-century observers would have found puzzling and distasteful. But above all, Senior's maps show with particular clarity the way that Chatsworth lay at the centre of a landscape devoted to the production of exotic foods, denied to the generality of the population: the house was surrounded by great ponds stocked with carp and other fish, by an extensive rabbit warren, and by a vast park full of deer. These were necessary to sustain the lifestyle of a great household. But they also served to display to the world at large the status of the Cavendish family, as much as their elaborate gardens and their imposing mansion.

The development of the gardens under the first three earls

Elizabeth of Hardwick died on February 13 1608 and, because she had no surviving children by her other husbands, Chatsworth and the other estates passed to her sons by her second marriage, William and Charles Cavendish.[50] It was William who inherited the Hardwick and Chatsworth portions of the estate. He had already been created Baron Cavendish of Hardwick in 1605, and in 1618 he was made Earl of Devonshire. The geographical element in this title, as in all such titles, had no significance. Indeed, the Cavendish family has never owned a single acre in Devon. William died in 1625 and Chatsworth passed to his son, the 2nd Earl, an individual who seems to have achieved little and, in the words of one historian, was 'notable merely for his extravagant way of life'.[51] He died three years later and the estate passed in turn to his son, the 3rd Earl, an individual more involved in national politics and, in particular, a prominent supporter of Charles I in the run-up to, and during, the Civil War. Like many royalists he went into exile following the defeat of the king, but returned in 1646 – having paid an appropriate sum to the revolutionary government for the return of his estates – and, at the Restoration of Charles II in 1660, was appointed Lord Lieutenant of Derbyshire and spent much of his life at court. He was, among other things, the patron of the philosopher Thomas Hobbes.[52]

It would be easy to assume that the gardens created by William Cavendish and Elizabeth of Hardwick survived largely unaltered until the 1680s when, with the extensive rebuilding of the house by the 4th Earl, vast new gardens, famous throughout the land, were created. But there is little doubt that the gardens continued to evolve under the 4th Earl's three predecessors, although the paucity of surviving documents from this period makes it impossible to chart their development in detail. The eighteenth-century copy of the mid seventeenth-century painting of Chatsworth, attributed to the Dutch artist Siebrechts, thus shows many of the features familiar from Senior's map,[53] but also suggests that the gardens to the south of the house had been remodelled in line with contemporary fashions. A simple parterre of grass and gravel now surrounded a central pond, an arrangement clearly in seventeenth- rather than sixteenth-century style. More extensive changes may have occurred under the 3rd Earl. John Walker, visiting Chatsworth in 1677, described 'a kind of hanging Garden cutt out in Walkes under ye Rockes with Basins, Jettos, and Fountains but as yet unfinished'.[54] But there is little doubt that it was only with the accession of the 4th Earl in 1684 that the serious transformation of Chatsworth, into one of the greatest gardens in England, was begun.

CHAPTER THREE

A Baroque Landscape:
Chatsworth under the First
and Second Dukes

Introduction

The mansion and gardens created at Chatsworth in the late seventeenth century were among the most magnificent in England. We are particularly fortunate in having a remarkably detailed depiction of them, in the form of an engraving published in Johannes Kip and Leonard Knyff's *Britannia Illustrata* of 1707 (Figure 22), itself based on a drawing made by Knyff in 1699. Like all the other engravings in that famous volume, this shows the landscape from an impossible aerial vantage point. Only from such an elevated perspective could the full scale of such a design be appreciated. This great ensemble was, as we shall see, the work of a host of architects, designers, sculptors, craftsmen, nurserymen and engineers. But it was above all a monument to the achievements of one man: William Cavendish, 4th Earl and 1st Duke of Devonshire.

Born in 1640, he acceded to the earldom in 1684. Unlike his two predecessors, he was neither a prominent courtier nor a staunch supporter of the Stuarts.[1] The 1680s brought further political crisis in England, for on the death of Charles II the throne passed to James, Duke of York – a Roman Catholic. As MP for Derbyshire, the Earl opposed his succession to the throne, and when James was crowned he was promptly fined the enormous sum of £30,000 by the new king. James was politically inept, antagonising Parliament and the political establishment in a number of ways; but he was old, and it was generally assumed that he would soon die and be succeeded by his Protestant daughter Mary, who had married the ruler (or *Statdholder*) of Holland, William of Orange. But in 1688, against all expectations, James had a son. He would be brought up a Catholic, thus threatening the re-establishment of a permanent Catholic monarchy in England. This was more than many in England were prepared to stand and a group of seven important political figures signed an invitation to William to come and take the English throne. One of them was William Cavendish.

William of Orange and his army landed at Torbay in Devon on 5 November

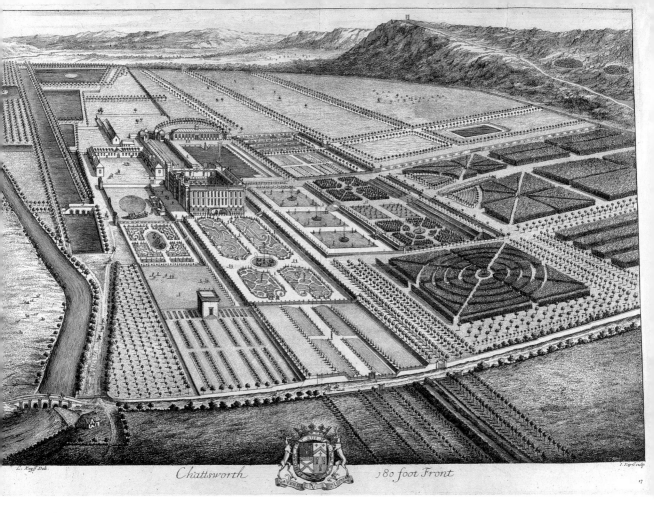

FIGURE 22.

This famous view of Chatsworth was drawn in 1699 and published in 1707 in Kip and Knyff's *Britannia Illustrata*. Although not apparent in the drawing, the Baroque mansion and its gardens were still under development: the Canal Pond has yet to be dug, the Cascade will soon be lengthened and the Cascade House constructed. The old Elizabethan West Front of the house can just be seen, contrasting sharply with the modern, flamboyant south facade, recently completed.

1688, and marched on London. James' forces melted away, James himself fled to France, and Parliament asked William and Mary to become joint king and queen. By the so-called 'Glorious Revolution' the powers of Parliament were secured by the Bill of Rights, which limited the power of the monarch in significant ways; while the subsequent Act of Settlement laid down that no Catholic could succeed to the throne, and that no monarch could marry a Catholic. The Earl reaped rich rewards from his timely support of William. He was made Lord Lieutenant of Derbyshire and, in 1694, Duke of Devonshire and Marquis of Hartington. He continued to be actively involved in politics.[2] He was, in particular, closely associated with a further Act of Settlement in 1701, which made the members of the House of Hanover heirs to the throne on the death of William: when William died in 1712 he was duly succeeded by Anne.

A passion for building

The Earl, later the Duke, began to rebuild the old Elizabethan house even before the triumph of William of Orange brought particular wealth and prestige to himself and his family.[3] Originally, it seems, he intended only to reconstruct the South Front in a more up-to-date style: and 'when he had finisht this Parte, he meant to go no farther'.[4] But in the event he embarked on a building campaign which continued intermittently for twenty years, and completely transformed the old mansion. Daniel Defoe, writing in 1720, wryly remarked how the house 'had received Additions, as it did every Year, and perhaps would to this Day, had the Duke liv'd, who had a genius for such Things beyond the reach of the most perfect Masters, and was not only capable to design, but to finish'.[5]

The late seventeenth century was a time of great change in architecture, a period in which England became particularly open to foreign influences, especially from France and the Low Countries. During the Civil War many landowners had fled to, or been exiled on, the Continent, where they had been exposed to the latest foreign fashions. Returning home, they were keen to copy what they had seen on their own estates. But in addition, the royal court – which still set the pace in matters of fashion – was now more than ever influenced by, and connected with, the royal houses of continental Europe. Charles II had been brought up in France, at the court of Louis XIV; James was a confirmed francophile (his Catholic leanings were really one manifestation of this); and William III was, as we have seen, a Dutchman.

The Civil War of 1642–49 thus marked a watershed in English architecture. After the Restoration of 1660 great mansions were no longer built in the old way, around courtyards. Compact, symmetrical designs, two or three rooms deep, variously influenced by French and Dutch models, were now the norm. The grandest were constructed in a style which architectural historians call the *Baroque*. This took Renaissance ideas, ultimately derived from classical models, but used them flexibly and dramatically, almost as a piece of architectural theatre. The massing of voids and spaces and the pattern of windows were contrived to particular effect, most notably to inspire awe and deference. Much use was made of flamboyant decoration – urns and statues littered rooflines, heavy key-stones added authority to doors and windows. The style had originated during the Catholic Counter-Reformation in the sixteenth century, but had then been adopted by the great royal houses of Europe for the design of their mansions and palaces. In the eighteenth century English writers and theorists rejected the Baroque, castigating it as a badge of foreign absolutism, and instead adopted a much more rigid interpretation of classical architecture – 'Palladianism'.[6] But in the 1670s and 80s it did not carry this kind of intellectual baggage. It was simply the accepted style for the grandest houses, of royalty or great courtiers.

The Earl selected William Talman as architect for the new South Front (Figure 23). Talman was soon to become one of the greatest architects in

England but was at this time still in the early stages of his career. The Earl may have come into contact with him, or heard of him, because he was involved in the rebuilding of Thoresby in the neighbouring county of Nottinghamshire: it was, in turn, probably the prominence acquired through working at Chatsworth that, in 1689, helped Talman to obtain the post of Comptroller of the King's Works at Hampton Court. At Chatsworth a constellation of talented men worked under him, masters in their respective fields: Benjamin Jackson as master mason; John Cressell as master carpenter; the fashionable artists Antonio Verrio and Louis Laguerre; the modish French metalworker Jean Tijou; and the Danish sculptor Gabriel Cibber, who had also worked at Thoresby.[7] And working beneath *them* was a veritable army of local labourers and artisans. The new work was principally carried out using local Millstone Grit, which was mainly quarried from Bakewell Edge and Whicksop Edge, both west of Calton Pasture on land in Bakewell parish where the Vernon family, later Dukes of Rutland, were lords of the manor; but stone also came from smaller quarries at Beeley, Calton and at unspecified locations 'in the park'.[8] The 'marble' (polished limestone) used in the interior was acquired from quarries further afield, at Calver, about 5 km north of Chatsworth, and from Roche Abbey near Rotherham in Yorkshire.

Work was underway by the start of 1687, and proceeded swiftly and to plan: by 1689 Laguerre and Ricard were painting the revamped chapel. The great staircase, with the Grotto at its base, was begun in 1688 – there is some dispute over whether it was part of the original plan, or a subsequent addition, an example of the constant changes of mind to which the Duke was subject. The project, which included new state rooms and hall, was largely completed by 1692. By this time, however, work had commenced on the East Front, the range which contained the main service areas of the building – the kitchens, storerooms and the like (Figure 24).[9]

The Duke's decision to extend his building works was no doubt encouraged by the improvement in the family fortunes following the 'Glorious Revolution' of 1688. In the words of Kennet, the Duke's chaplain, in the oration which he made at his funeral in 1708, 'seeing Publick Affairs in a happier Settlement, for a Testimony of Ease and Joy, he undertook the east side of the Quadrangle, and rais'd it entirely new, in Conformity to the South'.[10] But the decision to rebuild may already have been taken as early as 1687, before the successful outcome of the Revolution was assured. Either way, construction began in 1689 and the sources make it clear that the work involved not simply alterations to the existing structure, but – as Kennet's words imply – wholesale demolition and rebuilding.[11] Indeed, the contract drawn up with Talman stipulates 'a certain building to be erected and built in a workmanlike manner on the East side of Chatsworth house ... being in front One hundred and fforty foot, or thereabouts, and Sixty foot in front on the North side of the said house'.[12] The principal room was to be a 'Gallery' on the first floor, now the Library, with 'two winding staircases of stone att each end'. Above the gallery was to be an apartment, now the Leicester Apartment; below, on the ground

FIGURE 23.

The South Front of Chatsworth House, designed by William Talman and completed around 1692. In the foreground is the Triton and Sea Horses fountain, by Caius Gabriel Cibber. The surrounding lawn was once occupied by the great parterre laid out by George London and Henry Wise in 1694. © THE DEVONSHIRE COLLECTION, CHATSWORTH. REPRODUCED BY PERMISSION OF THE CHATSWORTH SETTLEMENT TRUSTEES.

floor, the service rooms. The building was finally completed in 1696, after problems with money, and acrimonious disputes with a number of the master-craftsmen.

Two facades out of four had now been rebuilt in fashionable style: whether the Duke considered this a provisional situation, or whether he intended the contrast between the old Elizabethan North and West Fronts, and the modern South and East Fronts, to be a permanent feature, is unclear. He certainly made moves to provide some degree of harmony between the disparate elevations. A new forecourt was thus built immediately in front of the Elizabethan West Front. It comprised two large stone pedestals, surmounted by sphinxes and embellished with classical trophies, which were connected by an elaborate gilded iron palisade made partly by Tijou and partly by a London smith called William Marshall.[13]

After 1696 there was a pause in major building operations. In Kennet's words, the Duke 'seem'd then content to say, that he had gone half way through, and would leave the rest for his Heir. In this Resolution he stop'd about seven Years'.[14] But in fact the Duke continued, in a more modest way, to work on the house, and in particular to make further moves to soften the contrast between the styles of the various elevations. These included the construction, from 1696, of the terrace immediately below the West Front, on which the house still stands. This is the stage the house had reached when it was depicted by Knyff in his view of 1699: both the Duke's up-to-date South Front, and the Elizabethan West Front, complete with new terrace and fore-court, are visible (Figure 22).

The Duke soon turned again to more substantial building projects. For him, as for many great landowners of the seventeenth and eighteenth century, architecture was in effect a hobby: and each improvement made to the house invited and encouraged further refinements and alterations. In 1700 work duly began on the West Front, and continued until 1702 (Figure 25). He had now got rid of the various master-craftsmen with whom

FIGURE 24.
The East Front of Chatsworth House (centre), also designed by William Talman. The second of the house's elevations to be rebuilt by the 1st Duke, it was completed in 1696. To the right is Wyatville's addition of the early nineteenth century. © THE DEVONSHIRE COLLECTION, CHATSWORTH. REPRODUCED BY PERMISSION OF THE CHATSWORTH SETTLEMENT TRUSTEES.

he had been in dispute and employed instead a new set of men, mainly from the local area; and instead of, as formerly, paying lump sums to contractors, the work was now largely supervised directly by the estate.[15] William Talman was no longer employed as architect, and the designer of the West Front remains uncertain, although it was probably the Duke himself, perhaps advised by others, most notably the architect Thomas Archer. Archer was one of the few English architects who had actually studied Baroque architecture first-hand, in Europe, and his designs show an easy familiarity with the work of architects such as Bernini and Borromini. He was the principal architect of the final building campaign, the remodelling of the North Front. Work on this began in 1705 and was completed in 1708. The Duke had, however, died in the previous year: his will included a bequest of £200 to Archer, 'in acknowledgement of his favour and his care and trouble touching the building of my house'.[16]

The Duke's new gardens

Such an up-to-date house demanded appropriate gardens, and these were duly established. Indeed, work on the grounds began even before construction of the South Front commenced. But to understand the significance of the great design depicted by Kip and Knyff we need to first say something briefly about the wider cultural context. The late seventeenth century was a period in which French and Dutch influence was felt as strongly in the design of gardens as in that of houses: but in many ways this is a more difficult and problematic subject. Some garden historians feel confident in identifying distinct 'Dutch' and 'French' styles of garden design, and of seeing their influence in particular features of English gardens of the period. Put simply, seventeenth-century French gardens – as designed by André le Nôtre or André Mollet, and typified by the vast ornamental landscapes associated with the great palaces at Versailles or the Tuilleries – were larger than Dutch ones, less compartmentalised, and more integrated with the wider landscape. Avenues were prominent, often extending out across forests, parks and hunting ground; so too were cascades, fountains and other elaborate water features. Most displayed a clear and recurrent hierarchy of spaces and elements, derived ultimately from Italian Renaissance gardens. In the immediate area of the mansion were *parterres de broderie*, swirling arabesques defined by low-cut box hedges, the spaces between filled with bedding plants or – more usually – gravel or coloured earth. Beyond lay *parterres de gazon*, plain areas of turf fringed by topiary. Lastly, at a distance, were *bosquets* or ornamental woods, which in England were commonly described as 'wildernesses'. All these features, and areas, were arranged on either side of a strong central axis, focused on the main facade of the house, which was often extended as an avenue far into the surrounding countryside. But in the largest gardens the two sides of this main vista were not necessarily arranged in rigid symmetry. Instead, le Nôtre and other writers advocated the idea of 'balance' – forms and features on either side should be similar, but not necessarily identical.[17]

Dutch gardens, in contrast, were much more compartmentalised, a series of separate experiences – distinct 'outdoor rooms', defined by hedges or lines of trees.[18] They were usually clearly cut off from the surrounding countryside in a similar manner, or by wide moats – vistas did not extend out through parks or forests, which were rare in the Low Countries. Although in some gardens (such as Honslarsdijk) there was a strong central axis, with the various compartments arranged either side with strict symmetry, in most there were several axes, equally strong. Terraces and avenues were of minor importance and cascades and fountains of negligible significance, although canals and moats were important. Extensive topiary, and displays of flowers, were prominent, the latter often arranged as *cutwork parterres*, geometric designs in which the pattern was defined by shaped flower beds, cut into the turf. In some gardens the old Renaissance tradition of using pergolas and arbours, or tunnels of vegetation trained on trellis work, was continued; sometimes entire pavilions might be constructed in this way.[19]

Both French and Dutch gardens drew on a common heritage of design, derived ultimately from Renaissance Italy, and the differences between them were less dramatic than many historians – and indeed, the above account – might suggest. We must avoid what one scholar has described as the 'confusions which can be caused by being too specific about French and Dutch influences on English gardens'.[20] While some thus see canals – linear areas of water – as an essentially 'Dutch' feature, others have emphasised their importance at classic French sites like Versailles. Such differences as there were between French and Dutch garden styles largely reflected the particular characteristics of the nations concerned. Seventeenth-century Holland was a Protestant Republic which had thrown off the authority of Spain, and which was ruled by an elite of gentry and merchants which had grown rich on international trade. Densely populated, it lacked the land necessary for large parks, extensive forests and chases. The level polderlands, moreover, made it difficult to construct terraces, cascades, or fountains, and at the same time required the provision of drainage canals and sheltering hedges. France could scarcely have been more different: a centralised absolutist monarchy dominated by a rich court aristocracy. French gardens were created by the king and his leading courtiers and ministers – men with land and money to spend.[21]

To some extent aspects of 'French' and 'Dutch' style can be picked out in the gardens of late seventeenth century England; but only to some extent. Even in their homelands, the two styles – in so far as they had ever been distinct and separate – begin to mix and blur in the middle and later decades of the century, especially in Holland where the increasing power of the *Stadtholders* was reflected in the growing magnificence of their gardens and in the adoption of many classically 'French' features, such as *parterres de broderie*. The gardens created by William of Orange before he came to England at his great hunting seat of Het Loo, while still retaining the divided, compartmentalised form of

the traditional Dutch garden, were replete with avenues, extensive displays of *broderie*, and cascades. Indeed, during the second half of the seventeenth century ingenious methods were found by Dutch engineers and garden designers to overcome the absence of natural gradients which, in French gardens, usually provided the necessary heads of waters for water features and fountains. At Soestdijk, for example, the two fountains in the north garden were driven by a windmill.[22] William of Orange was particularly interested in waterworks and fountains; as early as 1671 he was personally involved in the reconstruction of the water supply system at the palace of Honselaarsdijk.[23] There were, as already noted, elaborate cascades at Het Loo, and fountains and waterworks featured at William's other Dutch residences. He inherited the hunting lodge at Dieren from his father and remodelled it extensively, with terraces, lakes, grottoes and fountains. One visitor, in 1696, described how 'The bouling Green, Arbour of Venus round a great Pond, the Grotto, a Cupid drowning in a fountain, are all very entertaining. There are alsoe several Pretty Inventions for wetting Gentlemen and Ladies'.[24] In 1689, the year after he became king of England, William made Hampton Court – just outside London – the main royal residence and revamped the gardens in a style which was more French than Dutch. The Great Fountain Garden, laid out in 1689, featured extensive *parterres de broderie* designed by the Frenchman Daniel Marot (one of the key architects of the Franco-Dutch style), and thirteen fountains, as well as a 'goose-foot' arrangement of avenues. The overall designer was William Talman, the architect of Chatsworth. Nevertheless, while French ideas and features were increasingly adopted in Dutch gardens in the later seventeenth century, the overall layout of space continued to differ. Well into the 1690s, 'Dutch' gardens remained more compartmentalised, more a series of green rooms than a single, awe-inspiring experience.[25]

In many ways the gardens at Chatsworth, as illustrated by Kip and Knyff (Figure 22), epitomised the mixed Anglo/French/Dutch style dominant in the last decades of the seventeenth century, with parterres of box, formal arrangements of trees, terraces, canals, *bosquets* and elaborate waterworks. The waterworks were not only French in inspiration, but were actually designed by French engineers; some of the sculpture was by French artists, some by Dutch; the great parterres were in the French fashion but designed by English gardeners; and the greenhouse reflected an enthusiasm for horticulture which derived more from Dutch than from French traditions.

The Earl began to work on the gardens soon after his accession in 1684, spending the incredible sum of £4,325 on them in 1686 alone.[26] This phase of the work involved vast amounts of earth-movement and, in particular, alterations to the elaborate complex of ponds shown on Senior's map of 1617 in the area to the west of the house.[27] The southernmost pond, the central pond and the western sections of the two northern ponds were thrown into a single long canal, flanked by tree-lined walks (described in the accounts as the 'New Walk' and the 'Sycamore Walk'). This rivalled in size the canal built two decades later to the south of the house, which is still a major feature of the gardens. The work was completed in 1685.[28] Next, in 1688, a contract was drawn up with George London for the creation of a parterre in the area immediately to the south of the new forecourt, an area which had originally formed a corner of the New Park.[29] George London was the most important designer and nurseryman in late seventeenth-century England. He had originally worked as gardener to Henry Compton, Bishop of London, who had been tutor to Mary II and officiated at her wedding to William of Orange; Compton's garden at Fulham contained one of the richest horticultural collections in Britain. London left Fulham in 1689 to take up the post of gardener at Hampton Court. But, as well as being retained by these great establishments, he also worked as a nurseryman on his own account, and with three others founded the famous Brompton Park Nursery in London in 1681 (it covered some 40 ha in the area where the South Kensington museums now stand). In 1688 he went into partnership with another famous gardener, Henry

Wise, and together they provided designs and plants for all the greatest gardens in the land, including Castle Howard, Longleat, Canons, as well as the royal residences of Kensington Palace and Hampton Court. By the late 1690s Wise was concentrating on the royal parks and gardens – becoming, from 1702, master gardener to Queen Anne – while London ranged more widely across the kingdom, advising and planting at innumerable great residences.[30] In the words of Stephen Switzer, the early eighteenth-century garden designer and writer, 'The planting and raising of all sorts of trees is so much due to this undertaking that 'twill be hard for any of posterity to lay their hands on a tree in any of these kingdoms that have not been a part of their care'.[31]

The Chatsworth contract describes how 'George London, gardiner' was to 'make or cause to be made one peace of ground for the Rt Honble ye earle of Devonshire ... wich peece of ground is scituate on ye west side of ye great parterre'. London was to lay out the work and set out the 'turfe gravell or sand', although these materials were to be brought to the site 'at the Rt Honble ye earle of Devonshire's charge'. After this, the parterre was to be finished 'fitt for planting'.[32] For all this London was to be paid the sum of £120. Between August 1690 and March 1691 a large number of plants was 'sent out of Brompton parke': 5000 'slips' of green lavender, 5000 of white lavender, 3000 lavender 'spike', 1,000 Roman lavender, 2000 'common lavender', ten striped (i.e., variegated) hollies, six striped phylleria, six striped box, ten scorpion sena, ten standard scorpion sena, 40 standard white lavender, 40 green standard lavender, 20 standard Roman lavender, unspecified quantities of 'firs' and 'three sortes of time', and one scarlet honeysuckle.[33] What proportion of these plants was destined for the parterres is unclear; for example, the nineteen peaches, four apricots, and three plum trees purchased in March 1690 from the nursery were presumably intended for the orchard grounds or kitchen garden.

In 1688, the same year in which London started the western parterre, the old bridge over the river by the south-west corner of the gardens was rebuilt; we do not know if this was due to its bad state or, alternatively, to improve coach access and perhaps to enhance the visual appearance of the approach route to the house and gardens. Six years later, in 1694, a contract was drawn up for another new parterre, this time in the area immediately below the new South Front, which by this time was nearing completion. Some kind of formal design evidently existed here already, perhaps created by the 3rd Earl before 1684 and shown on Siberecht's painting of c. 1680. Indeed, the previous contract, of 1688, describes the area then to be designed by London as lying *to the west of the great parterre.* The new contract was made not only with George London but also with Henry Wise, his partner.[34] This parterre was to be 473 feet (144 m) long, north to south, and 227 feet (69 m) wide. The 'middle line walk' was to be of gravel, 'near 414 feet long [126 m] and near 30' [9 m] broad'. Another north–south walk (the contract refers to a plan, now lost) was to be 440 feet (134 m) long and 24 feet (7 m) wide. The 'cross walk next the house' was to be 179 feet (54 m) long and 30 feet (9 m) wide, as were the 'Crosse walk

at the fountaine' and the 'crosse walk next the Iron worke at the head of the
garden'. The parterre was thus divided into four sections or 'quarters'. These
were of unequal size, however, for the contract states that those nearer the
house were to be 'near 227 foot [69 m]' long, implying those further away
(allowing for the width of the cross paths) were to be around half this length.
This arrangement, confirmed by the evidence of Kip and Knyff's illustration,
may perhaps have been intended to create a 'false perspective' effect, making
the gardens appear rather larger than they really were when viewed from the
windows of the house (Figure 22).

The larger quarters near the house were to have borders 5 feet (1.5 m) wide,
'of good Earth fit to receave such a Collection of hardy Ever-greens and
flowering trees, Shrubs and flowers as his Grace hereafter shall be pleased to
order to be collected'. Around the borders there was to be a 'division of Sparr'
(perhaps calcite or fluorspar from the local lead mines) 'of near 4 foot [1.22 m]
broad'. The two southerly quarters were different. These, too, were to have
planted borders but 'the quarter is to be of that worke called cutt worke in
grasses, with centres of two statues and four trees in cases, the cutts in grasses
are to be covered with ye brightest sand as is near that place'. At the corners
of the quarters large pots of plants were to be set. The fountain, placed 245
feet (74 m) away from the house at the intersection of the central walks, was
to be 56 feet (17 m) in diameter. The contract states that the 'fountain which
now stands within [blank] foot of ye House shall be taken up, that is all the
materials as stone worke, Lead, Iron, Pipes and Figures, all wch are to be
brought to the Place where the new fountaine is designed and placed, and
there to be completely finished in six weekes time after ye worke is begun, all
wch worke is to be finished at his Grace's expense'. The term 'figures' presumably refers to the Triton and Sea Horses fountain, which still stands here,
carved by Caius Gabriel Cibber in the years from 1688 to 1691 (Figure 23).[35]
The new parterre cost £350, but further work – apparently changing the
ground level within it – was carried out later in the year by the Brompton Park
partners, at an extra cost of £150.[36]

The activities of London and Wise were limited, so far as the evidence goes,
to the layout of the two great parterres near the house. But the wider landscape was also being transformed. Through the late 1680s and early 1690s the
area of the gardens was massively expanded: the rest of the New Park, and part
of the main deer park, were now brought into the grounds and systematically
landscaped. The Bowling Green, which lay to the south of the western
parterre, was created between 1688 and 1699.[37] In 1688 the 'gravell walke that
goes to the bowling green' was made, and earth removed from the area of the
New Park, as this was being levelled, used to level the site.[38] In the following
year the foundations for the walls were dug, and between 1692 and 1699 the
walls themselves erected.[39] The 'Bowling Green House' – a substantial stone
structure in imitation of a classical temple, probably designed by William
Talman – was built between 1693 and 1695 (it can clearly be seen on Knyff's
engraving, on the south side of the Green itself); bowls was a game at the

FIGURE 26.
Flora's Temple,
originally called the
Bowling Green House,
was built between 1693
and 1695. Kip and
Knyff's engraving
(Figure 22) shows it
standing in its original
position, beside the
bowling green to the
south-west of the
House. It was moved
to its present location
around 1750.

height of fashion at this time, and all houses of any status had a bowling green in their grounds.[40] The building, renamed 'Flora's Temple', was later moved to a new site, and now stands at the public entrance to the gardens (Figure 26). North of the entrance courtyard at the West Front of the house a range of ornamental bird houses was erected between 1697 and 1699, together with new stables and offices.

At roughly the same time – between 1694 and 1696 – the great Cascade, designed by the Frenchman Monsieur Grillet and perhaps the most impressive of the many waterworks at Chatsworth, was constructed to the south-east of the house.[41] This preceded the feature which we see here today and was a shorter yet, in some ways, more complicated affair, to judge from the description made by Celia Fiennes in 1697, shortly after it had been completed:

Beyond this is a bason in wch are ye branches of two Artichock Leaves wch weeps at ye End of Each Leafe into the bason wch is placed at ye foote of Lead steps 30 in number. The Lowest step is very deep, and between Every 4 stepps is a half pace all made of Lead and are broad on Each side. On a little banck stands blew balls 10 on a side, and between Each ball are 4 pipes wch by a sluce spouts out water aCross ye stepps to

Each other like an Arbour or arch. While you are thus amused suddenly there runs down a torrent of water out of 2 pitchers in ye hands of two Large nimphs Cut in stone that Lyes in the upper step wch makes a pleasing prospect ...[42]

In 1697 the area of the Old Orchard, lying immediately to the north-east of the house, was brought into the new gardens and the great Greenhouse was built.[43] This still survives, albeit altered in later years and re-erected on a slightly different site. It is built of stone, with twelve sash windows ranged symmetrically around a central door. This, too, may have been designed by Talman. Such buildings were first developed in Holland at the start of the seventeenth century and were called 'greenhouses' because they were originally used to house tender 'greens', or evergreens, during the winter. They were also often referred to as 'orangeries', because they were used in particular to grow citrus species and similar plants which could survive the

FIGURE 27.
The 1st Duke's Greenhouse was erected in 1697 but, like Flora's Temple, was moved to a new site around 1750. It was altered on a number of subsequent occasions but remains one of the most important seventeenth-century greenhouses surviving in England. © THE DEVONSHIRE COLLECTION, CHATSWORTH. REPRODUCED BY PERMISSION OF THE CHATSWORTH SETTLEMENT TRUSTEES.

northern winters only if provided with a minimum temperature of around eight degrees centigrade. They spread to France in the first half of the seventeenth century but only began to appear in English gardens after the Restoration (William had a particularly fine example at Hampton Court). The 1st Duke's Greenhouse is one of the largest and best-preserved in the country, and was evidently used, in the customary way, for tender and half-hardy plants: both oranges and myrtles were purchased for it in 1698 as it neared completion (Figure 27).[44] As Knyff's 1699 drawing shows, the building originally had a substantial rectangular pond – the 'Greenhouse Pond' – immediately to the south, with a central fountain: this was removed in the following century, and has left virtually no trace. The drawing also shows what appears to be a kitchen garden immediately east of the Greenhouse Pond, which may well have been created or remodelled in the late 1690s. It was removed in 1709–10 when new kitchen gardens were built beyond the edge of the formal gardens to the south-west (pp. 77–8).

The documents make a number of references to statues and fountains in the grounds. The famous Willow Tree Fountain was erected in the mid 1690s, judging by the accounts, which record a number of payments to the sculptor Josiah Ibeck 'for an Artificial Tree of brass for a fountain'.[45] Ibeck came to Chatsworth as Grillet's assistant and was probably also a Frenchman. The feature was plumbed in 1695: it was an example of an *automata*, or water-trick, of the kind which had been very popular in the Renaissance gardens of the sixteenth and seventeenth centuries and which continued to find favour, in Dutch gardens especially, into the late seventeenth century (Figure 28). Celia Fiennes described it in operation:

> There is another green walke and about the middle of it by the Grove stands a fine Willow tree, the leaves barke and all looks very naturall, the roote is full of rubbish or great stones to appearance, and all of a sudden by turning a sluce it raines from each leafe and from the branches like a shower, it being made of brass and pipes to each leafe but in appearance is exactly like a willow.[46]

Another visitor, in 1725, described it as a 'merry conceit wetting the unwary'.[47] It can just be seen, standing in the centre of a circular pond, on Kip and Knyff's engraving. The pond still survives, now called the Ring Pond, but it no longer has the tree at its centre (Figure 29). There were several other ponds and fountains – indeed, fountains and waterworks were the features which most impressed visitors. The 'Neptune Fountain', the 'Boreas Fountain', the 'Fountain in the New Garden', and the 'Greenhouse Fountain', are all referred to in the accounts. The most striking, however, was 'Triton and the Sea Horses', erected in the south parterre in 1691 and retained when this was remodelled by London and Wise three years later.[48] Sculptural fountains were not common in England at this time, so the array at Chatsworth, and Triton in particular, must have seemed particularly impressive. Most were cast or carved by Ibeck, Caius Gabriel Cibber and his assistants, Samuel Watson,

Nadauld, and Richard Osgood; but it was the sculptor Jan Nost who was responsible for the statue of Flora, for which he was paid in 1694.[49] This still survives but, like so much else from the seventeenth-century gardens at Chatsworth, in a different position. It originally stood in the centre of 'Flora's Garden', which occupied the area between the south parterre and the east–west public road, Holmes Lane, which at this time bounded the gardens to the south (it can clearly be seen in this position on Knyff's engraving).

The accounts for the early and mid 1690s show a mass of other activity in the grounds. There was much digging and levelling to make new terraces, or extend old ones: some had painted perspectives at their ends.[50] There was much planting of 'wildernesses' (ornamental woods) and other formal arrangements of trees, on the rising ground to the east of the main garden areas, towards the foot of the escarpment. These included the 'new scotch fir wilderness' made in 1695, which featured '300 Scotch firrs', purchased for 12d each.[51]

Like other gardens created in the later seventeenth century, those at Chatsworth were intended to complement the architecture of the house, to delight, amuse, and impress. To judge from the accounts of most visitors, they succeeded. Celia Fiennes visited in 1697 and described the gardens with infectious enthusiasm:

> Before ye gate there is a Large parke and Severall ffine Gardens one without another with Gravell walkes and Squares of Grass with stone statues in them, and in ye middle of Each Garden is a Large ffountaine full of Images, sea gods and Dolphins and sea horses which are full of pipes which spout out water in the bason and spouts all about the Gardens. 3 gardens just around the house. Out of two of ye Gardens you ascend by Severall Stepps into other Gardens which have some Gravell walks and squares like ye other with Statues and Images in the bason. There is one bason in the Middle of one Garden thats very Large and by sluces besides the Images Severall pipes plays out ye water – about 30 Large and small pipes altogether, some fflush it up that it ffrothes Like snow. There is one Garden full of stone and brass statues. So the Gardens lyes one above another which makes the prospect very fine. Above these gardens is an ascent of 5 or 6 stepps up to a green walk with groves of firrs and a wilderness and Close arbours and shady walks. On each end of one Walke stands two piramidies full of pipes spouting water that runns down one of them – runns on brass hollow worke wch looks like rocks and hollow stones ...[52]

True, there were some dissenting voices, often from individuals politically hostile to the Duke. One in 1690 complained that the gardens had 'nothing extraordinary but their situation, nothing wonderful but their cost, and nothing unusual but their solitariness'.[53] But on the whole, visitors were clearly overwhelmed by the scale of what they saw.

Although the design of the Chatsworth gardens is often attributed to London and Wise they evidently provided designs only for the parterres. As

FIGURE 28. (*opposite*)
The first Willow Tree Fountain was made in the mid-1690s and was immensely popular with seventeenth- and eighteenth-century visitors. This is not the original fountain, but a nineteenth-century copy, and stands in a different position.

FIGURE 29. (*above*)
The Ring Pond is a survivor from the seventeenth-century gardens. It originally lay in the middle of a formal *bosquet* or wilderness, with the Willow Tree Fountain at its centre: it can be seen to the right of Kip and Knyff's aerial view (Figure 23). The *herms*, stone busts on columns, were designed by William Kent in the eighteenth century and were only placed here in 1893. They originally stood in the gardens at Chiswick House. The beech hedges were added in the 1950s.

already noted, the water-features were under the control of the otherwise obscure Grillet. From 1687 to 1706 one Monsieur Huet seems to have been in overall charge of construction work, but there is no evidence that he was the actual designer of the grounds.[54] Indeed, it is possible that no single individual – other than, perhaps, the Earl himself – was really responsible for these magnificent gardens, although William Talman may well have had some hand in the overall design while involved in the construction of the house between 1686 and 1696 (he was, after all, responsible for the design of the royal gardens at Hampton Court); while between 1696 and 1700 his role may to have been taken over by 'Monsieur Audias the French gardener'. Whoever was responsible, the gardens typified – as we have seen – the mixed French/Dutch style which dominated in the grounds of great mansions in the last decades of the seventeenth century. But, in spite of the prominence of French designers like Huet, Grillet and Audias, there is much about their overall layout which appears to owe more to the Dutch than the French tradition. In particular, there is no strong, dominant axis of symmetry, and the gardens were divided into a number of distinct areas, echoing the compartmentalised appearance of gardens in Holland. This is clear not only from the aerial view produced by Kip and Knyff but also from the accounts of visitors like Celia Fiennes, which emphasise not the overall grandeur of the design, but rather the magnificence of the various parts: she talks of 'Severall ffine Gardens one without another', almost like a series of separate rooms. The importance of covered walks and arbours in the wildernesses, so clear from the engraving, is also notable in this context.

The gardens depicted by Kip and Knyff were first considerably modified, and eventually swept away, in subsequent phases of Chatsworth's development and, in spite of their vast scale, relatively few traces of them survive. Of the great terraces which formed such a major feature of the gardens, only the two lowest remain, and in modified form: that on which the house stands, extending south to form the western side of the South Garden and the northern section of the margins of the great platform on which the Canal Pond now sits; and that which lies immediately to the east of the house, and which forms the western edge of the Broad Walk. The line of others can still be detected as very faint earthworks in the Salisbury Lawn. Further hummocks and disturbances to the north probably represent the site of the Greenhouse Pond. A number of other features from the seventeenth-century gardens have, however, survived to the present, although many of these have been altered, moved, or both during the intervening centuries.

Triton and Sea Horses remains in its original position. The Ring Pond also survives, although without the Willow Tree. The Jack Pond – a small pool in the far north-east of the gardens – also seems to date from the 1690s, and was perhaps originally a supply pond for the waterworks further down the hill. The Bowling Green House survives, although it no longer stands in the position shown by Kip and Knyff. It was taken down, stone by stone, in 1749, and re-erected in its present position at the end of the long north–south gravel walk laid out before the East Front. It now forms one of the entrances to the gardens. The statue of Flora has also been moved, for the position it occupied on the 1699 illustration was, as we shall see, soon to be taken by a magnificent new canal. It now stands within the Bowling Green House (thus renamed 'Flora's Temple') and had apparently been placed here before that building was erected on its new site, for an entry in the accounts for 1711, detailing work carried out on the Bowling Green House, refers to 'Repairing ye figure call'd Flora'.[55] The 1st Duke's Greenhouse has likewise been moved and altered in a number of ways. It was given a new roof in 1718;[56] reconstructed on a new site, slightly to the south and the east, in the middle of the eighteenth century (it originally stood roughly where Flora's temple now stands); and considerably modified by Paxton in the nineteenth (below, page 139). Two other features which appear at first sight to be among those illustrated by Kip and Knyff, or described by contemporary visitors, turn out on closer inspection not to be quite what they seem. The present Willow Tree Fountain is a copy (possibly a copy of a copy) made in the early nineteenth century to replace the original, which had become decayed, and it occupies a different position to the original. And the Cascade, although occupying in part the line of Grillet's original construction, was considerably altered and extended shortly after the engraving was made.

People often ask whether the engravings in *Britannia Illustrata* and similar works exaggerated the scale of great Baroque gardens like Chatsworth in order to flatter their owners. In many cases the extent to which these great landscapes have been destroyed makes it hard to answer this question. But at Chatsworth enough remains on the ground to allow us to relate the details of the engraving to the present landscape. The gardens evidently covered a rather smaller area than the present grounds: their southern limits can be identified with some certainty, for the uphill continuation of the public road which Kip shows as forming the southern termination of the gardens – Holmes Lane – survives in part as an earthwork in Stand Wood. But they nevertheless covered a very large area of ground and clearly were as vast, and as awesome, as the engraving suggests.

However, while the engraving may accurately portray the extent of the gardens, it has the potential to mislead in other ways. In particular, it is easy to assume that all of what we see was created by the 1st Duke. Yet this is clearly not so. A number of features were inherited, and reused, from the landscape shown on Senior's Map of 1617:[57] the complex of fish ponds to the west of the house; the Stand; Queen Mary's Bower; and the Greenhouse Pond, which seems to represent only a slightly expanded version of the large area of water which Senior shows in the centre of the 'Ould Orchard'. There is also some evidence, as we have seen, that the Duke's predecessor, the 3rd Earl, had already begun carrying out extensive improvements to the grounds. But the engraving conveys a misleading impression in a more important way. It presents an air of completion and finality, whereas, in reality, work on the gardens continued unabated into the early decades of the eighteenth century.

The gardens in the early eighteenth century

That work continued in the gardens is hardly surprising, given that work was still continuing on the house, with the West Front under construction between 1700 and 1702 and the North Front between 1705 and 1707. The first major change in the gardens was the excavation of the great canal, or 'Canal Pond', to the south of the Great Parterre (Figure 30). This was laid out through the middle of Flora's Garden and into new ground taken into the gardens following the diversion of Holmes Lane to the south. The accounts contain numerous references to the canal's construction, which spanned the years

FIGURE 30. (*opposite*)
The impressive Canal Pond does not appear on Kip and Knyff's 1699 illustration, for it was a later addition to the gardens, dug between 1702 and 1703. Its construction involved the removal of Flora's garden, shown to the south of the great parterre on Kip and Knyff's aerial view. ©FRAN HALSALL.

FIGURE 31. (*above*)
A Cascade is shown on Kip and Knyff's illustration, but this was remodelled and extended in the early eighteenth century, and the Cascade House erected at its summit, to designs by Thomas Archer. © THE DEVONSHIRE COLLECTION, CHATSWORTH. REPRODUCED BY PERMISSION OF THE CHATSWORTH SETTLEMENT TRUSTEES.

71

1702–3: 'Digging clay for the canal, making a new slope about the canal, and digging the earth in the new way'.[58] In 1703 the final touches were made: levelling was carried out at the ends, where the earth had sunk, and payments were made for 'finishing the great slope'.[59] There were pedestals with figures both around, and within, the canal (they were repainted in 1722)[60] and it was bounded on its southern side by a 'pallisade', presumably an open fence of some kind.[61] The canal, right from the beginning, suffered from problems of leakage; as soon as it was completed £10 was spent to remedy the problem, while in 1718–19 Robert Rowland and partners were paid:

> Ye further Sum of Twenty pounds, being the remaining part of ye money agreed to be paid for Securing ye Canall in ye Garden Except ye Sum of Twenty pounds more to be paid at ye end of three years provided ye sd canal stands firm for ye said time and doth not loose water.[62]

The construction of the canal involved a substantial amount of earth-movement in order to create a level area of sufficient extent, a project referred to in the accounts as 'the filling up of the Great Slope'. The land-forms here had probably already been altered before 1699, for Kip and Knyff's illustration suggests that the area of 'Flora's Garden' comprised a broad, artificially levelled space. But the new arrangements required further earth-moving and levelling, which also served to improve the view south-wards from the mansion. Sir Godfrey Copley described in a letter of 1703 how 'The Duke's chief work hath been the levelling a hill ... by which he hath gained a distant prospect of the blue hills and made on the same level with his house and garden a canal'.[63] Defoe similarly described in 1722 – with some exaggeration – how the Duke 'removed and perfectly carried away a great mountain that stood in the way and interrupted the prospect'.[64]

The other great project carried out in the first decade of the eighteenth century was the reconstruction of the Cascade (Figure 31). This feature had only been completed in 1696: but already, in 1697, Celia Fiennes reported that there were plans to improve it. However, she either misunderstood the char-acter of the proposals, or else a more ambitious scheme than that actually executed was originally mooted, for she described how it was:

> ... designed to be enlarged and steps made up to the top of the hill which is a vast ascent, but from the top of it now they are supply'd with water for all their pipes so it will be the easier to have such a fall of water even from the top which will add to the Curiositye.[65]

Either way, work began in 1703 and had been largely completed by 1708, when John Ingham and Thomas Harris were paid 'Ye remaining part in full of there bill ffor 1277 yards 2 feet of Paveing in ye 23 Spaces or falls of water in the Cascade'.[66] Work on the supply pond, the Cascade Pond, which lies a little higher up the hill to the east, continued until 1712, when there were payments for taking stone 'from Baley [Beeley] Moor to the head of the cascade'; for ten days' work 'casting earth and clay at the pond for the cascade';

and for 'the labourers bill for the pond at cascade (the most of it being made before viz £24.11.6)'.[67] To judge from the Kip and Knyff engraving, the new Cascade was nearly twice the length, and substantially wider, than the old. But the new feature was more impressive in another way: at its summit stood the Cascade House, designed by Thomas Archer. This is one of the finest surviving features in the gardens, perfectly complementing the Cascade itself (Figure 32).

There are numerous references in the estate accounts to the construction of this fine building, which seems to have spanned the years 1703 to 1712. In 1711, for example, £200 was paid 'Upon ye Cascade Account' for bringing stone to the site 'for ye seafish heads', squaring stone, 'Paveing in ye cascade House' altering the 'old circular steps' at the Cascade, and for:

> Working and setting a neck and Bull upon the Llanthorne Ffor imbossing and putting up 4 [?] lyon heads putting up 4 shells in ye frieze in ye inside and hanging 2 Dolfins on ye outside.[68]

The carving was carried out by Samuel Watson and Nadauld. The building continued the established tradition of using water in amusing ways, to surprise and delight visitors, one of whom, in 1725, reported how jets within the building 'throw up several streams and wett people' (the spouts in the floor are still there).[69]

When first completed the Cascade may have featured a more elaborate display of waterworks than today. Since at least the late eighteenth century the spouts and fountains have been restricted to the Cascade House and its immediate vicinity. But an undated early eighteenth-century painting of Chatsworth hanging at Ombersley Court in Warwickshire (Figure 33) suggests a more complex arrangement, with a whole series of spouts running all the way down the sides of the Cascade. This is curiously similar to the character of the waterworks described by Fiennes *before* the Cascade was revamped, with her description of fountains spouting out water 'aCross ye stepps to Each other like an Arbour or arch'. The painting is of considerable interest for a number of other reasons, confirming the existence of features shown on the Kip and Knyff engraving but showing them from another angle, and also revealing a number of additional ones, most notably an avenue, aligned on the house, on the western side of the Derwent.

Impressive though the Cascade undoubtedly was – and indeed, still is – there is evidence that even more grandiose schemes were considered at this time. One visitor in 1703 was told that the Duke planned:

> To take the Current of ye River Derwent ½ a mile above & turn it into his Great Canall which is below the house & hath a bridge over it, & then let it fall in a Great Cascade & go again into its own course below the House.[70]

The extension of the Cascade and the creation of the Canal Pond necessitated alterations to the water supply system. The waterworks were fed from ponds located in the deer park above the gardens. A number of ponds, or

remains of ponds, still exist in the eastern part of Stand Wood and the nearby fields, together with various leats and channels (Figure 34), but their eighteenth-century history is obscure and uncertain. There are five artificial lakes, one of which is now empty and disused. Three – the Emperor Lake, the Ring Pond and the Open Pond – were created in the nineteenth century but the others are older. In December 1700 labourers were paid for 'digging a place to make a pond in the parke to keep a stock of water for the new canal', probably signalling the construction of Morton Pond, now within the gardens but then within the deer park, and well-placed to supply the new canal (the Grotto Pond nearby may be of a similar date).[71] Old Pond is probably that referred to in the estate accounts for 1723, as the 'little pond on ye top of ye parke'.[72] This is indeed the smallest of the ponds in this area, and now dry: it was created by damming a minor valley. Originally it was probably filled from the small stream that runs down the valley but – presumably at a later date – the supply of water was augmented by the construction of the artificial watercourse now known as the Harland Sick leat. The Old Pond was, as its name suggests, probably the first to be created, for an area of water must have existed in the park in the 1690s, if not before, in order to supply the Cascade and other water features. Swiss Lake is slightly later: it is probably the 'Great Pond in the Parke' which was begun in 1710. It is located in the same valley as the Old Pond but is considerably larger. Work on its construction continued through 1711 and 1712, when it was excavated and lined with clay, and into 1717. It was, and still is, retained by a substantial L-shaped earth dam – the 'pond wall' – whose construction is noted in the estate accounts. It may originally have been fed by the Harland Sick leat. However, in 1719 a channel was opened to bring water from 'Humberley Spring to the pond in ye parke'.[73] This still survives, a broad watercourse following the contour to the scarp top above the ponds, running for over 1.5 km from Umberley Brook, adjacent to Umberley Well – eighteenth-century documents sometimes refer to it as the 'Great Canal

FIGURE 33.
This undated painting, which hangs at Ombersley Court in Warwickshire, is of immense importance in understanding the development of the Chatsworth landscape in the early eighteenth century. It shows many of the features depicted by Kip and Knyff, but also the new Cascade and Cascade House. In the wider landscape it shows the avenue aligned on the west front of the house, climbing the hillside to the east of Edensor village. The coach in the foreground may be using the coach road running through the deer park which was created in 1710–11. © THE DEVONSHIRE COLLECTION, CHATSWORTH. REPRODUCED BY PERMISSION OF THE CHATSWORTH SETTLEMENT TRUSTEES.

Aqueduct'.[74] It was presumably the Swiss Lake which Daniel Defoe described in 1722, although he somewhat exaggerated its size:

> On the top of that Mountain, that is to say, on the Plain which extends from it, is a large Pond or Basin of Water, spreading, as I was told, near thirty Acres of Ground, which, from all the Ascents around it, receives, as into a Cistern, all the Water that falls, and from which again by Pipes, the Cascades, Waterworks, Ponds, and Canals in the gardens, are plentifully supplied.[75]

It seems likely that one of the main reasons for creating this new pond was to supply additional water to the Cascade and other garden waterworks, and possibly the fountain in the Great Canal. Whether this fountain was created at the same time as the Canal remains unclear: the first possible reference to it comes in 1719, immediately after the Umberley Brook leat's completion, when plumbers were paid for 'casting and laying 50 yards of pipe for ye Great Fountain'.[76] There are further references to laying pipes in the garden in 1720, but some of these were perhaps to take water from 'Springs in the parke' to the 'upper pond in the Canal Walks', as the Duke requested in 1720:[77] certainly, it is only in 1727 that the first explicit references appear, when £10 was paid for 'casting and laying the Great pipe to ye Fountaine in ye Canal', £10 for enlarging the pond 'Wch playes the fountain in the canal', and no less than £47 for the piping from the pond to the canal.[78] It may be that the Swiss Lake was first connected to the Great Canal fountain at this date, and that it had previously supplied a fountain elsewhere in the gardens.

The creation of the new Canal Pond to the south of the house, the remodelling of the Cascade, and the building of the Cascade House were the most dramatic changes in the gardens in the first decades of the eighteenth century. But the accounts show that much else was going on, and that in a number of other ways the gardens depicted by Kip and Knyff were being steadily altered. Numerous changes were made to the planting in the various gardens, and repairs and alterations were made to the fountains and pipes; flower pots, tubs, 'ffigures', chairs, seats and pallisades were painted.[79] In 1702 the Willow Tree was removed from its position in the centre of the wilderness 'to some other place' and replaced with a new fountain.[80] Plants were purchased, some from London, including in 1702 12,000 hornbeam and, in 1710, 1,110 'eweplants', the former presumably and the latter certainly for new hedges.[81] The 2nd Duke, who inherited in 1707, continued to elaborate, and to develop upon, the great schemes initiated by his father. In 1715 there were payments for 'Repaireing the railes and bannisters that were blown down upon the terras wall'. Arbours were also repaired and four new circular ones erected; an 'earthe House' – presumably the ice house by the Canal Pond – was built and thatched in 1728.[82] The hedges within the gardens were so tall that a 'scaffold' was required to clip them. The complex of ponds and canals to the west of the house was not neglected: they were regularly dredged, the sluices repaired, and in 1723 new 'pallisades' were erected beside the walks there, and also alongside the river.

FIGURE 34. The complex waterworks in the Chatsworth gardens are supplied from a series of ponds, mostly on the level shelf above, which were themselves fed by leats running across the moorland. The water supply system developed over a long period of time, from the late seventeenth century onwards, as shown here (A: Old Pond; B: Swiss Lake; C: Morton Pond; D: Round Pond; E: Emperor Lake; F: Open Pond).

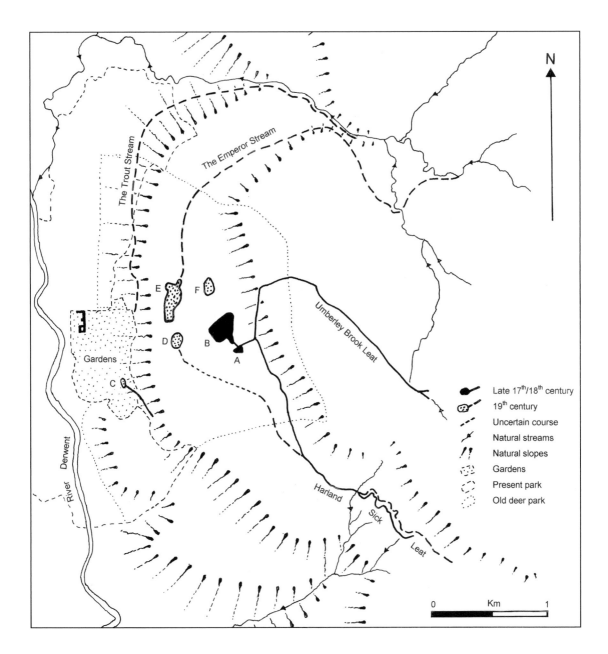

The ponds were still used in the traditional way, stocked with fish. New stews (holding ponds) were dug here in 1720, nets were purchased, and quantities of pease brought specifically 'for feeding carp'.[83] More importantly, 7000 box plants were bought in 1713 'for the garden before the South Front', suggesting that the old pattern of cut work, sand and borders was at this time being replaced by a pattern of box work.[84]

As work began to slow in the main area of ornamental gardens, increasing attention was paid to the productive kitchen gardens. In the 1690s, to judge from Kip and Knyff, these had covered a relatively small area immediately to the east of the Greenhouse Pond, and were thus integrated into the overall design of the gardens. By the early eighteenth century such a location was becoming increasingly unfashionable, and they were therefore moved to the far south-west of the garden areas, in the area below the Bowling Green. Numerous payments were made for the construction of new walls, both in the main gardens and, in particular, in the area of kitchen gardens to the south-west. In 1709 alone 100,500 bricks were purchased for walling. New walls were made 'in the garden' (1709); in the 'low garden' (1710) and 'at the head of ye Holmes ground' and 'along Holmes Lane' (1710).[85] From 1711 many of the entries in the accounts relating to the gardens seem to be concerned with walls – some of stone, some of brick. These included an 'Artificiall Wall', 'Furness Wall' or 'Fire Wall', presumably a hollow, heated wall – an unusual feature at so early a date – which was altered in 1719.[86] In 1719 the 'Nursery below the mill' was enclosed.[87] Further activity occurred in the 1720s: in 1721 there was more walling in the kitchen gardens, while in 1722 63,000 bricks were carried to 'the new wall in the low garden', and an additional fire wall was built here.[88] The gardens were evidently elaborate and complex, and included extensive hot frames. Yet further walls were built here in 1729.[89]

But walling also continued in the main area of ornamental gardens. In 1710 payments were made for 'Cutting stone and Walling ye Wall at ye end of ye Walk by ye Canal', while in July 1711 £70 was paid for 'walling 77 rods [388 m] of a slope wall in ye gardens', and a little later 41 rods [206 m] of walling were made 'against ye slope Wall in the garden'.[90] In 1711 the pheasant yard and low garden were walled, and in 1715 there were payments for getting 'stone and clay and walling about ye Canal in ye garden'. The pheasant yard was presumably an area for displaying ornamental birds: it may, like the bird houses mentioned in the seventeenth-century documents, have been located to the north of the house, but it could have occupied the area of the 'Peacock Yard' shown in the south of the gardens on George Barker's survey of 1773,[91] in an area probably newly brought into the gardens in the early eighteenth century after the diversion of Holmes Lane (in 1722 'paycocks and henns' were brought to Chatsworth from nearby Haddon).[92]

Ornamentalisation of the landscape beyond the gardens

Although most of the references in the accounts in the early eighteenth century are to work in the gardens, activity was also taking place in the deer park. For example, in 1704 there were payments to labourers involved in 'digging up ye earth amongst the rock in Chatsworth Parke and planting Acors Berrys and Seeds', while in 1705 a further 4,000 unspecified 'plants' were planted in the 'lower part of Chatsworth park', followed the next year by the planting of 4,000 'young plants' in the 'New Enclosure in the Park'.[93] Planting continued intermittently over the following decade: in 1718 labourers planted 3000 'yonge Plants in the Inclosure in ye Parke' and made 6000 holes 'in ye Rock for Scotch firs', probably adding to the planting on the escarpment. In 1720, 250

FIGURE 35.
The view towards
Edensor from above
the gardens. The
avenue, aligned on the
west front of the
House, has a complex
history. It was
originally planted in
the early eighteenth
century, but later
removed, probably in
the 1760s. In the 1820s
it was reinstated, but
removed again in 1860.
In the 1980s its line
was re-established by
removing trees in the
ridgetop plantation. A
few of the original
eighteenth-century
trees, sweet chestnuts,
still remain in the fields
below the plantation.

holes were dug in the 'inclose' in the north end of the park, and a further 750
holes 'to plant trees' were dug somewhere here.[94]

One exciting discovery made during the archaeological survey concerns the
avenue which nineteenth-century sources show existed to the west of Edensor
village, aligned on the West Front of the house (Figures 35, 57). This was
apparently created in the mid 1820s,[95] and took the form of two parallel strips
of closely-planted trees. Cartographic evidence suggests that this was an
entirely new feature – an estate map of 1785 shows only fields here, the western
ones enclosed by a grid of narrow shelter belts lying on a quite different alignment.[96] But field survey has revealed five massive sweet chestnuts with girths
consistent with an early eighteenth-century planting date, apparent survivors
from an earlier double-planted avenue running along this same line. The nineteenth-century avenue thus appears to be a reinstatement of a much earlier
feature, although whether its creators knew this is uncertain. There are also

low, fragmentary earthworks which flank the centre line of the avenue. These comprise two broad banks, set about 30 m apart, each with a planting trench along its crest, presumably designed to hold a hedge or near-continuous line of decorative shrubs. The centre of the avenue, between the two banks, is slightly dished, probably indicating some kind of drive. This feature continues westwards, even across areas where later land use has succeeded in levelling the parallel banks, as far as the public road leading from Pilsley to Bakewell. However, its eastern end appears to have stopped well short of Edensor village, at about the point where, because of the lie of the land, the avenue would have disappeared from view from the house: the banks and central depression are completely absent here, although numerous other earthworks have survived, including one boundary lynchet which probably pre-dates 1785 – as it crosses the line of the avenue, it would have been levelled if the drive had been extended to here. While it is tempting to attribute these features to the same phase as the chestnut planting, they seem more likely to relate to the nineteenth-century *re*planting. Certainly, an undated plan by Unwin, made in the second half of the 1820s,[97] shows a drive in this position, which has been carefully painted out: work on a drive here was paid for in 1826 (p. 174). The most plausible explanation is that the earthworks relate to an abandoned nineteenth-century scheme, begun but never completed. The early eighteenth-century avenue of chestnuts was probably only ever a visual feature, planted on the upper slope visible from the house but never intended to flank a drive.

A further stretch of avenue existed in the early eighteenth century on the same alignment, but lying to the east, between Edensor and Chatsworth House, within what was then the rabbit warren. As noted above this is shown on the early eighteenth-century painting of Chatsworth which now hangs in Ombersley Court (Figure 33): its eastern termination is also shown on Knyff's drawing of 1699 (Figure 22). It ran from the river to the crest of the ridge just short of Edensor village; as the avenue started at the riverbank this was again evidently a purely decorative feature rather than an approach to the house. While this feature has, likewise, disappeared without trace, presumably cut down when the landscape park was created in the 1760s, it is curious that there are two old sweet chestnuts growing in the parkland near to, but not quite on, its line. If this stretch of avenue had been planted with the same species as that lying to the west of Edensor, then perhaps these trees, which are significantly younger that those to the west, are self-seeded descendants. While it is tempting to see the two sections of avenue as having been created at the same date, prior to 1699, there are problems with this interpretation. The Ombersley Court painting does not show the western stretch, although the area to the west of Edensor is clearly visible, suggesting that it is a later addition, perhaps created between about 1710 and 1740.

These two avenues were not the only ones at Chatsworth. The Knyff drawing shows another major example, comprising multiple rows of trees aligned with the South Front of the house and starting at Holmes Lane beyond the southern end of the gardens, as well as others, running through areas of 'park-like' grassland to the north-east of the house (Figure 22).

The wider landscape

Beyond the house, gardens and deer park of seventeenth- and early eighteenth-century Chatsworth, the working countryside continued to evolve. Preserved in the parkland turf, particularly in the area to the west of the Derwent, are the earthwork traces of this functional landscape, mainly in the form of low banks which mark the line of former field boundaries (Figure 36). Such earthworks are of great interest, for they give an exceptional glimpse of a complex agricultural landscape evolving over time before being fossilised by successive expansions of the park between 1760 and 1830. Many define fields which were created by the gradual consolidation and enclosure of open-field strips, often followed by further piecemeal modification: these include a series of small closes around Edensor village and alongside the riverbank to the south. Elsewhere, larger and more rectilinear fields are evident. On the Chatsworth side of the river, numerous boundaries defining small rectangular fields of seventeenth- or early eighteenth-century date survive to the north of the house, amongst which are traces of a farmstead or small hamlet which was evidently contemporary with them. Still further to the north, within Baslow parish (and thus in an area which remained outside the Chatsworth estate until the nineteenth century) a complex network of boundaries, some again created by the piecemeal enclosure of open fields, corresponds well with the field pattern shown on the earliest surviving map of the area, surveyed in 1799.[98] To the south of the house, in contrast, the earthwork remains of field boundaries are more fragmentary.

One of the most significant contributions made by the archaeological survey was the discovery that some of the large, undivided areas shown on Senior's map of 1617[99] had been subdivided into smaller enclosures before the mid eighteenth century, when the boundaries were again removed to make way for the landscape park. This is a particularly important discovery as no maps of these areas survive from the period between 1617 and the late eighteenth century. The archaeological evidence, in other words, shows a landscape in a constant state of flux, and reveals radical changes of which we would otherwise remain unaware. The areas in question include the lower parts of the old deer park, the warren and the demesne sheepwalk extending onto Calton Pasture. In addition, examination of the earthworks elsewhere in the park also reveals that many of the large fields shown by Senior (Figures 10, 14) had been subdivided before emparking took place; in many of these areas straight and relatively narrow ridge and furrow shows that the land was periodically used for arable, although the documentary sources show that livestock husbandry remained the cornerstone of the local economy and a major source of income for the estate. The accounts reveal how, up until the end of the 1750s when the landscape park was created, four areas were regularly rented out under

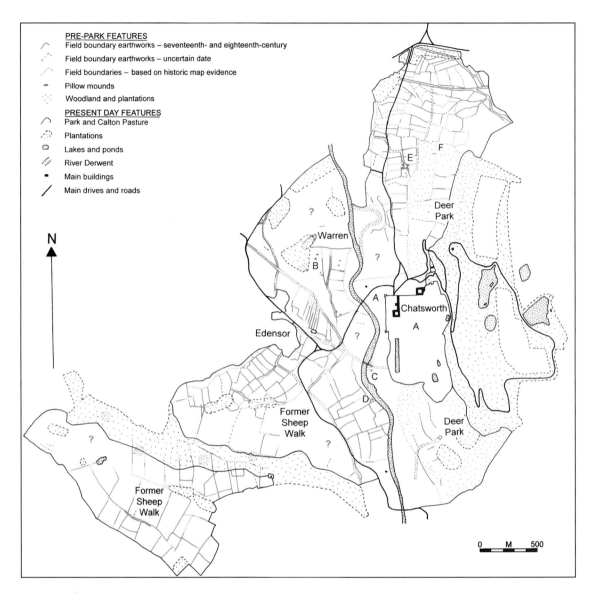

The legend of the map reads:

PRE-PARK FEATURES
Field boundary earthworks – seventeenth- and eighteenth-century
Field boundary earthworks – uncertain date
Field boundaries – based on historic map evidence
Pillow mounds
Woodland and plantations
PRESENT DAY FEATURES
Park and Calton Pasture
Plantations
Lakes and ponds
River Derwent
Main buildings
Main drives and roads

N

Warren

Deer
Park

B

E   F

A
Chatsworth
A

Edensor

C

D

Former
Sheep
Walk

Deer
Park

Former
Sheep
Walk

0   M   500

FIGURE 36.

Chatsworth Park and the adjacent area of Calton Pasture contain numerous earthworks which provide important clues about the way the agricultural landscape beyond the park and gardens developed in the course of the seventeenth and eighteenth centuries. They show that fields depicted on Senior's map of 1617 were later subdivided; that the open sheepwalk was enclosed; and that the warren, and parts of the deer park, were also divided into fields, perhaps to grow fodder for the rabbits and deer (A: site of formal gardens, orchards and outbuildings, B: site of warrener's lodge, C: site of corn mill, D: site of stable, E: site of farmstead, F: the boundary between Chatsworth and Baslow).

'joysts', or agistment agreements, for winter and summer pasture or as summer hay meadows. A typical example, from the 1756–57 accounts,[100] perhaps indicates the relative size of the main areas concerned:

Calton summer and winter joysts	£184
Chatsworth Park joyst	£73
Warren joyst	£21
Cracknewls joyst	£17

A rare survival of a Joyst Book, for 1745,[101] indicates that while Cracknowls – a large pasture elsewhere on the estate, north of Bakewell – was grazed by cattle, sheep and horses, the others were used in more specialised ways. Chatsworth deer park and the summer grazing at Calton were for cattle, while the latter was used in the winter for sheep; grazing in the warren was restricted to cattle and horses. The intensive use of these grazing areas presumably explains the subdivision into large fields indicated by the earthwork evidence at Cracknowls, Calton Pasture, in the Warren and perhaps in the lower parts of the deer park. It is possible, however, that the large straight-sided fields within the area of the rabbit warren have another explanation. They may have been used to grow fodder for the rabbits, a development recorded on warrens elsewhere in England in the early eighteenth century. These enclosures evidently post-date the Ombersley Court painting, which shows the warren as internally undivided.

The superficially mundane archaeology of post-medieval field boundaries adds to the story of the landscape in intriguing ways. When Senior's map was surveyed in 1617 the deer park extended further down the slope than Stand Wood does today, its edge coinciding roughly with the line of the later upper drive running through the Park to the north of the house, and with a similar contour to the south.[102] What is particularly interesting is that there are earthwork traces of rectangular fields in the deer park above this line, evidently created some time between 1617 and the 1760s. These may represent encroachments into the area of the park made some time in the seventeenth or early eighteenth centuries. Alternatively, they may be special fields created within it for the cultivation of fodder crops, such as turnips, for the deer.

The deer park was also used for industrial activity at this time. Millstone production was one of the principal medieval and early post-medieval industries of the Peak District and the quarries around Baslow, centred at Gardom's Edge, were one of two main production centres in the region, the other being around Millstone Edge above Hathersage. Although some millstones were used locally, the majority were transported eastwards across the moors to inland ports at Bawtry and Stainforth. Production started at least as early as the fourteenth century, reaching its peak in the sixteenth and seventeenth centuries, and ceasing in the early nineteenth century as the consumption of white bread became more common – for the grit from the peak stones turned the bread an unpalatable grey colour.[103] At Baslow, millstone makers are recorded from the fourteenth[104] to the seventeenth centuries, although documentation seems

FIGURE 37.
On Dobb Edge in the
far north-east corner of
park are the remains of
several millstone
quarries. A number of
domed millstones can
still be seen lying
around, discarded at
various stages of
production.

to suggest production here had tailed off by the end of the sixteenth century. But it is likely, from their character, that some of the larger quarries whose remains survive around Baslow are of seventeenth- to late eighteenth- or even early nineteenth-century date. One John Rotherham is known to have leased a millstone quarry in the Chatsworth deer park, high above the house to the east, between 1695 and 1745. A surviving estate account book for 1743 records that the annual rent was £4, suggesting a substantial operation.[105] The making of millstones was observed somewhere near Chatsworth by the Browne brothers in 1662 and by Defoe in the early eighteenth century, who noted quarries, presumably Rotherham's, on the top of the scarp to the east of the Chatsworth House.[106] There are no signs of these today but they probably lay somewhere in the northern part of Stand Wood and were comprehensively backfilled with waste material from the coal mine shafts dug here in the second half of the eighteenth century. A draft agreement to set up Chatsworth Old Park Colliery, dated 1765, specified that this should happen.[107]

At Dobb Edge in the far north-east corner of the landscape park there are several surviving millstone quarries, although these are not the ones rented by Rotherham as the Chatsworth estate did not acquire the land in this area until the early nineteenth century. There are seven conjoined face-quarries, as well as smaller delves. A number of domed millstones can still be seen lying around, discarded at various stages of production, presumably because they broke or because a flaw in the stone was identified (Figure 37); there is even one unfinished and abandoned stone chocked for dressing, as if the quarrymen intended to come back the next day but never did. The quarry appears to have been disused by the time this area was incorporated into the landscape park in the 1820s and 30s, although it was later reopened by Paxton to provide stone for the rockworks in the gardens (pp. 143–5).

The deer park may also have been used for a short time for coal mining in the early seventeenth century. The estate accounts record payments of £110 1s 6d for working coal mines 'at Chatsworth' in 1623–4 and 1624–5, and to the sale of coal for £82 16s 9d:[108] it is unclear if this short-lived venture thus ran at a loss, or whether only coal not needed by the estate was sold. While coal certainly outcrops in the deer park, it is possible that the mining was on nearby Beeley Moor where the estate also held the mineral rights by the early eighteenth century. A smaller quantity of coal was certainly mined in the Park, costing £13 14s 0d to extract, when just over 100 packhorse loads were obtained between 1656 and 1659.[109]

The medieval and later landscape fossilised within the park and its environs does not consist only of agricultural and industrial features. The earthwork remains of numerous abandoned routeways are also represented. In the Peak District, evidence for pre-nineteenth-century communication routes largely takes the form of sinuous and often 'braided' – that is, interlinking – hollow-ways on land that was once open waste and common, where a succession of alternative routes could be taken to avoid the worst of the boggy ground. Such features are particularly common on the gritstone moorlands of the region, where erosion has given them considerable definition – as, for example, those on the moorlands high above Chatsworth House to the east.[110] However, in the agricultural land below, the movement of traffic was restricted to defined routeways by the existence of fields and boundaries. Here abandoned early roads are often only intermittently visible. They are generally most obvious on steeper slopes as sunken lanes, created by water erosion once the vegetated surface was broken by traffic. Elsewhere their course is indicated by the earthworks of the flanking hedges that separated them from the adjacent fields.

Taken together, the traditional routes around Chatsworth formed a complex interconnected network, some merely running to and from local settlements and their fields and commons, others providing access to more distant villages and market towns such as Bakewell, and to the industrial production centres to the east centred on Sheffield and Chesterfield. Some formed parts of long-distance routes, such as saltways, which cross the Peak District from the east and west. Many may well have medieval or earlier origins, although this is often difficult to document with any certainty; much of their physical remains, resulting from heavy erosion along the routes, may well be the result of increased traffic in post-medieval times, consequent upon the growth in the scale of production of manufactured goods and raw materials. Much of the commercial traffic using these various routes took the form of strings of pack-horses, although wagons were certainly employed on some, if only with difficulty. One of the most important products coming out of the Peak was lead ore destined for smelters on the East Moors, or in the valleys of the Coal Measure foothills to the east; similarly, smelted lead from smelters nearer the orefield was transported to ports to the east. Other exports included millstones and other quarry products, and agricultural produce such as cheese, hides and wool. Imports included manufactured items from potteries, ironworks and other workshops lying in the lowland regions to east and west.

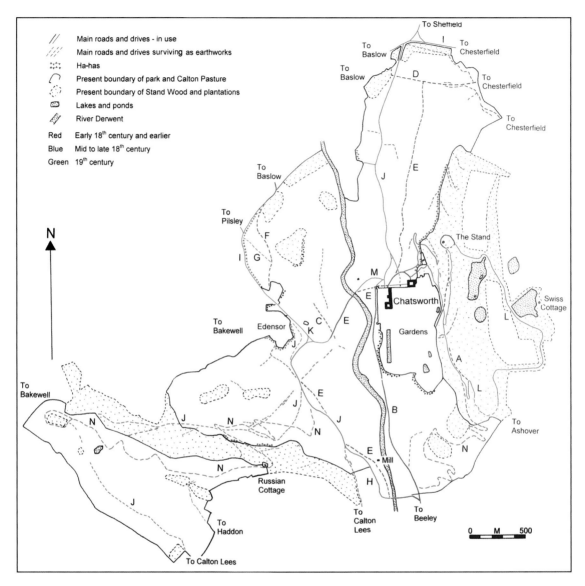

FIGURE 38.

The roads and drives within the park were altered and added to on a number of occasions
through the eighteenth and nineteenth centuries: they often follow entirely different lines to
pre-park routes, traces of which can still be found (A: the 1710–11 coach road (and later drift
way), closed in 1759; B: the 1739 turnpike from Bakewell to Chesterfield, closed in 1759; C:
the public road to Pilsley and Baslow, closed in 1759; D: the 1759 turnpike from Baslow to
Chesterfield, diverted in the 1820s; E: the new roads and drive built through the park in c.
1760; F: the 1760s road from Edensor to Baslow; G: the 1812 Edensor to Ashford Turnpike;
H: the 1818 road diversion near One Arch Bridge; I: the 1820s road diversions to the new
park edge; J: the new roads and drives built in the park in the mid 1820s; K: new drives built
in 1836 after the demolition of the eastern half of Edensor; L: new drives in Stand Wood
built in 1839; M: new drive to House built in 1842–43; N: the serpentine drives constructed in
the 1850s).

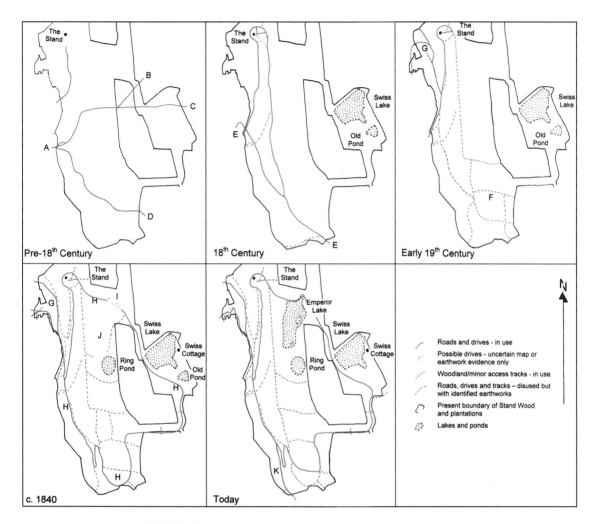

FIGURE 39.

An example – at Stand Wood – of how cartographic and archaeological evidence shows that the pattern of roads and drives changed dramatically in the course of the eighteenth and nineteenth centuries (A: Holmes Lane leading to Chatsworth Bridge; B: route through the deer park to Sheffield; C: route through the deer park to Chesterfield; D: route through the deer park to Ashover; E: 1710–11 coach road through the deer park, leading from Chatsworth towards Ashover; F: access tracks into new plantation here; G: new early nineteenth-century drives from the park and stables; H: Paxton's 1839 circular drive; I: presumed original course of H, diverted in the mid 1840s with the creation of the Emperor Lake; J: access tracks into new extensions to the plantations; K: the top end of the late 1850s serpentine drive).

East of the Derwent the course of a number of old roads can still be made out, mostly leading to and from the medieval bridges over the Derwent at Baslow and Chatsworth (Figure 38). These include one running south-eastwards from Baslow Bridge, which can be traced through the north-eastern part of the park as a lane between fields, and on the higher ground above as a sinuous braided hollow-way, heading to Chesterfield via the Baslow Colliery coal shafts on the shelf above. By 1617, when Senior mapped the deer park,[111] some braids of this route had been blocked by the park pale at the north-eastern corner of the deer park, and travellers were forced to skirt its edge. Prior to the creation of the park a branch from this road ran south-westwards to Chatsworth Bridge, and deep hollow-ways along its route can still be seen running diagonally down the scarp in the northern part of Stand Wood. By 1617 the route had been diverted southwards, through a gate in the park boundary, to pass along a hollow-way running diagonally through Stand Wood to Holmes Lane beyond the southern edge of the gardens, thus giving added privacy to the house (Figure 39). This route may well have been for traffic from Chatsworth Bridge heading for Sheffield, while a branch in the upper park shown on Senior's map led directly east towards Chesterfield. A second route leading from the top of Holmes Lane is shown by Senior, heading in a south-westerly direction. This continued beyond the deer park as a major braided route, passing the sites of medieval lead smelting bole furnaces around Harland Edge, and heading towards Ashover and then on to Hardwick Hall, the other main residence of the Cavendish family in the region. In 1710–11 this road was improved as a coach road, although it was in part re-routed in order to reduce the gradient on the scarp slope, and diverted southwards on the lower slope because of the expansion of the gardens around the house. This route was superseded for wheeled vehicles in 1739 when a turnpike road was built through the riverside fields, following the river southwards from Chatsworth Bridge before ascending onto the moorlands above. However, some public traffic still followed the old route until this was formally closed in 1759, at the time when the landscape park was created.

The evidence for old routeways is more fragmentary to the west of the Derwent but again several can be identified, leading from Chatsworth Bridge towards Bakewell, Pilsley, Hassop and places beyond. The main road to the market town of Bakewell ran up the main village street of Edensor and then westwards, through fields to the north of the park. However, an alternative route existed, which avoided the village by skirting it to the south, and this can still be traced in part through the park as a braided hollow-way leading to both Bakewell and Haddon. It cuts obliquely across medieval ridge and furrow and probably only came into use during later-medieval or early post-medieval times, after this area had become an open sheepwalk. This land was enclosed probably in the seventeenth century, and by this time the route had presumably gone out of use, except near the river, where part perhaps still survived as a lane giving access to fields. A second route skirted the village to the north, running to Pilsley, Hassop and Baslow, and again a stretch of this can be traced as a hollow-way in the park. A further sinuous hollow-way can be traced between Edensor and Calton, although its line is largely obscured by a drive laid out along its length after the landscape park was created. In the early seventeenth century this ran along the edge of the open sheepwalk but it later became a bounded lane as the land up the slope, to the west, was enclosed into fields.

In one sense the working countryside of the estate was quite separate from the aesthetic landscape of the park and gardens. But the avenues running out into the countryside served to integrate the two visually, while some of the changes in field patterns evident from the archaeological evidence may, at least in part, have had an aesthetic motivation: the creation of new patterns of fields, and the reorganisation of the old, signalled the Cavendishes' ownership of, and active involvement in, the management of the productive estate landscape.

Reading the designed landscape

In some ways it could be argued that the changes in the Chatsworth gardens in the early decades of the eighteenth century served not only to make the gardens more magnificent, but also to change their character. The box parterres before the South Front, the larger and more elaborate Cascade, and perhaps above all the creation of the Canal Pond and the consequent strengthening of the axis leading south from the house – all these increased the *French*, as opposed to the *Dutch*, character of the grounds. The creation of the Canal Pond was particularly important in this respect. Linear canals, axially aligned on the mansion, had long been a prominent feature in the great French gardens. It is noteworthy that around this time – in the first decade of the eighteenth century – there was a similar 'radical alteration in the careful … balance between French and Dutch elements' at Hampton Court and other royal sites.[112]

Among the tight-knit group of courtiers and leading politicians who effectively ruled post-Revolutionary England, fashions set by the royal family were quickly and eagerly followed. Familiarity with the latest styles in architecture and garden design, and possession of the capital required to carry them out, were a necessary badge of status. But there was more to the layout of great garden landscapes than simply 'fashion'. Their design embodied philosophical and, at times, political ideas. Baroque gardens exuded wealth and power, but at another level embodied ideas about science, technology and the perfectibility of nature. Fountains and waterworks made beautiful and amusing experiences but they also conveyed lessons about mathematics, hydraulics, and gravity, and showed how nature could be tamed and improved. Topiary, which usually took the form of neat globes and pyramids, could similarly be viewed as an improvement on the irregular growth patterns otherwise exhibited by trees and shrubs: or, in terms of contemporary Neoplatonic thought, was a practice which served to bring out the ideal forms to which the fallen works of nature were always striving to return. What made Chatsworth such an iconic place, viewed in these kinds of terms, was its location: visitors went out of their way to draw attention to, and sometimes exaggerate, the wild and irregular appearance of the surrounding countryside in order to emphasise the structured beauties of the gardens, and the well-farmed landscape of the Derwent valley. Cotton, writing at the time of the 3rd Earl, described how house and gardens were:

Environ'd round with natures Shames, and Ills,
Black Heaths, wild Rocks, bleak Craggs, and naked Hills
And the whole Prospect so inform, and rude,
Who is it, but must presently conclude?
That this is Paradise, which seated stands
In midst of Desarts, and of barren Sand.[113]

Roger Gale visited around 1694 and described the walks around the 'noble canal … where as from heaven, one may survey the distant horrors of the kingdom of Erebus, in the dismal country round about us'.[114] John Dodd compared Chatsworth to 'a Diamond set in black [which] seems to take a Lustre from the wretched Country it is situated in … The Gardens about this house are wonderful Charming', while Joseph Taylor described the places as a 'heaven', from which 'one may survey the distant horrors of a hellish country'.[115]

But it is possible that, as well as embodying such widely shared *philosophical* notions, the Chatsworth landscape also expressed some more immediate *political* ideas. The unusually strong 'Dutch' character of the gardens before c. 1700 may have served to emphasise William Cavendish's crucial role in bringing William of Orange to the throne, as well as symbolising his loyalty to him. Orangeries – of which that at Chatsworth was one of the country's largest – were widely seen as symbols of support for the house of *Orange*. The exhedra – the curving arrangement of trees which Kip and Knyff show prominently positioned at the foot of Grillet's Cascade – mirrored those at William of Orange's palaces at Zorgvliet, Heemstede and Het Loo, described as 'theatres' and used, as apparently at Chatsworth, to display exotic plants, especially oranges.[116] Even the statues in the gardens may have had a political significance, in an age steeped in reading such messages. The strong nautical theme – Neptune, Triton, sea horses – may reflect something more than just the importance of water in the garden. The salvation of Protestant freedom had, after all, come from across the sea.

This, perhaps, is a speculation too far. What is certain is that by 1720 the gardens at Chatsworth were among the grandest, and the most admired, in all England. But over the next half century they would be transformed again, and altered beyond recognition: and, with them, the wider landscape of Edensor and Chatsworth.

CHAPTER FOUR

Kent, Brown, and the
Making of the New Park

The progress of a dynasty

Changes in the style of designed landscapes are intimately related to broader developments in society, politics and the economy; and changes in *particular* gardens and parks are closely connected with the fortunes of the individuals and families that owned them. No apology, therefore, is given for the brief account that follows of the changing political system of early eighteenth century England, and – more importantly – of the Cavendish family's place within it.

The Restoration of 1660 and the Revolution of 1688, in which the 1st Duke had played so important a part, did not sweep away the power of monarchy in England and create 'democracy' in the modern sense of the word. Instead they marked the start of a system in which the Crown, while continuing to be an active player on the political scene, was to varying extents controlled by an elite of large landowners, represented in a parliament elected by only a relatively small proportion of the population.[1] Political struggles to control parliament, and to gain the ear of the monarch, were waged under the banners of 'Whig' and 'Tory'. In very simple terms, the former were the party of the 1688 settlement and, subsequently, of the Hanoverian succession: they supported a measure of religious toleration, and (after 1722) a foreign policy that avoided major conflicts. They were the party of the greatest landowners, of wealthy merchants and powerful City interests. The Tories, in contrast, were the party of old-fashioned paternalistic values, staunch supporters of the high church and – initially at least – of the Stuart succession. Their leaders were drawn from among the ranks of the great landed families but their political core was the minor local gentry, the backwoods squires of the 'shires'. But we must be very careful with these terms. They often masked more complex alliances and oppositions, and from the 1730s especially their meanings shifted in complicated ways. Great families like the Cavendishes strove to attain positions of authority at court or in parliament, partly for ideological reasons but also for the wealth and influence, and the prestige, that such things conferred. Above all, this was what great families did – it was the very reason for their existence. Elections were, as often as not, dynastic clashes between rival magnates, rather than arguments over public policy.

The Cavendish family continued its staunch support of the Whig cause, and – with occasional reverses – it continued to reap rich rewards. The 2nd Duke of Devonshire, who succeeded his father in 1707, was soon created Lord Steward of the Household and Lord Lieutenant of Derbyshire, and while he lost both posts following the victory of the Tories in the general election of 1710 he regained them with the accession of the Hanoverian George I, and the return of a Whig administration, in 1714. George's succession to the throne ushered in a new political era: the Whigs, under the astute politician Sir Robert Walpole, ran England as a one-party state for the following three decades.[2]

The 2nd Duke was active in politics but the 3rd Duke was a much more important figure on the national stage. Walpole regarded him as one of his most loyal supporters, and his close relatives held high office. The Duke of Newcastle, his cousin, was secretary of state and Henry Pelham, the latter's younger brother, was Walpole's lieutenant in the House of Commons. The Duke served as Lord Privy Seal between 1731 and 1733; as Lord Steward of the Household from 1733 to 1737; and as Lord Lieutenant of Ireland from 1737 to 1744. Only in 1749, following an acrimonious disagreement between Pelham and Newcastle concerning the conduct of foreign policy, did the Duke withdraw from the court and, in effect, from politics.[3]

Meanwhile his son, later the 4th Duke, had been making a political career of his own. Lord Hartington (the courtesy title of the Duke's eldest son) entered the House of Commons in 1741 as MP for Derbyshire but the following year Walpole resigned from office over the War of the Spanish Succession, in spite of Hartington's strenuous efforts to rally support for him in the Commons. After a period of political confusion, Pelham succeeded as Walpole's ultimate successor, as First Lord of the Treasury; and Hartington's fortunes rose steadily in spite of his father's retirement from politics. In 1751 Pelham had him appointed Master of the Horse, and in July of the same year he became Privy Councillor.[4]

Politics formed only one part of a great family's life, and was only one of the methods it could use to increase its power and wealth. Marriage was another, and in 1748 one of the most important alliances in the history of the Cavendish dynasty took place when Hartington married Lady Charlotte Elizabeth Boyle, daughter and heir of the 3rd Earl of Burlington – a figure of immense importance in the artistic and cultural world of early eighteenth-century England. Lady Charlotte was only seventeen at the time of the marriage (she had been born on 24 November 1731) and the marriage had, in fact, been arranged between the two families while she was still only a child. This was a time when such practices were beginning to be criticised by more progressive members of society, and Hartington's mother is said to have been so incensed by the arrangement that she separated from the Duke for over a year. But the match was designed to enhance the status and wealth of the Devonshires, and in this it certainly succeeded. Lady Charlotte was Baroness de Clifford in her own right as well as being heiress to her father. Up to this time the Cavendish family had, by some way, been the largest landowners in Derbyshire, but their estates had been almost entirely restricted to that and the neighbouring counties. Hartington's marriage now brought them far-flung estates: Bolton Abbey and Londesborough in Yorkshire, together with the right to return two MPs for the borough of Knaresborough; various properties in London; Chiswick House in Middlesex; and a huge estate centred on Lismore Castle, County Waterford, in Ireland.[5]

Lady Charlotte died in 1754, only eight years after her marriage, and was buried beside other members of the Cavendish family in All Saints Church in Derby, leaving behind four children. Despite this, her husband's political career continued to prosper. He was made Lord Lieutenant of Ireland by the Duke of Newcastle in 1755; in December of the same year the 3rd Duke died and he succeeded to the dukedom; and he eventually became First Lord of the Treasury in a compromise administration which was acceptable both to Newcastle and his arch-enemy Pitt, who was thus able to prosecute the Seven Years War. He continued to be a central figure in politics until 1762, but then his fortunes waned rapidly. He resigned from office shortly after the accession of George III. In 1764 he was dismissed as Lord Lieutenant of Derbyshire, the post which had been in his family since 1714. In October he suffered a stroke, and went to Spa in Germany, where he died on November 1764 at the age of 44. His body was brought back to England and he was buried with his wife at Derby.[6]

Whig landscapes

Political ideology and the design of polite landscapes and buildings were much more closely connected in the early eighteenth century than they are today. Following their acquisition of power in 1712 some great Whig landowners began to patronise a new style of architecture – 'Palladianism'. Whereas Baroque architects like Archer and Talman had used classical features in a flexible, imaginative way, for dramatic effect, the new theorists adopted a purist approach. The various forms of pillar, pediment, entablature and so on now had to be combined in the correct ways, sanctioned by classical precedent, and rooms and elevations designed to a number of set proportions, as cubes, squares, double cubes, etc. The new architects drew directly on the writings and drawings of the sixteenth-century Italian architect Andreas Palladio for their principal inspiration, and on the relatively few works of his seventeenth-century English imitator, Inigo Jones. Whig theorists explicitly contrasted their new pure form of classicism with the decadent Baroque, a style forged by the Catholic church and adopted by foreign absolutist monarchs. Palladianism was the style for a new age, for a Protestant Britain ruled by enlightened patricians which was taking its place in the world as the New Rome. But other factors were probably equally or more important in the development of the new taste. This was a period in which more and more young gentlemen were undertaking the 'Grand Tour', and seeing first hand the classical ruins and Renaissance architecture of Italy – and enjoying the climate and scenery there. And when they returned to their English country seats, they were keen to imitate what they had seen.[7]

Changes in architecture in the first half of the eighteenth century were, not surprisingly, accompanied by changes in landscape design. The compact, elegant lines of the Palladian villa looked wrong when surrounded by enclosed gardens featuring complex topiary and fussy parterres. Under the influence of writers and designers like Charles Bridgeman and Stephen Switzer, garden geometry was progressively softened and simplified. Plain grass lawns replaced complicated cutworks and *broderie*: this fashion was in part set by Queen Anne herself, who removed the complex box scrollworks in the Fountain Garden at Hampton Court and replaced them with plain lawns. For a while flamboyant displays of topiary continued to be popular but in time these, too, fell from favour, and walls were reduced in number. Indeed, from the 1720s perimeter walls were sometimes banished altogether and replaced by a sunken fence or 'ha-ha', which allowed uninterrupted views from the garden out into the surrounding parkland. By the later 1720s, at the most fashionable residences, gardens were simple and elegant in their outlines, with clipped lawns, subdued topiary, gravel walks, and sloping turf terraces.[8]

In the course of the 1730s and 40s, however, still more radical ideas were pioneered by William Kent. Kent was an artist and interior designer deeply imbued with Italian ideas who was patronised by a small circle of Palladian enthusiasts centred on Lord Burlington, and who became increasingly involved in architecture and garden design. He began, in the 1730s, to lay out gardens or (more usually) sections of gardens in an irregular, 'naturalistic' way, without straight lines, with casual groupings of trees and scattered temples, in imitation of the landscape of the Italian *Campagna*, or of the paintings of idealised classical scenery produced by artists like Claude Lorraine or Poussin.[9] Such grounds formed the ideal accompaniment to Palladian houses designed, in effect, in imitation of Italian villas. But, to contemporary Whig theorists, they had another significance. The grand lines and rigid geometry of French gardens, they argued, represented the centralised power of an absolutist monarchy for which control – of nature, and of men – was everything. The irregular and serpentine lines of the new English gardens, in contrast, were a reflection of the political order which, begun with the Glorious Revolution, had been further elaborated in the early decades of the eighteenth century: an order in which the power of the monarch was balanced by that of Parliament, and which steered a middle course between absolutism and democracy.

Lord Burlington was the key figure in all the stylistic developments of the 1720s and 30s. In 1725 he began to rebuild his house at Chiswick to designs by Colen Campbell: it was modelled on Palladio's Villa Capra near Vicenza. As already noted, Burlington was Kent's principal patron and Kent, together with Charles Bridgeman, laid out innovative gardens around the house, complete with vistas leading to temples, columns, and rustic houses, terraces, an exhedra, and a river with a cascade and a rustic bridge. The design was full of echoes of Italy, complex and diversified: Alexander Pope praised the Earl in his poem *Epistle to Burlington*, of 1731, as being the first landowner to 'consult the genius of the place' when laying out his grounds.[10]

The 3rd Duke's garden

It is usually stated or implied that the elaborate Baroque gardens laid out by the 1st Duke and completed by the 2nd Duke at Chatsworth survived, more or less intact, until they were completely swept away by the 4th Duke in the late 1750s, under the direction of Lancelot 'Capability' Brown. In part this notion of stasis is the result of an old-fashioned view of garden history which sees the geometric garden as something essentially static and unchanging in the first half of the eighteenth century, effectively marking time until the new ideas, pioneered by Capability Brown, came along to sweep it away. Even the noted historian of Chatsworth, Francis Thompson, was able to state with confidence how:

> After the 1st Duke's death, not unnaturally, a long period of great activity and great expense was followed by a long lull. For fifty years Chatsworth stood still. So far as is known, the 2nd Duke made no alterations at all, either in the house or in the gardens. The 3rd Duke (born 1698; succeeded 1729) made none in the house, and outside the house only two of note.

The two alterations Thompson mentions were the extension of the gardens slightly to the east and the rebuilding of the greenhouse.[11] In reality, as we have seen, the 2nd Duke not only saw through to completion all the projects begun by his father but also continued to make significant alterations to the gardens. More importantly, a careful examination of the evidence leaves no doubt that the 3rd Duke also made major changes and that most of the formal, geometric gardens created by his two predecessors had been removed long before Brown appeared on the scene. Indeed, it would have been most remarkable if this had not been so. The Duke, as a great political figure, could hardly have stood aloof from the changes in contemporary taste, especially given his close contacts with Lord Burlington. While there is no evidence that the house itself – so recently completed – was at all modified in line with the new fashions, its grounds unquestionably underwent some of the stylistic changes which we would expect at a residence of this importance.

The available evidence suggests that the gardens remained relatively unchanged into the 1720s. William Stukeley, in 1724, thus described how 'The Gardens abound with green-houses, summer-houses, walks, wildernesses, oranges, with all the furniture of statues, urns greens etc. with canals, basons, and waterworks of various forms and contrivances, sea-horses, drakes, dolphins, and other fountains'.[12] Peter Tillemans painted a distant view of the house and gardens, probably in the mid 1720s, which seems to show the gardens largely unchanged, with fountains, statuary, parterres and complex wildernesses and arbours extending up the slopes to the east of the house (Figure 40). But alterations were begun even before the 2nd Duke died. In 1728 the accounts record payments for 'hacking and wheeling away 134 roods of earth in the gardens where the arbour was', and at the same time John Sale, Robert Pennistone and their partners were paid for 'levelling, getting Turfe, and laying it down in ye Garden before the South Front (or parterre)', clearly suggesting that the complex boxworks here were being replaced with smooth grass lawns.[13] Work continued apace under the 3rd Duke. In 1731 Pennistone and his men were paid for 'stubing a Rowe of Limes, levelling and turfing the Slope at side of Canall' in the garden; in 1732 they felled no less than 2,340 trees there; and in 1733 were paid for felling more trees, and for 'stubbing up all the Fir trees in the Gardens', presumably signalling the destruction of the Scots pine wilderness planted in 1695. There are also payments for 'removing the figures in ye Gardens'.[14] In 1735 more trees were felled in the gardens by Pennistone's men.[15] There were still some formal elements – in 1728 '135 hedge ewes, 34 ball ewes' were purchased – and the various waterworks were maintained and indeed improved, with, for example, payments in 1731 for 'inlargeing the Pond at Cascade'.[16] In 1738 an 'Annanus House' – that is, a heated building used to grow pineapples, a novel delicacy – was built at a cost of £134 18s 1d (the following year were payments for 'Fetchin pots for the pine Apple plants from Sutton in Ashfield').[17] But the overall impression is that the gardens were beginning to be simplified.

Still more drastic alterations came in 1736 and 1737, and are recorded in a special account in the archives with the telling title: 'An Account of the Charge of Altering the Gardens to the East Front and Raising the greenhouse Pond'. This details payments for large amounts of earth-moving by different teams of labourers. The nature of the changes is sometimes unspecified, but one entry refers to the movement of earth 'from the slope next the East Front to the Greenhouse Pond', and another to 'removing Earth to make part of the Slope below the Cascade steps'. There are also payments to Robert Pennistone and his partners for 'soughing [draining], levelling and turfing in the gardens'.[18] Evidently, major alterations to the contours were taking place in these years on the rising ground immediately to the east of the house.

The most important piece of evidence, however, for the scale of change in the gardens in the late 1720s and 30s is a distant view of Chatsworth painted by Thomas Smith of Derby, some time around 1743 (Figure 41). Distant view it may be, but even without the aid of a magnifying glass it is clear that the upper two terraces of the seventeenth-century gardens, which Capability Brown is usually credited with destroying around 1760, had by this time already been largely removed. Only the lower terraces remained intact – those that survive today. The Cascade and Cascade House, Canal Pond, and some fountains remained but the area above the second terrace (that is, to the east of what is now the Broad Walk) had been completely transformed. Straight gravel paths, topiary, geometric plats and formal arrangements of trees had been removed wholesale: in their place were gently sloping grass lawns rising to areas of natural-looking woodland which were evidently the remains of the *bosquets* of the previous century, now half a century older. Thus the Salisbury Lawn, so often attributed to Brown, was already well established when he came to Chatsworth. Hidden away within or behind the areas of woodland two small pools remained – the Jack Pond and the Ring Pond (they still survive). But the other small garden ponds and fountains, with the exception of that pond surrounding the Triton and Sea Horses fountain on the South Front, had been filled in and taken away. Some signs of terraces can, it is true, just be seen behind the house – in the vicinity of the Greenhouse Pond and the First Duke's Greenhouse – both of which still survived although out of sight from this position. But Smith's fine painting leaves no doubt that, more than fifteen years before Brown arrived at Chatsworth, most of the old formal gardens had been removed. It is in this context that we need to consider several further pieces of evidence. Given the Cavendish family's close ties with Lord Burlington it is, perhaps, not surprising to find William Kent at Chatsworth some time in the 1730s, preparing designs for improvements, which still survive among the Devonshire collection.[19] The most striking shows the rising escarpment to the east of the house.[20] The slope is planted with pines, and a waterfall comes steeply downhill, dividing, re-uniting and passing through two grotto-like arrangements of arches flanked by pavilions with pyramidal roofs (Figure 42). At the top of the slope, placed a little to the right in the view, is a domed, circular temple. In the words of one prominent garden historian, the design embodies 'an anthology of Italian reminiscences'. The domed temple 'recalls the so-called Sybill's Temple at Tivoli'; the cascade itself is modelled on those 'in the upper gardens of the Villa Aldobrandini'; while the flanking pavilions are 'an eclectic concoction of famous Roman remains'.[21] There are number of other suggestions for improving the escarpment, with temples and rocky cascades.[22] Another of Kent's drawings for Chatsworth shows a domed temple in front of a square pond, set against the backdrop of the rising escarpment which is again extensively planted with conifers. The pond may well be the Jack Pond which, as already noted, still survives in the gardens to the north of the Cascade.[23] We are on safer ground with a further drawing, which depicts what is unquestionably the Canal Pond, flanked by trees and terminated with two diminutive classical pavilions.[24] Other Kent sketches in the collection may relate to Chatsworth, although many are proposals for Chiswick or sketches of idealised landscapes.[25]

It is usually assumed that none of Kent's proposals were implemented by the Duke, and this may be true. But we should be cautious here. It is by no means impossible that the great designer had an influence on the development of the pleasure grounds around the house. Much of Kent's work was essentially ephemeral. His buildings were sometimes of wood rather than stone and his planting made much use of quick-growing but short-lived species like birch, larch and pine. The next detailed plans of the pleasure grounds date to the 1770s,[26] and the informal pattern of paths and planting which these show

FIGURE 40.

Peter Tillemans' distant view of Chatsworth, painted in the 1720s, shows the gardens much as in the Ombersley Court painting, made more than a decade earlier (Figure 33): still replete with fountains, statuary and parterres, and with complex wildernesses and arbours extending up the slopes to the east of the house. But the extensive kitchen gardens, just visible behind the watermill, were new; and in the foreground, to the west of the Derwent, several fields had been thrown together to create an extensive horse pasture, partly ornamental in character. © THE DEVONSHIRE COLLECTION, CHATSWORTH. REPRODUCED BY PERMISSION OF THE CHATSWORTH SETTLEMENT TRUSTEES.

FIGURE 41. (*opposite top*)

Thomas Smith's painting of c. 1743 is one of our most important sources of information for the development of the Chatsworth landscape in the first half of the eighteenth century. Like Tillemans' earlier view (Figure 40), it shows an extensive area of semi-ornamental pasture in the foreground, to the west of the river: here elegant ladies and gentlemen peruse the thoroughbred racehorses. The mill, and Chatsworth old bridge, are still in place. But the gardens around the House are greatly altered. Many of the fountains and sculptures have gone, the formal wildernesses have been made more irregular and 'naturalistic', and large sections of the terraces have been removed. The smooth expanse of the Salisbury Lawn, running up the slopes to the east of the House, is usually attributed to the activities of Capability Brown in the years around 1760 but the painting makes clear that it had been created many years earlier, possibly with the advice of William Kent. © THE DEVONSHIRE COLLECTION, CHATSWORTH. REPRODUCED BY PERMISSION OF THE CHATSWORTH SETTLEMENT TRUSTEES.

is generally attributed to Lancelot Brown or his associate Michael Millican who did so much at Chatsworth in the years around 1760. But much of what is shown was clearly in place by 1743, to judge from Smith's distant view: might the creation of the Salisbury Lawn, and the winding paths and casual groupings of trees elsewhere in the gardens, owe something to Kent? This is certainly a strong possibility.

Some 'Kentian' changes were certainly made to the wider landscape around this time. The estate accounts record a large amount of planting in the late 1720s and 30s. There was tree planting 'on Calton' in 1728; in 1729, 4,400 fir trees were planted 'upon Lindup' and 13,000 trees were planted 'on Lees Moor' nearby.[27] The following year 10,000 'young firrs' were planted in the park and on Lindup.[28] In 1733 an enclosure in the park was built 'to plant with wood' and 10,000 trees were planted 'at Calton Plantation'.[29] Further work occurred at the end of the decade: in 1739 £52 was spent on 'planting the hill side in Calton', and an area called Spring Wood was fenced and

FIGURE 42.
One of several designs
by William Kent for
the grounds of
Chatsworth. This one
shows proposed
improvements to the
steep escarpment to the
east of the House: pine
trees, a waterfall and
classical temples would
have created the kind
of romantic, idealised
Italian scenery
fashionable in the
period. This scheme
was never executed,
although some of
Kent's other ideas were
possibly adopted.

planted.[30] Some of this planting was clearly within the park, probably on and below the escarpment. But much was further afield on the other side of the river, on the slopes and hilltops flanking the Derwent valley to the south-west of the house, and visible in the far distance. In this context it is noteworthy that maps surveyed later in the century – in 1773 and 1785 – shows a number of small circular clumps on the rising ground now occupied by New Piece Plantation (Figure 48).[31] The latter area of woodland was planted by Capability Brown in the early 1760s, so the clumps, which would have appeared as prominent features on the south-western skyline when viewed from the house, are evidently related to some earlier landscaping scheme. They are very similar to distant, skyline plantations which Kent created at a number of other places where he advised, such as Holkham in Norfolk. The writer Horace Walpole was later to describe Kent's use of 'loose groves' to crown an 'easy eminence with happy ornament'.[32] It is noteworthy that in three short sections the boundary wall of New Piece Plantation is hidden behind a low bank – an unusual form of ha-ha, lacking an accompanying ditch (Figure 93). As the sections in question are associated with, but do not encroach upon, one of the skyline clumps (now subsumed within Brown's plantation), it is possible that the wall *predates* Brown's plantation and originally formed a field boundary which, lying like the clumps on the crest of the hill when viewed from the house, needed to be kept hidden in this way. Significantly, in this context, Kent was a noted early exponent of the use of the ha-ha.

Rather similar clumps are shown in a number of places within the park on these later maps, most notably in the area to the north-east of Edensor village, again crowning a low eminence in full view of the house within what was then the warren. In addition, boundary earthworks of a small oval plantation survive high on the ridgetop to the west of Edensor, again in view of the house and now subsumed in the much larger Paddocks Plantation, created in the 1860s. No oval plantation appears here on estate maps from 1785 onwards, by which date a small wood of similar size but square in shape had been integrated with shelter belt plantations created in the mid eighteenth century. All these oval plantations may well have been established in the 1720s–30s, and perhaps under Kent's direction. Either way, the appearance of these clumps, and the more extensive areas of woodland a little further south, is a clear sign that under the 3rd Duke's guiding hand more attention was being paid to the main view from the house, westwards across the Derwent valley.

There is also another, albeit minor, indication that greater aesthetic attention was being paid to the far bank of the river. Both Tillemans' painting of the mid 1720s, and Smith's of 1743, show in the foreground a park-like pasture for thoroughbred horses, sited just west of the river and immediately south of the road to Edensor, entered via an ornamental gate. This appears, from the archaeological evidence, to have been created by the removal of a number of field boundaries some time in the first two decades of the eighteenth century.

The evidence thus suggest that a number of important changes were made to the landscape and gardens around Chatsworth in the late 1720s and 1730s, changes shown perhaps most clearly by Smith's painting of 1743. Further modifications were made after the date of the painting; in 1743 attention turned to the canal and its associated 'slope', probably that to the south rather than west of the house, and work continued through 1744 and 1745. This was extensive, involving levelling, turfing, 'claying the bottom', and 'removing the slope by the side of the canall'.[33] In 1745–6 there was more felling of trees and earth-moving; and in 1749–50 the Greenhouse Pond was altered and enlarged, a new summer house erected, and both the Greenhouse and the Bowling Green House removed and re-erected in their present positions.[34] The 3rd Duke noted in a letter, written in the spring of 1749, that 'The Green House is down'; and in March of the following year, 'they are at work on the Orange House and will soon have done'.[35] The enlarged Greenhouse Pond was short-lived and appears to have been removed before Brown came to Chatsworth. Although the precise nature of the changes under the 3rd Duke remains obscure, it is clear that a great deal of activity occurred during the late 1720s, 30s and 40s. These were *not* years of inactivity.

Nor was the deer park neglected in this period. Indeed, the records from the first half of the eighteenth century show that it was intensively managed. The state of the grass was improved by regular, large-scale applications of lime, by removing rushes and 'rubbish', and by burning bent grass;[36] breaches in the walls were repaired every year, as were the drives, causeways and 'hunting ways', and the deer houses were kept thatched.[37] Foxes, moles and other vermin were systematically eradicated,[38] and the deer were regularly fed on hay and other fodder, and 'brousewood' was cut for them from the shreds and pollards.[39] The fawns were culled, and new stock were brought from Hardwick.[40]

But when the 4th Duke inherited in 1755 the park was still entirely restricted to the eastern side of the river, and much of it lay out of sight on the gritstone shelf above the house. More importantly, the house still looked out across a jumble of functional, productive and geometric features. True, the old ice house beside the Canal Pond had probably gone out of use by this time – a new one was constructed in a more secluded location in the Roe Park, to the north of the house, in 1734 (its site is now occupied by the Game Larder).[41] But to the south-west of the house the kitchen gardens lay in close proximity and, to judge from a plan made by Samuel Brailsford in 1751 (Figure 43), were extensive and complex.[42] The plan shows other things that would by now have been considered unsightly, unfashionable, or both, including the formal canal and old complex of fishponds; the 'Cana Deerpond', a large pond for ducks and other wildfowl; the barns and outbuildings to the north-west of the house; and the water mill to the south-west. Beyond the river – and beyond the area covered by Brailsford's plan – the 'Cunigre', or rabbit warren, continued to function. In 1756–7 there were 335 breeding couples recorded.[43] By the 1750s such a setting was no longer considered at all appropriate for a house of Chatsworth's grandeur.

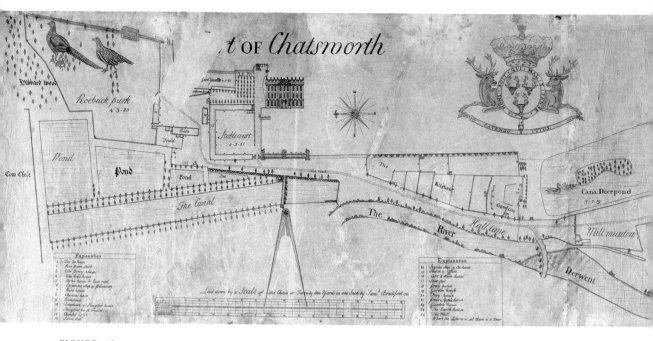

Capability Brown and the landscape park

In the 1750s and 60s, the stylistic developments of the 1730s and 40s pioneered by Bridgeman, Kent and others were taken to their logical conclusion.[44] The boundary between garden and park was now largely dissolved, so that the mown grass of the former appeared to merge with the grazed ground of the latter – although, in reality, the two were often separated by a discreet ha-ha. Ideally, all avenues, walls, terraces and geometric planting were removed, and kitchen gardens and other functional features of the estate landscape discreetly hidden away from view, so that the mansion appeared to sit, 'solitary and unconnected', in a 'naturalistic' and irregular landscape of grass and scattered trees, interspersed with circular or ovoid clumps. Where an owner had the money and the terrain was suitable, the design would include a lake of irregular or serpentine form. The whole ensemble was usually surrounded, in whole or part, by a perimeter tree belt. Designed landscapes of this type, thought of as nature idealised but in fact worlds apart from what nature would create if left to its own devices, became popular in the 1750s and spread rapidly throughout the estates of the landed classes. Looked at in one way, they were the kind of irregular, Italianate picture-painting landscape espoused by

William Kent, but writ large – made, as it were, the sole setting for the house, rather than one part of it. The clumps, temples and scattered trees that had occupied fairly small areas in the grounds of grand houses like Stowe or Holkham were now spread across a much wider area of ground. But we can look at the landscape park – as its name implies – in another way: as the final triumph of the *park*, an irregular landscape of grass and scattered trees, over the *garden*, as the primary setting for the mansion.[45] Chatsworth, as we have seen, was in many ways unusual among great mansions in that prior to the 1760s it had only a small area of well-treed parkland beyond the walled garden. The main area of 'park' was far less picturesque in character, a bleaker and rougher tract of ground, quite out of sight of the house. At most residences of Chatsworth's status the creation of a fashionable landscape park simply involved the demolition of walled gardens and terraces and the removal of formal planting, so that an existing park could be extended up to the walls of the mansion. It was generally only at lesser residences – the homes of the local gentry, individuals who seldom aspired to the expensive luxury of a deer park – that parks had to be created from scratch, out of the raw material of the working countryside. But the unusual earlier development of Chatsworth's landscape ensured that this, as we shall see, is to a large extent what happened here.

Landscape parks, like all styles of landscape design, were not entirely divorced from other aspects of life: from social practices, political beliefs and the like. It was only because the style fitted the spirit of the age that it became so popular. The middle decades of the eighteenth century saw the development of less hierarchical relations among the landed and professional classes. Earlier, the Dukes of Devonshire, as paramount leaders of county society, would have been treated with appropriate deference and awe. The structure and geometry of their house and their gardens both reflected, and formed a setting for, the stiff formality of social engagements, in which rank and status were reaffirmed in an almost ritual fashion. But in the course of the eighteenth century deference was replaced by an easy affability, by an emphasis on social skills honed at urban assemblies and at great spa towns like Bath. The owners and rulers of the land – from great magnates, through wealthy merchants and local gentry, down to the professional classes – began to meet on more informal and more equal terms, forming a single 'polite society'. And at the same time, they became more clearly marked off from the farmers, labourers and others who lived around them.[46]

Parks were the shared badge of this new society. They were landscapes of seclusion, excluding close-up views of the local population or their homes and providing their owners with a measure of privacy, as well as offering some protection for the game with which the larger parks, at least, were usually well stocked. Yet at the same time they were places for 'polite' recreation, and most of the larger parks were open to the 'public', in the contemporary sense of the respectable members of society. The removal of walled gardens, moreover, was also accompanied by the destruction of nutgrounds, orchards, dovecotes, fishponds, and farmyards – all the productive clutter with which landowners had once been happy to associate themselves. This, too, made an important statement: that the owner was distanced from the humdrum practicalities of domestic production, and was a member of a class quite distinct from the farming and labouring population. The removal of formal gardens also emphasised the superiority of the landed elite over the expanding middle classes who, of necessity, given the size of the plots at their disposal, continued to lay out structured and often fairly geometric gardens. In a polarised yet socially complex world the landscape style flourished because it required the one resource which only the established elite, and those wealthy enough to join it, possessed – land in abundance.[47] Today, we associate landscape parks with the famous designer Lancelot 'Capability' Brown; and although it is true that there were other important landscape gardeners working at the time, all to some extent developing the new taste, Brown was by far the most famous and successful. And not surprisingly, it was to Brown that the 4th Duke turned when he decided to create a more suitable and fashionable setting for Chatsworth.

Brown began his career as a gardener in Northumberland, moved to the south of England in 1739, and by 1741 was being employed by Lord Cobham at Stowe in Buckinghamshire. He was periodically 'lent out' by his employer, supplying advice to friends and associates, such as Lord Denbigh at Newnham Paddox and Richard Greville at Wooton, and after Cobham died in 1749 he moved to the outskirts of London and set up in business as a landscape gardener. His career blossomed: he produced designs for Packington in Warwickshire and Croome Court in Worcestershire in 1750; for Petworth in Sussex in 1751; for Kirtlington Park and Moor Park in Hertfordshire in 1752; for Beechwood in Hertfordshire and Belhus in Essex in 1754; and for Ingestre in Staffordshire in 1756. In 1757 he was at work at Longleat and the following year began commissions at Harewood in Yorkshire, Ragley in Warwickshire, Wrest Park in Bedfordshire and Shortgrove in Essex. His involvement with Chatsworth probably began in the same year.[48]

Brown continued to work until his death in 1783, so Chatsworth came quite early in his career. But his reputation was already well established, his working methods well refined, and his style mature and accomplished. This said, Chatsworth must, in many ways, have been a challenge to the great man. This was rougher terrain than he was used to, and whereas most of his earlier commissions had involved transforming an existing deer park, integrating the experience of park and pleasure ground, here – as already noted – there was very little parkland in the normal sense in view of the house and, in effect, an entirely new park had to be made, at the expense of a large area of working countryside, on both banks of the Derwent.

The making of the new park

It is probable that the removal of the old-fashioned clutter in the vicinity of the house – the ponds, outbuildings, yards, kitchen gardens and mill – was first contemplated by the 3rd Duke as early as 1751, as the next stage in his progressive modernisation of the grounds. The survey made by Samuel Brailsford in that year shows Chatsworth House and some of its immediate surroundings – but, surely significantly, *only* those features which were to be swept away at the end of that decade (Figure 43).[49] If such a change had indeed been mooted as early as this nothing came of it immediately. It was only with the 3rd Duke's death, and the accession of his son as the 4th Duke, that the immediate surroundings of the mansion were transformed and the creation of the new park begun.

The decision to start work in earnest in 1759 may have been influenced by the promise of significant income from the Duke's copper mines at Ecton in Staffordshire. These had been leased to two successive companies of 'adventurers' since 1723 and the second lease was to run out in 1760. In the early 1750s rich ore deposits were found here and by 1759, as they were followed downwards, they were discovered to be exceptional; the mine promised to continue to be very productive. The Duke decided that the lease would not be renewed, as a great deal more money could be made by running the mine 'in-house'. This was a prudent decision; by 1790, when the main ore deposit at depth had been largely worked out, it had proved to be one of the richest copper mines in Britain and had earned the estate a total of over £290,000 profit.[50] It is ironic that the creation of the idealised landscape of the new park – like the various other changes made to the setting of the house between the seventeenth and the nineteenth centuries – was largely funded by the great mineral wealth on the Duke's estates, including lead and copper in the Peak District and coal and iron in north-east Derbyshire and Staffordshire. For, in making these splendours, significant amounts of money were obtained by the creation of (from our perspective) extensive industrial, heavily-polluted, and less than idyllic landscapes.

Work on the new landscape began in 1758. The old rabbit warren was the first feature to be targeted. A note in the accounts records that 'The Warren was destroyed 1758, sold all the rabbits': the following year there are references to 'Pareing, burning and ploughing ye Warren'.[51] Next, a writ of *Ad Quod Damnum* was called in the court of Chancery, confirmed by an enquiry in January 1759, which closed or diverted a number of local roads.[52] This was the normal, although legally rather cumbersome, method of closing and diverting public highways before legislative changes in 1773.[53] In theory, all freeholders dwelling within the hundred in which the changes were to take place were invited to the site and asked to agree with what was proposed (it would have been a rash man indeed who was prepared to oppose the wishes of the Duke in such a matter).

Three roads were terminated by the 1759 writ (Figures 38, 39): a 'drift way' running from 'south of the park at Randalls Gate', over the Chatsworth bridge across the Derwent, and thence to the inn at Edensor (a packhorse route through Stand Wood, in part probably following the then disused 1710–11 coach road, then skirting the southern end of the gardens to the bridge); a 'carriage way' leading from Beeley, over the old bridge, to the inn (the turn-pike or toll road, created in 1739, which ran from Bakewell, via Ballcross and Edensor, to Chesterfield, following the valley bottom to the east of the river); and a public way leading from the inn to a 'guide post at the top of Gunnell Lane' (a route skirting north of Edensor village, to Baslow).[54] These were replaced by new roads and drives which are essentially those which exist in and around the park today, although with a number of later modifications. The intention of these changes can only in part have been to secure a greater degree of privacy for the Duke and his family, for although public access was removed from the immediate vicinity of the mansion, roads still ran through the park west of the river, as of course they do today. An equally important aim was to provide a more imposing approach to the house, one which displayed its new setting to greatest advantage.

It is noteworthy that the changes to the road system in and around Chatsworth Park occurred at the same time as a wider programme of improve-ments to the transport network in the Peak District, which for the first time provided a linked infrastructure of good-quality roads, many of which are still in use today.[55] In 1758 the estate accounts record the construction of a new coach road across Harewood Moor, on the high moors to the east of Beeley. This was a private drive for the use of the Cavendish family and their visitors which provided a more direct route from the southern end of the Park through to Chesterfield, and one from which the vast extent of the estate (which began to the east of the moors) could be proudly displayed.[56] This still exists as a track across Harewood Moor, branching off from the 1739 turnpike. The latter had been the first public toll road built in the area. Burdett's map of Derbyshire, printed in 1767, suggests that it probably followed a route from the south end of the park, via Beeley Hilltop and thence to Chesterfield.[57] This road was made redundant for through traffic in 1760, when another turnpike, running from Rowsley Bridge to Stone Edge, was constructed, allowing easy passage to Bakewell via Haddon, rather than Edensor. The Harewood Moor route was left as a more exclusive drive to and from Chatsworth. This new turnpike was one of several created at this time around the estate, including the East Moor to Wardlow (via Baslow and Hassop) Turnpike in 1759 – the original line of which can still be traced as an earthwork in the north-eastern part of the park, for it was partly rerouted in the 1820s when the park was extended northwards. An estate road from Edensor to Baslow was also improved in the early 1760s, presumably to provide better links with Chatsworth House – this was also moved in the 1820s when the park was expanded. As so often in the eighteenth and early nineteenth centuries, 'private' improvements were thus closely integrated with wider 'public' under-takings: indeed, the line was very blurred in this still-deferential age.

According to the terms of the roads closure of 1759, the principal new road through Chatsworth Park, which ran on a similar line to the present main road from Beeley to Edensor, was to cross the river Derwent by means of 'a sufficient bridge', and the estate accounts duly record its construction in that year.[58] This is Beeley Bridge in the south of the park (described as 'a Bridge with one Arch' in the accounts for 1759).[59] The accounts record the work carried out between 1759 and 1760 on 'makeing a road from Edensor Church to the new Bridge' and beyond.[60] Stone was brought to the site, broken up to make the surface, and covered with gravel; some levelling also took place.[61] The total cost was around £350. In 1760–1 various other roads and drives were constructed, at a total cost of over £288,[62] and at the same time construction work began on new stables, and on the 'new bridge near Chatsworth' – that is, the elegant Chatsworth Bridge, which carries the main drive to the house across the river.[63]

Not only the bridges, but also the new stables and a new water mill located in the south of the park, were designed by the architect James Paine. He was born in 1716 and was, with Sir Robert Taylor, perhaps the most significant of the 'second generation' of Palladian architects working in Britain in the middle and later decades of the eighteenth century.[64] Indeed, it was said of the two men that they 'neatly divided the practice of the profession between them, for they had few competitors before Mr Adam [Robert Adam] entered the lists'.[65] Both Paine and Taylor were much less concerned with the 'correct' use of ratios and orders than the 'pure' Palladians of the previous generation – Burlington, Campbell, or Kent – had been. Instead, they used the ideas of Palladio and his English imitators in flexible, sensible ways.[66] Paine thus believed that certain features of the style, most notably free-standing porticoes, were 'very ill-adapted to our climate, still worse to our present mode of living', and should not therefore be slavishly imitated.[67] He was most noted as an architect of country houses, which he designed throughout the whole of his career, from the mid 1740s to the late 1770s. But he was also responsible for a variety of other buildings, including five major public bridges (and seven in private landscapes). The Duke had probably come across Paine in his capacity as Master of the King's Horse, for the architect worked as Clerk of Works at Newmarket. As well as being employed at Chatsworth, the Duke seems to have secured him the commission to design the new Cavendish Bridge over the Trent near Derby (which was destroyed in the floods of 1947), a project with which, as the name of the structure implies, the family were closely involved. Paine's association with the Devonshires continued even after the Duke's death in 1764, for he was retained by the 5th Duke as 'Surveyor': Paine dedicated his book, *Plans, Elevations and Sections of Noblemen's and Gentlemen's Houses*, to him.[68]

Paine made a number of changes to Chatsworth House itself, creating the present entrance in the north bow out of earlier kitchens and providing a new service range to the north (which was demolished in the nineteenth century when the present north range was built by the 6th Duke).[69] But it was his buildings in and around the park which are most striking. The stables which he designed, to the north-east of the house, has been justly described as 'one of the grandest' to be built in eighteenth-century England (Figure 44).[70] As was often the case, Paine drew heavily on the work of earlier Palladian architects, in this case William Kent. The entrance, in the form of a triumphal arch, the central cupola and other details are taken directly from Kent's design for the Royal Mews at Charing Cross, while the pyramidal-roofed angle towers are strongly reminiscent of those at Holkham Hall in Norfolk. But although Paine was happy to draw on earlier work in the 'correct' tradition, he was no slavish imitator. The rustication – that is, the lower courses of stone work, made to resemble crudely-cut blocks (a standard element of Palladian designs) – was much heavier than in anything which Kent or Campbell would have designed, more reminiscent of the work of the Italian architect Serlio; while in general the building is much more richly ornamented than almost any other contemporary stable block. Paine exhibited the proposals for the new building at the Royal Academy in 1763.[71]

For the design of the two bridges at Chatsworth he drew more heavily on Italian prototypes. In the absence of Anglo-Palladian precedents for such structures (with the exception of an unexecuted design by Colen Campbell for a new Westminster Bridge), he was obliged to base his design for the park bridge on one of Palladio's projects, as well as on the Roman bridge at Rimini. Both had niches for statues, but at Chatsworth these are empty and instead the statues were placed above the parapet: they were figures by Cibber, reused from the gardens.[72] Perhaps the most intriguing feature that Paine designed for the Duke, however, is the mill, which was erected between 1761 and 1762 in the far south of the park.[73] This is a striking classical structure, built of sandstone ashlar, with a mill wheel on the north front displayed beneath a massive round arch under a pitched slate roof (Figure 45). In part this was a utilitarian structure – a replacement for the old mill which stood close to the house, and which was demolished as part of the wider 'improvements' to the landscape. It was used, as the earlier mill had been, to grind corn from the estate farms: its large wheel was powered by a narrow channel, or leat, fed from water ponded back by a weir across the river, which was constructed, according to the estate accounts, in 1760 and 1761 (not the present feature, which is the result of a rebuilding in 1838) (Figure 46).[74] But in part the mill was also an ornamental structure, for the design of which Paine again drew heavily on Italian precedent, and in particular on the facades designed by Palladio for Roman churches. As we shall see, the building played a key role in the design of the new landscape and, while Paine was responsible for its design, its precise *location* must have been decided by Brown.

The mill was not the only functional feature cleared away from the vicinity of the great house. In typical fashion, the kitchen garden was demolished and rebuilt between 1760 and 1765 some 700 m to the north, secluded and distant from the house. The new site (now occupied by the Nursery and the caravan park) was levelled and cleared of trees in 1759 and 1760, and in the same year stone and bricks were brought there.[75] In 1761 more materials, including more than 333,000 bricks, were carried to the site.[76] Work proceeded fast and seems to have been largely completed by 1765. The bricks are said to have been fired in a kiln beside Brickhill Pond, a small area of water which still survives in the parkland some 400 m to the east (the pond is marked on Barker's survey of 1773).[77] Probably contemporary is the ice house, with associated pond and earthworks, which lies some 200 m to the south: this supplemented and eventually replaced the earlier ice house in Roebuck Park, which is still labelled as such on Barker's map.

These new structures – stable, bridges, mill and kitchen garden – striking and important though they are, formed only a relatively small part of the great landscaping project. Of far more significance were the vast schemes of earth-movement and tree-planting which continued for more than eight years. The estate accounts record in meticulous detail the work involved in landscaping the new park. 'Chatsworth New Park Wall' was begun in 1759 and largely completed by 1761.[78] At the same time, vast amounts of labour were expended, in the usual way, on 'levelling and stubbing old hedges and fences', work which was mainly concentrated in the years from 1760 to 1763, but which continued sporadically into the late 1760s.[79] The hallmark of the landscape style was extended panoramas over uninterrupted turf: walls or hedges would make the landscape look like the working countryside, and were invariably removed by park-makers with single-minded zeal. Yet while walls and hedges had to go, many hedgerow trees were allowed to remain, providing instant timber to grace the new parkland. Chatsworth was no exception to this rule, as we shall see (p. 121). Much of the park was also 'soughed' or drained, and some of the land here was newly laid to pasture.[80] In 1761 there were payments for 'Ploughing in ye Headfield to lay it down with Grass', in 1762 there were substantial purchases of grass seed for the 'new laid down ground', and in 1763 hay seed and clover were bought 'to sow the new ground with'.[81]

The accounts reveal, not surprisingly, that vast quantities of new trees were planted. Unfortunately, they are also rather vague about the precise locations, often simply listing payments for unspecified 'work in plantations'. But the broad pattern of planting is clear enough. The main effort seems to have been directed towards the rising ground on and beyond the south-western fringes of the new park. In 1758, two thousand Scots pine were planted on Lindup, well outside the park to the south-west but in view of the house, and unspecified ploughing, digging and walling continued here over the next few years.[82] At the same time, there was much activity along the ridge to the west, in Calton Pasture, where a number of small skyline clumps had already been established, as we have seen, as early as the 1730s. Large areas of ground were pared here in 1758–9, and ditching and planting at Calton, 'now the New parke', continued throughout the 1760s. All this marks the establishment of the long belt of woodland now known as New Piece Wood or Calton New Piece Plantation.[83] There was also much planting in the area of the Stand, and (probably) all along the escarpment to the east of the house, augmenting the existing areas of woodland here.

Not all the planting recorded in the accounts in the 1760s took place as part of Brown's landscaping. Some areas of woodland far from the park were also

FIGURE 44.

The stables, built to designs by the architect James Paine in the early 1760s, were as much an ornamental feature in the new landscape created by Brown as a functional necessity. © THE DEVONSHIRE COLLECTION, CHATSWORTH. REPRODUCED BY PERMISSION OF THE CHATSWORTH SETTLEMENT TRUSTEES.

FIGURE 45. (*opposite top*)

The mill in the far south of the park was designed by James Paine and built in the early 1760s. It served as a replacement for the old mill, which had stood to the south-east of the house, and which was removed when the new landscape was created by Capability Brown. But Paine's elegant building was also a decorative feature, terminating a long vista southwards from the pleasure grounds around the house, and ornamenting the approach road from the south.

© THE DEVONSHIRE COLLECTION, CHATSWORTH. REPRODUCED BY PERMISSION OF THE CHATSWORTH SETTLEMENT TRUSTEES.

FIGURE 46. (*opposite*)

The south weir in Chatsworth Park fed water into a leat which supplied Paine's new water mill. The weir was rebuilt in 1838 and forms an impressive decorative feature when viewed from One Arch Bridge.

established, or augmented, at this time, in what was evidently a period of frenzied afforestation: 'Burchells', planted in 1760–1, lies to the north-west of Edensor; 'Yarncliffe Wood', to the north-east of Grindleford, and 'Burnt Wood', south-east of Beeley, were planted in the late 1760s and early 1770s.[84] The accounts for 1758–9 also refer to 'walling and planting some clumps on Beeley Moor', and to the planting of 'nine squares with ash, wiggin, oler, poplar and willow'.[85] These flanked the new drive across Harewood Moor whose construction was noted earlier: the walled square enclosures still remain but the clumps themselves have largely disappeared. In 1764 a further 22,000 birch and other trees were established in a new plantation on Beeley Moor, just outside the southern boundary of the old park. Although the accounts imply that some of the trees used in these planting schemes were grown on the estate, large quantities were also brought in from outside. In 1760–61, for example, 71,800 thorns, 15,000 mountain ash and birch, 10,000 oaks and unspecified numbers of spruce were purchased.[86] Some of the trees came from local suppliers – the 10,000 oaks came from Matlock – but sometimes the estate was forced to look further afield, as in 1764, when there were payments for 'fetching oaks out of Leicestershire'.[87]

All this activity was undertaken by labourers or contractors directly employed by the estate. But the accounts also include a number of very large payments made to 'Mr Millican', and the particular tasks undertaken by him are not itemised, beyond the general description of 'moving earth'.[88] His name first appears in 1760, when he received £313 in twelve separate payments; in 1761 he received a further £637; from December 1761 to October 1762, £635; and from November 1762 to November 1763 no less than £710. The final payment – of £715, made for the period from 1763 to 1765 – is described as 'cash paid to Mr Millican on Mr Brown's account'. In all, the accounts suggest total payments to Millican of around £3,010 over a period of five years. This final payment to Millican contains the only reference to Capability Brown in the estate accounts.[89] Yet we can be sure that he was, indeed, the principal designer of the new landscape. Horace Walpole, visiting Chatsworth in 1761, specifically refers to the various works under way 'under the direction of Brown'.[90] 'Millican' is evidently Michael Millican or Milliken, one of several individuals who worked closely with Brown over the years and who are usually described as his 'foremen', although perhaps better considered as contractors or associates. He had been working for Brown for some time, for the latter's bank account records payments made to him as early as 1755.[91] But he settled into life at Chatsworth to such an extent that in 1764 he married a local girl, one Mary Lees, at Edensor. He continued to work at Chatsworth until January 1765, when Brown secured for him the post of Royal Gardener at Richmond Park. The letter sent by Brown to inform him of this appointment implies that the work at Chatsworth was by then nearly, but not quite, completed.[92]

Millican's activities, as already noted, are described in the accounts under the general heading of 'moving earth'. The fact that this particular activity was directly carried out by one of Brown's associates, whereas the rest of the work involved in creating the new landscape was undertaken by estate labour or local contract teams, indicates that it was in some way central to the execution of the design. Moreover, both the amounts of money paid, and the length of time involved, suggest that major alterations to landforms were involved. But where precisely was the earth being moved from or to? Some of Millican's endeavours may have been focused upon the area of the old formal gardens to the east and south of the house but, as we have seen, most of the terraces here had already been levelled before 1743, other than those which still survive today. Another possibility to consider is that, as at some of the other great landscapes on which Brown worked, areas of soil were being removed, and contours altered, in order to open up distant vistas. Here once again archaeology is of immense help in unravelling the history of the landscape. As we have seen, the surface of Chatsworth Park is covered by a more or less continuous carpet of earlier earthworks, including hollow-ways, field boundaries, and areas of ridge and furrow. There are few obvious *lacunae* in this rich continuum, where earth might have been 'shaved' to improve the landforms in this kind of way. The most important exception lies immediately north of the house, where the turf is smooth and featureless, and continuing into the area between the house and the river. A quick glance at Brailsford's plan of 1751[93] is enough to indicate the extent of the changes which must have been carried out to achieve this effect. Not only were the mill, stable yards, barns, farm yards, kitchen gardens, and Hall Lane removed and their earthwork traces systematically flattened, but the great canal and ponds lying to the north-west of the house were filled up and levelled so thoroughly that no trace of them survives today in the parkland turf: if we had no maps or plans of them, we would never guess that they had existed. The forecourt and bowling green to the west of the house, and the associated terrace, were also removed, and were replaced by a gentle slope. A similar degree of levelling seems to have occurred on the far side of the river, where the old road from Edensor once led to Chatsworth Bridge. It may well be that buildings at the easternmost end of the village were removed at this time; one is shown here on both Senior's 1617 survey[94] and Wilson's 1743 painting, and two can just about be made out on the early eighteenth-century Ombersley Court painting.

These changes not only provided the house with the isolated parkland setting demanded by contemporary fashion, here particularly striking as the house was approached from across the river, but also gave better views from the house down to the water: in all probability, the river had formerly been largely hidden. This is indeed confirmed by the comments made by Horace Walpole in 1761: that the Duke was 'making vast plantations ... *and levelling a great deal of ground to show the river* under the direction of Brown'.[95]

FIGURE 47. (*overleaf*)
This aerial view shows the two weirs in Chatsworth park: the south weir supplying water to the mill, the north ponding back the waters of the Derwent, transforming the river in front of the House and gardens into something like a narrow lake – a central element of Brown's design for the park. © THE DEVONSHIRE COLLECTION, CHATSWORTH. REPRODUCED BY PERMISSION OF THE CHATSWORTH SETTLEMENT TRUSTEES.

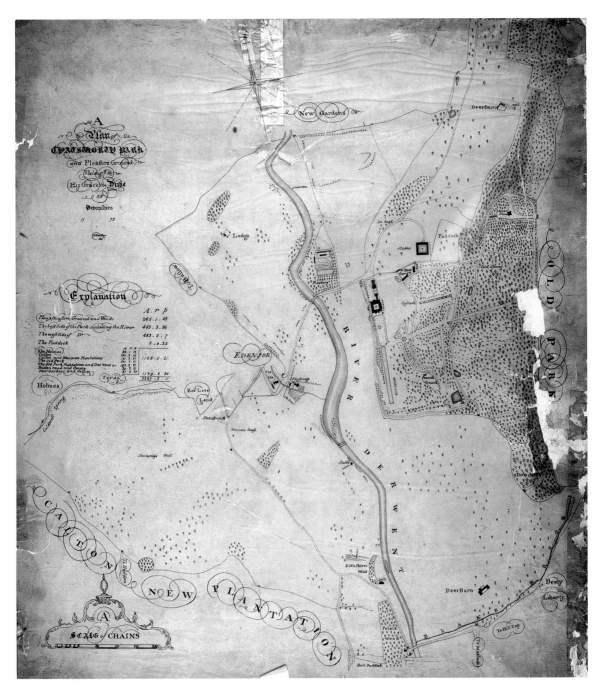

FIGURE 48.
George Barker's 1773 map of Chatsworth Park was probably made to show the newly-created landscape. All its main features were now in place. The roads, drives, weirs, mill, stable and bridges are shown, and the site of the new kitchen gardens, in the far north of the park, is indicated. Along the southern edge of the park the vast area of woodland planted by Brown, 'Calton New Plantation', is shown, together with at least one circular clump, perhaps created by William Kent in the 1730s. © THE DEVONSHIRE COLLECTION, CHATSWORTH. REPRODUCED BY PERMISSION OF THE CHATSWORTH SETTLEMENT TRUSTEES.

In addition a weir was installed some 700 m to the south of the house, ponding back the water and considerably widening the river; the effect appears to have been further enhanced by digging away the eastern river bank immediately upstream of the weir. Construction of this northern weir (in the sense that it lies to the north of the weir created for the new mill in the 1760s) is first specifically referred to in the accounts for 1772, when £239 12s 1d was spent on 'Building a new weir over ye River Derwent'.[96] But there is little doubt that this was a reconstruction of an existing feature – inadequate for the task at hand or damaged by flooding – which had been created by Brown and Millican and hidden in the accounts among the various substantial payments made to Millican in the 1760s. Walpole in 1760 described how 'The Duke is widening it [the river], and will make it the middle of his park', and it is hard to see how this effect could have been achieved simply by widening the channel itself. The use of dams and weirs to pond back the flow of streams or rivers, in order to create lakes or similar features, was a standard part of Brown's landscape package (Figure 47).

Although the new landscape was intended to function primarily as an ornamental setting for the house, deer were still kept within it. The estate accounts continue to record payments for feeding and managing the herds, and there were no less than three deer barns, for feeding and sheltering the deer in winter, of which one still survives in the south of the park, as well as a 'venison house' near Edensor, all of which are clearly shown on the map of the park surveyed by George Barker in 1773 (Figure 48).[97] Deer and other livestock were essential to maintain the grassland. The warrener's lodge at the heart of the old warren, which had stood since at least the beginning of the seventeenth century,[98] was also still standing at this time, although what it was used for after the late 1750s is not known (it was removed shortly after Barker's map was made).

It is noteworthy that, in spite of the scale and expense of all these changes, both of the sixteenth-century buildings which had survived up to this time – the Stand and Queen Mary's Bower – were allowed to remain. These were presumably now considered as picturesque incidents in the new landscape. It is particularly striking that the latter stood beside a small formal garden, secluded from the surrounding parkland by an area of woodland named by Barker as 'The Rookery' (Figures 18, 48). Indeed, the basic layout of this area – with a pond surrounding the Bower, and orchards to north and south – had remained largely unchanged since the sixteenth century, in strong contrast to the complete removal of the canal, ponds and tree-lined walks around it, which were systematically obliterated by Brown and Millican. There were, however, changes in detail. Barker's map shows a group of three small buildings in the northern area (by then cleared of trees) which nineteenth-century records suggest were hothouses;[99] and there was a ha-ha here (cleaned out in 1811 and filled in in 1822), which may be the 'sunk fence in the Canall Walke' which was walled in 1763.[100] The other boundaries seem to have been walled.[101] Why this small area of hidden formal gardens was retained is not clear, although it was not uncommon for secluded gardens in isolated positions to exist in this period, complete with ornamental buildings: they made pleasant destinations for short walks out from the mansion, across the parkland.

But this was not the only ornamental garden at Chatsworth (Figure 48). The extensive area to the south and east of the house continued to be used as such, as it had been for centuries. In the usual fashion it was separated from the park to the south and west by a 'sunk fence' or ha-ha, constructed in 1761–62.[102] Of this feature, the section running eastwards from the northern corner of the house was filled in during the early nineteenth century;[103] while another part running to the west of the house was presumably destroyed when the great terrace was built here around the same time. But it is possible that one stretch still survives on the boundary between the gardens and the park to the south of the house: the substantial ha-ha here has a retaining wall of large, regular and rectangular gritstone blocks, surmounted by wide flat slabs of gritstone. However, this may well be a later reconstruction, perhaps dating to the mid 1830s when the boundary between the park and garden was altered. Either way, both a plan of the pleasure grounds made in c.1770 (which survives only as later copy, perhaps by Wyatville (Figure 49)) and Barker's map of 1773,[104] provide much information about what lay inside this 'sunk fence'.[105]

The principal features of the grounds within the ha-ha, including Morton's Pond and the Grotto Pond, were connected by serpentine paths which meandered through areas of lawn, trees and shrubbery. These paths extended out into Stand Wood – indeed, some time in the 1760s or early 1770s the high wall between the formal gardens and the old deer park to the east was removed. There were a number of possible circuit walks. That which probably represented the main route started before the western front of the house and ran southwards, to the west of and below the canal, then followed the southern edge of the garden up to the Grotto Pond before returning to the house from the north-east. Near the two ponds, but further down the slope among the trees, paths led to a small enclosed area called the 'Peacock Ground' which, as noted above, had perhaps been in existence since the early eighteenth century. Barker's 1773 plan suggests that two of the 'paths', which came together at a small circular clearing in the trees just south of the Cascade, were designed as narrow open vistas through the woodland, one up to the Sowter Stone (a natural outcrop) at the crest of the scarp to the east, the other following the contour southwards; given the terrain, in all probability the first of these paths was not designed to be followed by anything other than the eye. Other walks led up to the Stand (also approached by a steep flight of steps) and to a 'Cold Spring' which existed some 200 m to the north-east of the Cascade House. This is shown as an L-shaped feature and was presumably a cold bathing pool, another fashionable feature of the period.

The archives suggest that the pleasure grounds were elaborately planted with a wide range of ornamental shrubs. The vouchers for 1760 record the purchase of '30 striped [i.e., variegated] hollies' and a 'parcel of flowering

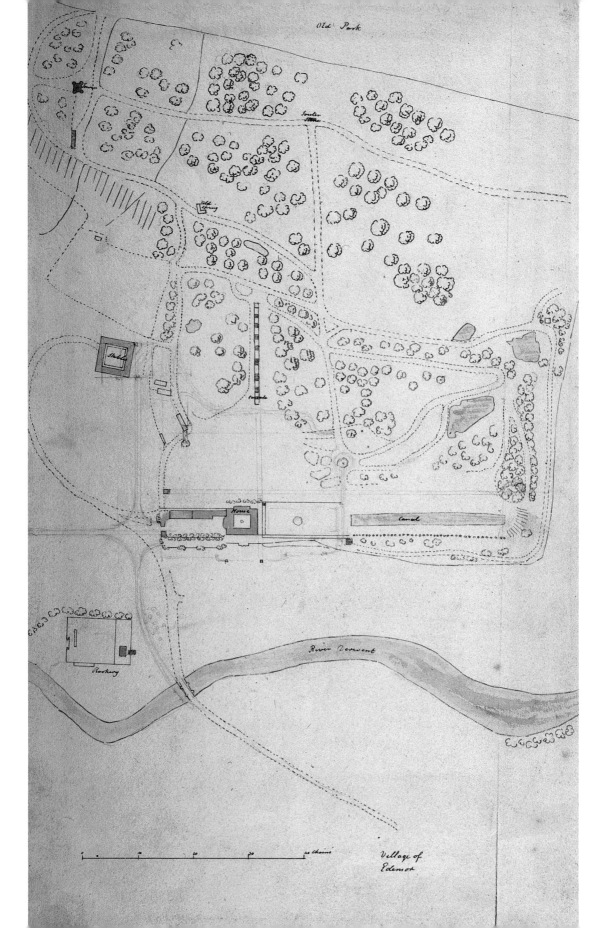

Old Park

South Lodge

Stables

House

Canal

Rockery

River Derwent

Village of
Edensor

chains

FIGURE 50.
View across Calton Pasture from the serpentine drive around Moatless Plantation. This large open area immediately to the south-west of the park, beyond New Piece Plantation, served as an 'outer park' in the eighteenth and nineteenth centuries, providing panoramic views westwards and southwards, towards Bakewell and Calton Lees. A pond, and the remains of a clump, still signal the area's aesthetic role.

shrubs', while in 1761 payments were made to one John Naylor for travelling to Londesborough 'for shrubs'.[106] In 1759 a phenomenal range of trees and shrubs was sent from Philadelphia by James Alexander – over eighty varieties in all, including tulip tree, hickory, swamp viburnum, 'blue beryd Cornus', and honey locust: 'these ar what I hav collected but would hav contained sum more varietys only for the nesesity I was of putting them up in such a hurry becaus of a vessel sudently and unexpectedly sailing ...'.[107] Some of these plants may have been grown in an area called the 'Green House Garden', located beside the 1st Duke's Greenhouse, but most must have been more widely scattered. The pleasure grounds were so extensive, however, that they were grazed by sheep in the summer rather than simply mown, and the accounts regularly record payments such as that made to 'Sam Furness and his boy for tending sheep in the Gardens', presumably to ensure that the more vulnerable areas of the planting were not immediately stripped by the flock.[108]

These plant purchases clearly suggest that the pleasure gardens were greatly modified around 1760. But as we have already noted, much of their basic structure may have come into existence more than two decades earlier, possibly under the direction of William Kent. Some even older features continued to exist within them. Although Walpole, visiting Chatsworth again in 1768, reported that the grounds had been 'much improved' by the removal of 'many foolish waterworks',[109] several – including the Cascade, the Willow Tree, and the great fountain in the Canal Pond – remained, and the estate accounts record numerous payments for the upkeep of pipes, channels and supply ponds.[110] This survival is, in some ways, slightly surprising, for by the middle of the eighteenth century many visitors seem to have found these features unfashionable and rather tasteless. Mrs Lybbe Powys for example, coming to Chatsworth in 1757, considered them 'more grand than pleasing', and noted disapprovingly 'a kind of triflingness ... in the copper willow-tree, and other contrivances beneath the dignity of the place'.[111] There were perhaps other ornamental features: Walpole refers to 'oaks and rocks' taken into the pleasure grounds, but nothing is known of them or their context.

The new landscape created at Chatsworth in the middle decades of the eighteenth century was, for the most part, self-contained and inward-looking. Yet it also provided opportunities to experience the beauties of the wider countryside. In particular, rides running through New Piece Plantation (shown on an estate map of 1785)[112] and following the line of an old road to Haddon (as indicated by Barker's 1773 map)[113] led to the extensive Calton Pastures, beyond the hilltop plantations to the south-west of the park. Here, to judge from the archaeological evidence, a pattern of enclosed fields put in place in the seventeenth or early eighteenth centuries was removed, probably in the 1760s, and made into a large sheepwalk (Figure 50). The area was given an ornamental, park-like appearance, with four stands of trees and a large pond. Although well out of sight of the house, it was evidently considered to be an outer park, designed to be visited while riding and perhaps for sport: the location provided magnificent views down towards Bakewell and Calton Lees.

The character of the design

Soon after the great transformation of the landscape has been completed, around 1770, William Marlow produced a fine painting, showing the house standing in the new park (Figure 51); and in 1773, George Barker produced his map of Chatsworth, perhaps to show the appearance of the completed land-scape (Figure 48).[114] The latter, in particular, shows all the alterations and additions so far noted, including the new mill in the south of the park, Paine's two bridges, the pleasure grounds containing serpentine paths and several of the old water features, and the newly-created parkland lying on both sides of the river. On the south-western edges of the mapped area the position of Calton New Plantation is shown, clearly engulfing the earlier skyline clumps (this arrangement is depicted with greater clarity on a slightly later map, of 1785, which shows only that section of the park lying in Edensor Parish to the west of the Derwent).[115] To the east, above the wooded escarpment and the pleasure grounds, the location of the 'Old Park' is carefully noted. The map also shows the substantial north weir which was constructed across the river Derwent, and the widened section of the river immediately upstream, in front of the house; and it marks the site of the 'New Gardens' – i.e., the walled kitchen garden – to the north of the house.

In short, by this time Chatsworth had acquired a fashionable parkland setting (Figure 52), the house looking out across the serpentine river and an extensive sea of grass. But the mansion did not stand 'solitary and uncon-nected'. As was generally the case in this period there were extensive pleasure grounds, containing lawns, trees and shrubs, in the area to the east and south of the house, nestling under Stand Wood, which had long been occupied by gardens. Despite the fashion for expansive parkland, people still enjoyed the relative intimacy of gardens, and the plants they contained, and were unwilling to sweep them away.

The 1773 map shows that a significant number of the trees within the new park grew in straight lines, indicating that they had originated as hedgerow timber, retained when the associated hedges were 'stubbed and levelled'. Many of these trees still survive, mostly oaks, but including some examples of ash and sycamore (Figure 53). This pattern is even more evident on the 1785 map of Edensor, a more accurate survey. A comparison of the surviving timber in the park with the trees shown on this map suggests that Brown added lime, beech, and sycamore, some sweet chestnut, and probably cedar, especially on the western bank of the river, to the north-west of the house. He also appears to have augmented the planting on the upper slopes in the south-eastern area of the park (Figures 3, 54).

While some of Brown's activities may have been directed towards the pleas-ure ground, this, as we have seen, was in part a creation of previous decades and his main activities were unquestionably directed towards the making of the new park. We can see how Brown adapted an already well-tried formula to slightly unusual conditions. As well as removing all the old-fashioned clutter

FIGURE 51.

William Marlow's painting of c. 1770 shows Brown's new landscape soon after completion. Mill, kitchen gardens and yards have been removed, the new stables and bridges built, and the area to the west of the Derwent transformed into a 'natural' landscape. The river has been widened, to form a narrow 'lake'. © THE DEVONSHIRE COLLECTION, CHATSWORTH. REPRODUCED BY PERMISSION OF THE CHATSWORTH SETTLEMENT TRUSTEES.

FIGURE 52. (*opposite top*)

The area covered by the gardens and park in c. 1780. By the late 1760s much of the new work transforming the ornamental landscape had been completed. However, by about 1780 several additional features, such as the two lodges, the New Inn, the Parsonage, and the drive to Beeley, had been added. The area of the Old Park above the escarpment still existed, but its days were numbered (A: pre-1760 skyline clumps; B: possible pre-1760 skyline clumps in the park; C: Buston Wood; D: The Stables; E: ice houses; F: the Rookery and garden; G: the new kitchen gardens; H: Brick Kiln Pond; I: deer barns; J: farmstead; K: the 1759 turnpike; L: Old Pond; M: Swiss Lake; N: One Arch Bridge; O: Paine's Mill; P: the weirs; Q: the 'lake'; R; the old stable; S: Three Arch Bridge; T: the old warrener's lodge; U: the venison house; V: Moatless Plantation; W: Wynne's Lodge; X: The New Inn and adjacent lodge; Y: Old Parsonage; Z: New Parsonage (on the site of the Devonshire Arms).

FIGURE 53. (*opposite*)

When the new park was created in the eighteenth century, and also when it was expanded to the north and west in the early nineteenth century, numerous existing trees, growing in hedges, were retained. Some, like these oaks in the north-east park of the 1820s, still grow in obvious lines.

Legend

- Park and garden boundaries – present in c. 1780 and today
- Park, garden and field boundaries – now gone
- Present park and garden boundaries – created since c. 1780
- Roads and main drives – present in c. 1780 and today
- Roads and main drives – now disused or little used
- Plantations - present in c. 1780 and today (often replanted)
- Woodland and plantations – now gone
- River Derwent – in c. 1780 and today
- River Derwent – course now changed
- Weirs - in c. 1780 and today (one now rebuilt)
- Canal, lakes and ponds – present in c. 1780 and today
- Ponds – now gone or disused
- Buildings – present in c. 1780 and today
- Buildings – now gone
- Edensor village
- Site of Old Parsonage removed in late 1770s

N

To Baslow
To Chesterfield
To Baslow
To Pilsley
To Calton Lees
To Beeley

K
W
J
H
E
I
G
C
B
T
B
Park
F
E
D
The Stand
Old Deer Park
X
B
S
Chatsworth
Stand Wood
M
Edensor
Gardens
L
Y
Z
I
U
Q
P
R
Park
Park
A
New Piece Plantation
A
A
P
A
O
V
N
Calton Pasture

0   M   500

of canals, ponds, service buildings and yards to the north and west of the house, he opened up views towards, and considerably widened, the river. Walpole makes it clear that the latter was a vital part of the design and its results are clearly visible on Marlow's painting and on Barker's map: it created, in effect, a narrow serpentine lake occupying the middle distance of the view from the main rooms of the house. At the same time, the relentless campaign of planting on the skyline to the south-west of the park, complementing woodland already present to the east at Stand Wood, created a particularly imposing version of the perimeter belts which were a feature of most of Brown's parks. The area between 'lake' and belt was scattered with trees in a superficially artless fashion. In slightly more undulating terrain than he often had to deal with Brown thus created a familiar – one might almost say, stereotyped – designed landscape. Indeed, as at Alnwick in Northumberland, where views of the distant moors were planted out and outcrops of rock on lower ground hidden, Brown seems to have gone out of his way to obscure anything wild or rugged. In effect, Brown brought an idealised *lowland* landscape to these upland sites.

Some historians have argued that Brown's designs were rather more carefully and rigidly structured than the above account might suggest, or than garden historians often assume: and a closer examination of the landscape at Chatsworth does indeed reveal the careful and considered organisation of space and vistas. The positioning of Paine's bridge – angled at about 45 degrees to the front of the house – both contributes to the visual impact of the approach and ensures that it can be clearly seen from the house, elegantly reflected in the river. But more striking – although for some reason, previously unnoticed – is the part played by Paine's water mill in the far south of the park. This simple yet elegant building evidently had an ornamental role. Of particular note is the massive wheel housing, under a huge round arch, on the north side of the building, which was clearly supposed to be viewed and inspected, presumably after a walk or ride along the river bank. But, more importantly, the building is carefully angled, and was originally framed by planting, in such a way that its north face would have formed the termination for a carefully composed view down the length of the Derwent, from the point where the perimeter path turns the south-western corner of the pleasure grounds. The use of a mill to terminate a distant view in this way is reminiscent of the arrangement created a few decades earlier by William Kent at the famous gardens of Rousham in Oxfordshire. Similarly, when approaching Chatsworth from the south, along the original carriage road from One Arch Bridge, the mill is a striking foreground feature. It is now a picturesque ruin (a tree fell on it in a gale in 1962) but the vista from the gardens has recently been opened up by the judicious felling of a number of riverside trees.

Like most parks created in this period, the design of Chatsworth was thus organised primarily around a series of contrived views which could be enjoyed from house, pleasure grounds, and immediate approaches. All this did not mean, of course, that the wider parkland, and less contrived views, could not also be enjoyed, on horseback or on foot; and as already noted, Calton Pasture

FIGURE 54.
As well as retaining
many existing trees,
Brown also planted
much new timber. The
substantial girth of this
beech tree, on the
rising ground near the
south-western edge of
the park suggests that
it was planted around
1760.

may have functioned as a kind of 'outer park', reached by a 'riding', which
provided panoramic views across the farmed and wooded landscape to the
south and west. For the most part, however, the landscape created by Brown
was enjoyed from the house, or the lower ground near to it, and turned its
back on the wilder scenery of the high moorlands to the east.

Various changes were made to the park, as we shall see, in the course of the
later eighteenth and nineteenth centuries, including its expansion northwards,
as far as Baslow, in the 1820s and 30s. More sweeping were the changes in the
gardens, where the various additions and alterations made by Jeffry Wyatt –
later Sir Jeffry Wyatville and Paxton for the 6th Duke radically altered the relationship of the house and park. Nevertheless, much of the essential framework
of the Chatsworth landscape remains that established by Brown and Millican
in the 1750s and 60s.

CHAPTER FIVE

The Sixth Duke's Garden

Introduction

Capability Brown, ably assisted by Michael Millican and James Paine, provided eighteenth-century Chatsworth with a vast 'naturalistic' setting of the kind demanded by contemporary taste. But much of what we see at Chatsworth today was in fact created in the nineteenth century. For under the 6th Duke the gardens and park were altered yet again, in line with further changes in fashions. The place acquired not merely national but international fame: it became one of the wonders of Britain.

Interlude: the landscape under the 5th Duke

So far as the evidence goes, relatively little was done to the park or pleasure grounds under the 5th Duke. But the archives suggest careful maintenance, and certainly not the neglect which has sometimes been assumed.[1] The kitchen gardens were kept well stocked with fruit trees, and some minor changes were made to the pleasure grounds, as in 1800, when labourers were paid for 'levelling and stubbing a piece of ground there'.[2] The waterworks were maintained, the ponds and channels kept clear of mud, and in 1800 new springs were tapped bringing water to the supply reservoirs; this may have involved the re-routing and extension of the Harland Sick leat which is indicated by the archaeological evidence (Figure 34).[3] Some substantial repairs seem to have been carried out on the Cascade, the total bill in 1809 coming to over £117. But the very survival of the Cascade, Canal fountain and Willow Tree into an age which found such things increasingly absurd and unfashionable is a clear enough measure of the Duke's inactivity. He spent much of his time in London and had, perhaps, grown tired of making changes to the landscape given that he had succeeded to the dukedom at the age of only sixteen and had been forced to oversee the final stages of his father's great landscaping project. Perhaps if the 4th Duke had survived longer the remaining waterworks would all have been swept away.

Certainly, by the last decades of the century most visitors seem to have thought them rather inelegant. Viscount Torrington was, in 1789, dismissive of the Cascade, which 'when dry, is a disagreeable sight, and not much better, when cover'd with the dirty water they lower from the hill'. The Willow Tree he thought 'worthy only of a tea garden in London'. Like many visitors, he hints that the grounds were in some sense uncompleted. He particularly disliked the survival of the broad terrace on which the Canal Pond sits: 'Nor cou'd I refrain from remarking what I suppose all others do, at the ground remaining unsloped to the vale and river; which the gardener said might be completely done for 2000£'. He went on:

> As for the river, of clear water, meand'ring through the meadows, it is now but a pitiful twine, which, under an owner of spirit wou'd be made equal, if not superior to the Blenheim Water; but here is no taste, no comforts display'd. All is asleep! More money may be lavish'd in follies, or lost in cards, in one year than wou'd render this park a wonder of beauty.[4]

Another visitor, William Bray, similarly noted the 5th Duke's reluctance to 'lay out his money in disposing his grounds according to the modern simple and beautiful stile' (and, rather bizarrely to modern eyes, for preferring to spend his money on the relief of local poverty).[5] Some of these criticisms appear unfair (it would have been impossible to transform the Derwent into a lake as wide as that at Blenheim) but the general consensus was clearly that the 'deformalisation' of the Chatsworth grounds remained uncompleted because of the Duke's lack of interest in such matters. In fact, the only significant addition in these years was the Grotto, located towards the south-western edge of the pleasure grounds, and even this seems largely to have been the responsibility of the Duke's wife, the Duchess Georgiana (Figure 55).[6] The estate accounts record much activity here in 1798 and 1799.[7] Masons, plumbers, and carpenters were all hard at work, and White Watson was paid for 'superintending the making of the Grotto ... in the Gardens 52 1/2 days at 10/6 per day'.[8] No less than £29 7s 6d was spent on 'fossils, stalactites etc.'.[9] The final touches seem to have been made in 1800, when one Daniel Hodkin was paid 'for a cabinet of Mahogany, fitted into a recess in the fossil room'.[10]

While the gardens were thus not entirely neglected by the 5th Duke this was, in relative terms, a period of stasis. And yet, paradoxically, this inactivity was critical in the development of the landscape at Chatsworth. Had the Duke been more interested in keeping up with fashion, he might have taken the work of 'deformalisation' begun by his father to its logical, fashionable conclusion, and removed the Canal Pond, Cascade, terraces and other relics from the seventeenth-century gardens – those features which are such key parts of the gardens today. By the time he died in 1811, at the age of 63, hostility to such artificial contrivances was fading. They thus survived, although – as we shall see – within a very different landscape.

Wyatville and the 6th Duke's early years

The 6th Duke inherited when he was only 21 years old. He was much less involved in national politics than his predecessors, although a staunch enough supporter of the Whig cause in the House of Lords. In part this lack of interest in public life was due to the early onset of deafness; but in large measure it reflects the fact that his real enthusiasms simply lay elsewhere, in art, architecture, and literature. He built up the collections at Chatsworth, augmented the library, remodelled the house and transformed the park and pleasure grounds.[11] He was in a peculiarly strong position to do all this as he had vast wealth at his disposal. Estates in Ireland, and in eight English counties, were bringing in some £70,000 per annum in the years 1813 to 1815. True, the estate was heavily mortgaged, partly through a spate of land purchases, partly though the cost of building the Crescent at Buxton, and partly through the extravagances of his father, his mother, and his father's various mistresses (Duchess Georgiana owed £109,135, much of it in gambling debts, on her death in 1806).[12] As a result, more than 40 per cent of estate income was taken each year in interest payments. But, unlike any of his predecessors in the eighteenth century – and unlike most contemporary landowners – he inherited an estate which was not 'entailed', tied up in such a way that he was unable to alienate portions at will. His father's unexpected death had occurred before the appropriate legal apparatus to achieve this had been put in place.[13]

In such a position, the Duke was free to borrow further, and indulged himself not only in transforming Chatsworth but also with extensive building projects at Devonshire House, his London home, and at two of his other country houses, Bolton Abbey (in the 1840s) and Lismore Castle (between 1849 and 1858).[14] The Duke had no family distractions, for he remained unmarried – hence the popular epithet, 'the Bachelor Duke'. But he formed deep friendships with two of the key designers of the new landscape at Chatsworth, Jeffry Wyatville and Joseph Paxton, both of whom must have encouraged further extravagance. The transformation of Chatsworth into one of the most remarkable spectacles in Victorian England was a consequence of his fortune, his vision, and his readiness to give these men a free hand in their work, while at the same time maintaining a keen interest in what they were doing.

Although the wonders at Chatsworth are usually – and quite correctly – attributed in large measure to Joseph Paxton, we must not underestimate how much had been achieved before his arrival here in 1826. These early changes were, once again, partly associated with alterations to the house itself. In 1815 the Duke began to convert the Gallery on the East Front into a library, but he soon decided on more ambitious schemes, and in 1817 commissioned Jeffry Wyatt to make extensive alterations and additions to the house. Wyatt submitted his plans in 1819; construction work began in 1820 and continued for twenty years.[15] Much of the interior of the existing house was remodelled but the most striking addition was the great north wing, built to replace the range of offices designed for the 4th Duke by James Paine. The new imposing structure contained – in addition to new kitchens and servants' accommodation – a dining room, a sculpture gallery, a suite of bedrooms, a ballroom/theatre, and an orangery.[16] Many great houses in Britain were extended in this period, in part because the increasing ease of travel encouraged regular house parties, necessitating both enhanced accommodation for visitors and servants but also additional entertaining rooms. But the new north wing was on such a scale that it completely changed the appearance and above all the size of the house, transforming it into a truly stately home.

Wyatville is most noted as an architect who worked in the newly fashionable 'gothic' mode, developing in part the ideas of his uncle, James Wyatt. He was a romantic medieval revivalist who transformed country houses into rambling pseudo-monasteries or castles, part of a wider reaction against the various interpretations of classical and Renaissance forms which had dominated English architecture during the previous two centuries. His greatest works include Ashridge in Hertfordshire, a vast gothic fantasy with the longest frontage in England – 1,000 feet (c. 300 m); and Windsor Castle, which he extensively remodelled for George IV from 1824.[17] But Chatsworth did not receive a gothic makeover. Instead, the architecture of the new north wing subtly echoed the design of the original house, but in a sufficiently subdued way so that, in spite of its vast scale, it does not detract from the original; in the words of the Duke, 'His aim was to restore in the character of the places he improved'.[18] This harmony was achieved partly because the new wing, although more than twice the length of the original house, was only around two thirds of its height; but in a masterly stroke, the new range was terminated by a massive tower which, while also in a restrained classical style, lends the whole a picturesque quality – not least because it is topped by a belvedere storey which recalls the prominent towers which were a feature of certain Elizabethan and Jacobean houses, such as Hardwick.[19]

Although the refurbishment and enlargement of the house absorbed much of the Duke's energy, the gardens were by no means neglected: indeed, he seems to have turned his attention to them immediately after his accession in 1811. Unfortunately, the wording of the estate accounts in this period is often rather vague, with a number of references to unspecified 'work in the garden', or to contractors paid substantial sums 'on account'. But in addition the Duke himself left an invaluable, if somewhat sketchy, description of his early activities in the gardens in his *Handbook*, published in 1845. This was a period in which, under the influence of Humphry Repton, William Sawrey Gilpin and others, it became fashionable to reintroduce more structured gardens in the immediate vicinity of the house, including formal parterres – a development in part associated with the growing enthusiasm for more romantic and antiquarian styles of architecture. And so it was that, in the year after his accession in 1811, the Duke began to lay out a new parterre immediately to the south of the 1st Duke's Greenhouse. This was ornamented with the statue of Flora, 'promoted from the temple'; statues from the temple at Carnac; and a 'white cistern ... from Carrar'.[20] In 1815 a new gravel walk was made 'from Stand to park', together with other new walks in the gardens.[21] The forty pounds' worth of shrubs purchased in the same year also shows an increasing interest in the pleasure grounds, as do the payments for roses planted in the 'borders' there.

FIGURE 55.
The Grotto was
originally constructed
in the late 1790s at the
instigation of the
Duchess Georgiana, but
was much altered by
the 6th Duke in the
1820s. It is built of
massive boulders and
contains a rectangular
room decorated with
stalactites; this is
surmounted by a rustic
timber summerhouse
with a conical slate
roof.

In 1820 major alterations were made to the Grotto. A total of £428 was spent on construction and materials, and a further £80 on masons' work, blacksmiths' work, on 'getting stone and reeds', paving stones, and for paying a night watchman 'to prevent depredations'.[22] To judge from the 6th Duke's *Handbook*, the alterations made principally affected the interior:

> I respected its exterior when the addition was made of a natural cavern, formed of crystals of copper ore that were discovered in Ecton mine, on the borders of Staffordshire.[23]

As noted earlier, Ecton Mine was owned by the Duke, and although previously a major source of his wealth, by the 1790s rich ore deposits had largely been worked out and the estate finally ceased managing it in-house in 1825.

A more important project of the Duke's early years was the creation of a great raised terrace to the west of the house, designed by Wyatville. Ever since Brown and Millican had swept away the late seventeenth-century forecourt immediately before the West Front, the two great stone pedestals, surmounted by sphinxes and embellished with classical trophies carved by Cibber, had remained standing, somewhat incongruously, in the open turf below the house. These were now reunited with the house by the creation of the new terrace, with a broad parterre, below the West Front. In the Duke's words, 'This space, flanked by two large bastions, from its size was difficult to fill and adorn, but Sir Jeffry Wyatville's most ingenious architectural parterres have gone a long way towards it'. The Duke added: 'There stand two imperial trees, planted by Nicholas and Michael Paulowitsch: the first, a Spanish chestnut, promises to be of surpassing beauty'.[24] The accounts for 1818 duly record payments for 'Making pallisading round the trees planted by the Grand Duke Nicholas'.[25] The Grand Duke was a close personal friend of the 6th Duke: he had visited England in 1816 and spent much of his time in London in the Duke's company, and had stayed for several days at Chatsworth. Much later, in 1826, the Duke of Devonshire was chosen as England's ambassador-extraordinary when Nicholas was crowned Tsar.[26]

There were a number of other changes. The old steps from the lawn to the east of the house, down to the south garden, were probably moved, and the retaining wall between them (perhaps a relic of the old seventeenth-century gardens) was replaced by the present turfed slope.[27] Large amounts were spent on repairing and improving the waterworks, perhaps as much as £1,400, to judge from estimates submitted by contractors.[28] To this period (i.e., around 1820) we can also date the main north–south gravel walk running along the east side of the house southwards from Flora's Temple, one of the most important articulating features of the present design. In 1820 a total of £524 11s 0d was spent on this 'New Gravel Walk'.[29] It was designed by Wyatville, and later described by the 6th Duke as 'his first great hit out of doors ... that is so much use and ornament here' (several decades later an urn was placed at its southern end, dedicated to his niece Blanche, who died in 1840 at the young age of 28) (Figure 56). The east–west path which joined it at right angles, at a point a little beyond the South Front, and which continued the alignment of the Cascade downslope, was also probably created at this time. Certainly, both are shown, more or less as they are today, on the map of Chatsworth surveyed by George Unwin in 1831 (Figure 57):[30] an important source for the history of the landscape in this period and one to which we shall have cause to refer on a number of occasions. The construction of this latter path caused considerable problems, as the Duke was later to record in his *Handbook*:

> The temple-cascade is old, but the gravel path leading up to it is new; and when the two lines met, to the dismay of all beholders, an elbow, or long angle, presented itself to the eye, making it necessary to take up more than half of the flight of water-covered steps, and replace them true

to the lines of the South Front, and, consequently, to those of the gravel walk.[31]

Thus the Cascade was rebuilt, for a second time. Another feature probably created at this time was the Rough Walk, which comprised a straight north–south cut running parallel with the 'New Gravel Walk', southwards from the Salisbury Lawn, through the garden woodlands east of the Great Canal, and with the Ring Pond about halfway along its length.

The period prior to the arrival of Paxton at Chatsworth thus saw a number of important alterations to the gardens, accompanying the great changes being made to the house itself. Structure and formality began to return, with the creation of the raised terrace and parterre to the west, the gravel walks and Rough Walk to the east, and the new garden in front of the greenhouse. Some of these new additions, while clearly at the cutting edge of fashion, coexisted uneasily – and still coexist uneasily – with the features created by Brown and Millican in the 1760s. In particular, the carefully contrived views from the West Front of the house out across the Derwent, towards Paine's bridge – created at such vast expense – were now seriously disrupted and obscured by the great western terrace. Indeed, the river was no longer clearly visible from the ground floor windows of the house.

Enter Paxton

Although much had thus been achieved before 1826, it was the 25 years following Joseph Paxton's arrival which saw the real transformation of the pleasure grounds. Paxton was probably the most famous, versatile and energetic of the new Victorian breed of 'hero gardeners'.[32] Born the son of a Bedfordshire labourer, at the age of 15 he started work as a garden boy at Battlesden in Bedfordshire. He spent a short period employed at Wood Hall near Watton in Hertfordshire before returning to Battlesden. From here he went to the Duke of Somerset's house at Wimbledon, and then to the newly-opened gardens of the Horticultural Society at Chiswick, next to Chiswick House. It was here that his skill attracted the attention of the Duke of Devonshire: and thus it was that, at the age of 23, he came to work at Chatsworth, being paid the sum of £65 per annum.[33]

Important changes were under way in British gardening at this time. Gardens continued to increase in complexity, scale and importance; but as they did so there was a growing interest in scientific horticulture – indeed, the founding of the Horticultural Society in 1804, and the establishment of its gardens at Chiswick in 1821 on land leased from the Duke, was one important manifestation of this. New plants from the Americas, Africa and Asia had been arriving in Britain in increasing numbers during the eighteenth century but scientific plant-hunting expeditions were now something of a mania; there was considerable interest in plant and tree collections, and in the development of heated 'stoves' and greenhouses in which the new tropical and subtropical plants could be grown. But gardens were about art as much as science – about bedding plants arranged in complex ways, about dramatic incidents like waterfalls and rockworks.[34] And, with a middle class growing yearly in size and disposable income, this was a period in which a popular gardening press first came into existence, reporting on the gardens and great gardeners at leading country houses; on the activities of enthusiastic amateurs; and on the design of the new public parks which, from the middle years of the century especially, were seen by social reformers as an essential part of the landscape of the growing industrial cities. Gardens were now a central feature of popular culture in a way that they had never been before.

Paxton, to judge from his own account, hit Chatsworth like a whirlwind:

> I left London by the Comet coach to Chesterfield, arrived at Chatsworth at half past four o'clock in the morning of the ninth of May, 1826. As no person was to be seen at that early hour, I got over the greenhouse gate by the old covered way, explored the pleasure grounds, and looked around the outside of the house. I then went down to the kitchen-gardens, scaled the outside wall, and saw the whole of the place, set the men to work there at six o'clock; then returned to Chatsworth, and got Thomas Weldon to play me the water-works, and afterwards went to breakfast with poor dear Mrs Gregory and her niece: the latter fell in love with me, and I with her, and thus completed my first morning's work at Chatsworth before nine o'clock.[35]

Nevertheless, although his energy from the start is undeniable, the impression derived from the documents is that, to begin with, Paxton worked very much with the Duke and Wyatville on the ongoing alterations to the grounds. Additions were made to the Cascade ('Tuft stone' was brought there in 1828);[36] the walls of the kitchen garden were altered;[37] and a new orchard was created beside the kitchen garden.[38] Paxton began his first experiments with constructing glasshouses and later commented (in an article published in 1850) that 'in 1828 … I first turned my attention to the building and improvement of glass structures'.[39] A number of modifications were made to the existing glasshouses in the kitchen garden. He tried bevelling off the sides of the wooden framing bars in order to let more light into the buildings, and experimented with a new form of sash bar, grooved to avoid the use of putty. This was the start of an obsession with glasshouses which was to continue for most of his career.

The costs of maintaining the gardens rose from £505 to nearly £2,000 per annum between 1826 and 1829, and Paxton's own salary was increased in the latter year to £226 per annum.[40] He was getting on increasingly well with the Duke: they were becoming close friends, and as the Duke's own interest in horticulture burgeoned Paxton was given his head. His expansive (and expensive) horticultural activities are recorded under two separate heads in the account books: 'Plants Shrubs Seeds etc.', and 'Building Hothouses' – the latter within the kitchen garden. Between 1830 and 1835 no less than £2,732

FIGURE 56.
The Broad Walk,
designed by Jeffry
Wyatville and laid out
in 1820, runs dead
straight for nearly a
third of a mile and is
terminated by an urn
inscribed with the
name Blanche – Lady
Blanche Howard, niece
of the 6th Duke, who
died in 1840.

was spent on plants. Numerous flowers were bought for the hothouses and gardens: tulips, auriculas, carnations, camellias, dahlias, daphnias, roses, hyacinths, lilies, and primroses; as well as unspecified 'greenhouse plants'.[41] There were also numerous purchases of plants and trees for the kitchen gardens, including box edging, pineapples, vines, asparagus, figs and orange trees, as well as unnamed 'fruit trees'.[42] In 1830 Paxton's expenses for 'attending the removal of the Weeping Ash from Derby to Chatsworth' were recorded. This tree was already forty years old, with roots spreading some 28 feet in diameter. Moving it took forty labourers, more than six horses, and a special

lifting machine designed by Paxton himself and built by Strutts of Belpher. A large crowd gathered to watch its arrival and planting at Chatsworth: in spite of some contemporary scepticism, Paxton was successful and the tree still grows close to the north entrance of the house (Figure 58).[43] But the largest project in these years was the creation, between 1830 and 1831, of a new Pinetum in eight acres taken out of the south park, on the fringes of the existing pleasure grounds. Numerous trees were purchased, including cedar of Lebanon, spruce, Douglas fir, Norfolk Island pine, larch, a giant redwood, monkey puzzle and Japanese white pine, together with large quantities of shrubs, including heather, rhododendrons, laurel, Portugal laurel, aloes, and lauristinus. Paxton carried the seeds of the Douglas fir from London carefully protected in his own hat; the Norfolk Island pine was brought all the way from Ireland by Andrew Stewart, Paxton's foreman.[44] More than fifty species of pine were planted in the eight acres, intermixed with examples of thuja, cypress, and yew.[45]

The expenditure on new greenhouses and hothouses in these years was equally lavish – no less than £3,409 between 1830 and 1835. These years saw the erection of four large houses for pineapples, at least two peach houses, a strawberry house, three ranges of vineries 249 feet (76 m) long, a mushroom house, and cucumber and melon houses.[46] In 1832 Paxton began to turn the old 1st Duke's Greenhouse into a modern 'stove'. A new glass roof was added, Paxton adopting the 'ridge and furrow' principal for roofing first developed by

135

John Claudius Loudon. The interior was remodelled to create a series of terraces, upon which plants in pots could be placed. A basin, for aquatic plants, was added and the heating system improved, with four furnaces circulating heat through flues in the back wall.[47] Paxton's most innovative structure, however, was the new glasshouse built to house the Duke's rapidly expanding orchid collection. This was 97½ feet (30 m) long and 26 feet (8 m) wide, of 15 bays and with a roof supported by 16 narrow cast-iron columns: the front ones were hollow and took water, draining off the roof, into drains beneath the gravel walk outside.[48]

Paxton was going from strength to strength, encouraged by an employer who increasingly treated him as a close companion, taking him on visits to country houses and on a protracted tour of Europe, and giving him more and more responsibility for the overall administration of the estate. But the costs of building, gardening and general maintenance soared. The household payments had reached £36,000 per annum by the early 1830s, and the Duke was more than £700,000 in debt. This, it should be noted, was in spite of a whole series of large-scale alienations of property elsewhere in England: the sale of the Nottinghamshire estates in 1813, which brought in £229,727; of Burlington House in London in 1815, for £70,000; and of the Wetherby estates in Yorkshire in 1824, which netted more than £160,000.[49] But the Duke, nevertheless, continued to spend on an increasingly lavish scale. He was hungry for new, exotic plants: and so John Gibson, one of Paxton's gardeners, was dispatched on a trip lasting six and a half months to South America, South Africa, and in particular India.[50] The rare novelties he brought back to England on his return in 1837 included a banana tree, *Musa superba*, and the *Amherstia nobilis*, an evergreen tree from the forests of India with yellow and scarlet flowers which had never before been successfully transported to England. Gibson wrote to Paxton that 'I do assure you that such is the splendour and extent of my <u>collection</u> as to make it one of the richest collections that has ever crossed the <u>Atlantic</u> ... The Orchideae are splendid indeed and I don't hesitate in saying that I shall supply from 80 to 90 new species which are not in England'.[51] There were, indeed, over 10,000 exotic plants, including more than 100 species of orchid. But Gibson was not the only source of new plants. 'Seeds from Van Diemans Land' are mentioned in the estate accounts for 1836, and plants from St Petersburg, the Cape, Calcutta, Paris and Malta in 1839.[52] In February 1835 James Bateman of Knyppersley in the west Midlands informed the Duke about a large collection of orchids – one of the best in the country – which was being offered for sale by a friend of his, one John Huntley, rector of Kimbolton in Huntingdonshire. Paxton went down in person to inspect the collection and the accounts duly record the payment of £500 – the asking price – for 'Rev Mr Huntley's collection' and their carriage from Kimbolton.[53]

In 1835 the accounts record numerous payments for 'forming the arboretum and the new walks in the Pleasure Grounds'.[54] The Arboretum was one of Paxton's greatest contributions to the Chatsworth landscape, a vast collection of trees made in part by expanding the existing Pinetum at the south-eastern end of the pleasure grounds at the expense of more land taken in from the park. In 1836 labourers were busy 'cutting out a length of the sunk fence for enlarging the Pleasure Grounds', and 'levelling ground, forming and soiling the slopes of the sunk fence'.[55] But the new arboretum also covered large areas of the existing eastern portion of the pleasure grounds. It was a vast enterprise, involving among other things the diversion, along the Trout Stream leat, of a natural stream for more than two miles from its original course on the East Moor, in order to provide a suitably picturesque element in the design.[56] The upper slopes of the garden to the north of the Cascade were given a similar makeover towards the end of 1830s, when the main walk up the slope past Jack Pond was redesigned to follow a sinuous course and a summerhouse was built at the top: this work effectively completed Paxton's initial scheme for altering the upper parts of the gardens.

George Unwin's map of 1831 shows a disposition of paths and planting within the pleasure grounds little different from that depicted on Barker's estate map of 1773,[57] except in the immediate vicinity of the house, where the long north–south gravel walk, an east–west linking walk to the Cascade and the Rough Walk had been created, as we have seen, in the 1820s. A plan published by Paxton in an article in the *Gardener's Magazine* in 1835, however, shows a very different arrangement, in all essentials that which exists today. The old pattern of paths had been largely removed: a long, meandering path now ran all around the pleasure grounds, with a number of branching walks. This main path led through areas of planting grouped according to biological criteria. In all, some 75 orders of trees are noted – a total of more than 1,670 trees and varieties, many of which still survive.[58]

The Great Stove

Paxton's plan does not show, for it was not begun until the following year, the 'Great Stove' or 'Great Conservatory', one of the most remarkable buildings in Victorian England. This was a heated greenhouse so vast that it was capable of housing the very largest tropical species that the Duke might collect (Figure 59). It was conceived in 1835 and initially a scale model was built, the accounts of January 1836 duly noting payments to John Marples, the estate carpenter, for 'making the Model'.[59] Work began in the same year on clearing a site for the new building, in the woodlands of the pleasure grounds some way to the south-east of the house. The choice of a relatively secluded site was deliberate. Paxton believed that large greenhouses should be proudly displayed, not hidden away, and the Great Stove should be an object of particular beauty and admiration. But, at the same time, it should not stand too close to any other building, and particularly the house, for this might detract from its scale and singularity.[60] The building was raised above a basement in which there were eight boilers, running a hot water rather than hot air heating system: such an arrangement demanded large amounts of fuel and necessitated the

FIGURE 58.
The weeping ash, which grows on a low mound beside the north front, was brought to Chatsworth with great effort by Paxton from a house in Kedleston Road, Derby, in 1830. It was already a mature tree, and is still flourishing today.

construction of underground tunnels for coal trucks. It was set within a large embanked enclosure with walks and flower beds, which set it apart from the Arboretum. Decimus Burton, the architect who, at around this time, designed the new model farm at Edensor, later claimed that he was the designer of this monumental structure but there is no doubt that his role was a relatively minor one: the Duke himself, in his *Handbook*, referred to 'this extraordinary monument of Mr Paxton's talent and skill, in the execution of which he was cordially met and assisted by Mr Decimus Burton'.[61] Paxton's architectural assistant John Robertson, who was also much involved in the rebuilding of the estate village at Edensor, also played a part and may have designed the entrances to the building. But Paxton was unquestionably the building's main creator, and he employed in its design all the features of glasshouse construction which he had been developing at Chatsworth over the previous few years.

The building, begun in 1836, was completed in 1840, although the accounts suggest that fitting it out, and possibly altering it, continued for another three years. They record all the many tasks involved in its construction: 'excavating earth within the Great Stove'; 'Removing soil at the Great Conservatory'; and the construction of rock work there. Stone for covering flues was brought to the site, and payments made for 'cutting and wheeling slate from the Flower Beds and Terrace slopes at the conservatory'.[62] There are numerous payments for the movement of gravel to the site, presumably in part for the drives within the great building, so wide that two carriages could pass abreast.

The building was 276 feet 6 inches (84 m) long, 123 feet (37 m) wide and 63 feet (19 m) high, the largest glass building in England before the erection of Paxton's other great marvel, the Crystal Palace in London, in 1851. In order to ensure the greatest possible span Paxton used the ancient expedient of a central 'nave' some 70 feet (21 m) wide and two lower side 'aisles'. In all, the Stove covered just under an acre; the surface area of the roof was 52,287 square feet (4,857 square metres); the 24,560 sash bars, if laid end to end, would have stretched for around 40 miles (64 km). The vast roof was supported on 36 cast iron columns in 2 rows: each was hollow and acted as a drain for moisture which collected in special wooden gutters running in the 'furrows' of the roof, with a channel on the upper surface to catch rainwater, and a groove below to catch condensation. The rest of the framing was of wood. There were 75,000 square feet (6,967 square metres) of glass, with the panes laid at angles to the main frame. The building was heated by 9,509 feet (2,898 m) of 5½ inch (140 mm) piping weighing upwards of 200 tons (203 tonnes). The costs were immense: no less than £33,099 10s 11d is recorded in a separate account for the Stove in the archives in the period 1836–41, with subsequent additional sums in other accounts after this date.[63]

Many features of the building were new, even experimental. The sheet glass was supplied by Chance Brothers, a Birmingham manufacturer which had recently imported a new method of production, the 'cylinder process', from Europe: the panes, each 48 inches (1.22 m) in length, were the largest they had produced. The 6-inch (15 cm) panes on the roof were put in place using a wooden wagon whose wheels ran along the groove of the glazing bars. A. B. Granville described this, in a tantalisingly obscure manner:

> The ingenious contrivance (equally the invention of Mr Paxton's own mind) for glazing the flanks and loftiest slopes of this *Hill*, as well as for covering its ribs with paint ... Its merits are simplicity and complete success. I must leave my readers to guess how a dozen or two of painters and glaziers may be enabled to crawl spider-like, freely and nimbly, over a surface of such fragile materials, without either bending a single one of the slender ribs, or fracturing a pane of glass.[64]

Each winter, on average, the furnaces consumed 300 tons (304 tonnes) of coal and coke. The smoke was taken uphill, away from the building, by an underground flue to a tall chimney that still stands just outside the pleasure grounds: this kept the immediate area free of fumes and smells, and also supplied additional draught for the furnaces. Keeping them supplied with fuel posed particular problems, for a procession of wagons laden with coal would detract from the splendour, and mystery, of the spectacle. The solution was to construct a special drive which ran from near the kitchen garden, under the Cascade in a tunnel, and then through cuttings to the northern end of the Conservatory. Payments in 1838 for 'making a new road into the pleasure grounds' and, in 1840, for 'removing earth from the road to the great conservatory', probably signal the construction both of this impressive feature, which still remains, and of a formal drive from the base of the Cascade that allowed carriage access into the Stove.[65]

The Stove not only housed the many exotic plants which the Duke himself had collected over the previous decade or so; a number of enthusiastic plant collectors also donated specimens. An entire collection came from Wimbledon House; James Bateman gave the largest of his tropical trees; while Lady Tankerville bequeathed the large palm trees growing on her estate in Walton, Buckinghamshire (they were brought to Chatsworth with considerable difficulty, for the largest weighed over twelve tons). A variety of soils were laid out inside the building, with special compartments to contain the roots of the more vigorous specimens. A vast range of palm trees, ferns and flowering plants from all corners of the globe was displayed, and exotic birds flew freely among the foliage.[66] There were elaborate rockworks to hide the stairs, planted with ferns: the accounts of 1841 and 1842 record numerous payments for 'Getting Stones for the Rock Work at the Conservatory'.[67] Charles Darwin came in 1845 and described the contents of the Stove as 'more wonderfully like tropical nature, than I could have conceived possible'.[68] Queen Victoria visited the vast structure in 1843: it was lit with 14,000 lamps.[69] It was generally agreed to be the wonder of Chatsworth.

The Great Stove was not, however, the only greenhouse to be constructed at Chatsworth in this period: a number of smaller examples are mentioned under the 'Building Hothouses' account and were reported in the contemporary horticultural press. Most were erected in the old kitchen garden, in the north of the park. They included the Amherstia House, built to house the *Amherstia nobilis* brought by Gibson from India; and the Lily House, or the Victoria Regia House, designed to house the water lily *Victoria Regia* (now *Amazonica*) in a tank of circulating water: the plant flowered at Chatsworth, for the first time in this country, in 1849. When it outgrew its tank a larger building was erected, 18.6 m by 15 m, iron-framed and with ridge and furrow roof, containing a tank 10 m in diameter. Some glass ranges were erected within a new extension to the main area of the gardens, north of the Stables in what had previously been a large horse paddock. These lay within a new kitchen and nursery garden created as part of the larger scheme noted above

FIGURE 60.
The Conservative Wall, designed by Paxton, lies to the east of the house and is c. 5 metres high and c. 100 metres long. It was originally built in 1838: flues at the back kept the temperature high enough in the winter for half-hardy plants, while at the front there were projecting wooden panels from which protecting curtains could be hung in the coldest weather. The glass frames are a slightly later feature, added in 1848. © THE DEVONSHIRE COLLECTION, CHATSWORTH. REPRODUCED BY PERMISSION OF THE CHATSWORTH SETTLEMENT TRUSTEES.

to reorganise this part of the gardens, and contained a grid of narrow beds and glasshouses with access paths between, which were probably constructed in c. 1839–40. Leading up to them, from the house, was the heated or 'Conservative Wall', 300 feet (91 m) long and 15 feet (4.5 m) high, built in 1838 (Figure 60). This had fires and flues at the back, to keep the temperature high enough in the winter for half-hardy plants, while at the front there were projecting wooden panels from which protecting curtains could be hung in the coldest weather.[70] The glass frames were added later, in 1848. It is hardly surprising that expenditure on glasshouses and associated features soared to no less than £5,704 over the five years from 1836 to 1840 – and this excludes the vast sums spent on the Great Stove itself.[71] A notebook in the Chatsworth archives contains a list, probably drawn up in c. 1840, of the plants grown in the garden: more than 3,500 species, a high proportion of which were difficult and demanding hothouse plants.[72]

Rockwork and waterworks

Not all the projects carried out by Paxton were associated with the contemporary obsession with scientific horticulture and plant collecting. More romantic, picturesque and evocative features were also created. In the late 1830s the 'Ruined Aqueduct' was constructed on the high eastern margins of the pleasure ground (Figure 61). The 6th Duke's *Handbook* tells us that it was inspired by:

> One on a gigantic scale in the gardens of Wilhelmshoehe, by Cassel. Had I to build it again, it should not be true, as now, to the cascade, but, by taking a slanting direction, should show its arches to the West: for nothing can be more beautiful than the icicles formed by the dripping from those arches in fantastical shapes during the winter.[73]

The 'Aqueduct' was the centrepiece in a scheme of the late 1830s to ornamentalise Stand Wood. This project also included a smaller waterfall above the aqueduct, falling from the natural Sowter Stone at the scarp crest. A wooden bridge lay below it with stone steps running between cliffs nearby, on an ornamental woodland path leading to the Stand (Figure 62). A new carriage drive ran up through Stand Wood and wound through the woods on the shelf above, passing Swiss Lake; and the Swiss Cottage was built to be seen from this across the lake. The artificial stream for the waterfall and Aqueduct was brought from the Ring Pond on the shelf above; after passing over the Aqueduct it ran down the slope to the Cascade Pond. Either shortly before all these changes were implemented, or as part of the same scheme, all these new features were separated from the main area of pleasure grounds below by the construction of a high garden wall, running between the top of the Arboretum to the south and the new kitchen and nursery gardens to the north. It is unclear why, on the one hand, the gardens below were given added security and separation from the surrounding park and woodlands, while on the other Stand Wood above was given a carefully-orchestrated group of features. Perhaps the wall was intended to reinforce the feeling of wilderness experienced on the overgrown rough slopes of Stand Wood, with its impressive 'ruin' and romantic 'natural' features.

By the early 1840s, when the Duke wrote his *Handbook*, the last main feature of Paxton's pleasure grounds – an ambitious group of elaborate and entirely artificial rockworks – was still under construction. The Duke described how, though still uncompleted, progress on the project had been rapid. In 1842 there had not been a single rock there, but at the time of writing (1844) he was able to describe:

> The double flight of steps, with balustrades of yews, the Queen's rock, Prince Albert's and the Duke of Wellington's, last removed and grandest of all. The spirit of some Druid seems to animate Mr Paxton on these bulky removals.[74]

FIGURE 61.
The Ruined Aqueduct,
on the steeply rising
ground above the
gardens, was
constructed in the
late 1830s as part of
a wider scheme to
ornamentalise
Stand Wood.

He implies, however, that he himself had some input into the design, commenting on how 'the fountains have adopted the rocky character of the spot: so saw I them at Nymphenberg'. Paxton had definite ideas on the arrangement and location of rockworks, which were becoming increasingly popular in Britain in this period. He believed that they should be placed some distance from the main areas of flower garden, and towards the margins of the pleasure grounds, where they could make the greatest visual impact – especially if arranged in such a way that visitors came upon them unawares.[75]

The stone was brought from the abandoned quarries on Dobb Edge: the largest construction, the Wellington Rock, was 45 feet (13.7 m) high and had – still has, in fact – a waterfall running down it. In 1844 steps were made in the rockwork (Figure 63).[76] There was a veritable maze of paths threading round and beneath the rocks.

One old and familiar feature of the Chatsworth scene was given a new lease of life in this rugged setting. In 1844 the accounts record payments for 'excavating a new site for the 'Willow Tree' in the Pleasure Grounds';[77] in 1847, for 'excavating soil for the Willow Tree';[78] and in 1848, for 'Getting stone for the Willow Tree'.[79] These entries signal the movement of the famous fountain to its present site on the northern edge of the rockworks: prior to this, according to Paxton's plan of 1835, it seems to have stood several metres to the south. This was not, it should be emphasised, the original tree from the seventeenth-century gardens, but a replacement of early nineteenth-century date.

In 1842, work began on the excavation of the 'Bolton Stride' or Strid – a narrow chasm, filled with a rushing watercourse and surrounded by further rockwork. This was based on a real feature – the narrow chasm cut by the river Wharfe – close to the Duke's Bolton Abbey estate in Yorkshire. The surrounding rocks were planted with wild currants, bilberries and other plants brought from Fountains Abbey. This was one of the last major additions to the gardens and does not, therefore, receive a mention in the Duke's *Handbook* of 1844. Work in this area seems to have continued for several years; in 1847 there were payments for 'setting leaping stones'.[80] The smoother area of water to the south was used for growing a range of aquatic plants, and formed a pleasing contrast to the more rugged and turbulent scenes nearby (Figure 64).

The other great project of the 1840s was the making of the Emperor Fountain. There had, as we have seen, always been a fountain in the canal to the south of the house, which reached a height of 30 feet (9.14 m), later heightened to 50 feet (15 m) and eventually to 95 feet (29 m).[81] Even Walpole, in the 1760s, had commented favourably on the 'great jet d'eau', although he had disapproved in general of Chatsworth's 'foolish waterworks'.[82] In early 1844, however, when it became known that the Duke's friend Tsar Nicholas of Russia was to visit England, Paxton was given the job of improving this fountain. A trench for the 'Great Fountain pipe' was dug in the garden and the 'Great Fountaine Pond in the old park' was enlarged – probably the pond now known as Swiss Lake. The existing 'Great Canal Aqueduct' running from Umberley Brook to the Swiss Lake was also repaired. Later, in 1845, work began on a more ambitious project – the excavation of the Emperor Lake, an area of water covering some nine acres on the level shelf high above the gardens (Figure 65). The earth and rock were removed to a depth of between 7 feet (2 m) and 13 feet (4 m): some 10,000 cubic yards (7,646 cubic metres) of material were excavated. In 1847 and 1848 an ambitious aqueduct to the new reservoir was created across the moorland, later known as the Emperor Stream (Figure 34). The Emperor Lake was itself further enlarged to 11 acres (4.5 ha)

FIGURE 62.
The Sowter Stone is a natural outcrop on the escarpment to the east of the House which was modified to take a picturesque waterfall in the later 1830s, when paths and a variety of other ornamental features were laid out within Stand Wood.

FIGURE 63.
The Wellington Rock, c. 15 metres in height, is the most spectacular of the elaborate rockworks created by Paxton at Chatsworth in the early 1840s. The natural outcrop from the scarp above was cut into pieces and carefully reassembled in the gardens.

FIGURE 64.
The Strid, constructed in 1842, is a narrow artificial chasm, filled with a rushing watercourse, which is based on a natural feature of the landscape, cut by the river Wharfe, near the Duke's other residence at Bolton Abbey in Yorkshire.

in 1849.[83] The fountain was linked to the Lake by 828 yards (757 m) of pipe with a 15 inch (38 cm) bore, which came 400 feet (121 m) downhill: the pressure was enough to play the jet to a height of 276 feet (84 m), discharging 873 gallons (3,963 litres) a minute.[84] In the event, the Tsar never made it to Chatsworth, but the fountain remains to this day, one of Paxton's greatest achievements (Figure 66).

The spectacle

By 1850 the gardens were largely completed. The Arboretum and Pinetum had been planted, and a new pattern of paths laid out; the Great Conservatory erected; the elaborate rockworks formed; and the Emperor Fountain installed. The Duke was, by 1844, nearly a million pounds in debt, a colossal sum, and interest payments amounted to no less than £54,000 per annum, or 55 per cent of income.[85] But Chatsworth was magnificent, and it was becoming a magnet for visitors. Like almost all country houses in England it had long been open to the public on an informal basis. It was generally accepted that members of the 'polite' classes could turn up at major stately homes and, making the appropriate tips to housekeepers and gardeners, be shown the principal features of the house and grounds. In 1789, for example, the young Viscount Torrington visited Chatsworth and reported how 'the porter was so obliging as to find the gardener, and the housekeeper for us; who are always ready to attend strangers'.[86] But as the nineteenth century progressed, the number of visitors to country seats began to increase. The middle classes were growing in wealth and in numbers, and were keen to view the stately homes of England; and it was widely felt that the minds of the artisan and labouring classes might be suitably improved by exposure to the art and culture found at country houses. Many great landowners believed it was their duty to allow at least limited access. It was part of the *noblesse oblige* which, in this new and more complex society, the aristocracy were increasingly encouraged to show.[87] Under the 6th Duke visitors of all kinds seem to have been granted a welcome at Chatsworth (although no doubt only if they were regarded as 'respectable').

FIGURE 65.
The Emperor Lake covers an area of 11 acres on the shelf high above the gardens. It was excavated in the mid-1840s to supply water for Paxton's new Emperor Fountain and was further extended in 1849.

FIGURE 66.
The Emperor Fountain
was constructed in the
mid-1840s in
anticipation of a visit
from the Tsar of
Russia. The jet of water
rose to 276 feet (84 m)
when the valves were
fully open, discharging
873 gallons (3,963 litres)
a minute. In the event,
the Tsar never came to
Chatsworth, but the
fountain remains to
this day, one of
Paxton's greatest
achievements.

The writer and designer John Claudius Loudon penned, in 1831, a highly crit-ical article about the gardens but nevertheless praised the Duke for allowing the waterworks to be played to any visitor who asked to see them in action.[88] But before the advent of the railways the extent of country house visiting was inevitably limited: most of the largest country seats simply lay too far from the main centres of population. This was especially true of Chatsworth, to which only small groups usually journeyed; a notice drawn up in January 1841 announced to visitors that 'Parties of not more than eight persons are admitted to view the House and Gardens, between Eleven and Five O'Clock, every day except Sundays'.[89]

Everything changed, however, with the arrival of the railway line at Rowsley, a mere three miles away, in June 1849. Two weeks later a party of 500 'respectable, orderly and well-dressed' visitors came by a special excursion train from Derby. They were conveyed to Chatsworth by an assortment of coaches, omnibuses and carriages, and shown round the house in groups of twenty at a time: 'The playing fountains and flowing cascades in all directions gave indis-putable proof that none felt more happy or more anxious than the noble Duke himself did in dispensing so much happiness to others'.[90]

The visit was followed throughout the summer by others large groups – one, from Sheffield, totalling some 2,000 individuals.[91] They came from as far afield as Birmingham, Leeds and Leicester, many on tours organised by the new travel firm of Thomas Cook. In the 1850s an average of around 80,000 visi-tors trooped through the gates each summer (a number which rose still further

149

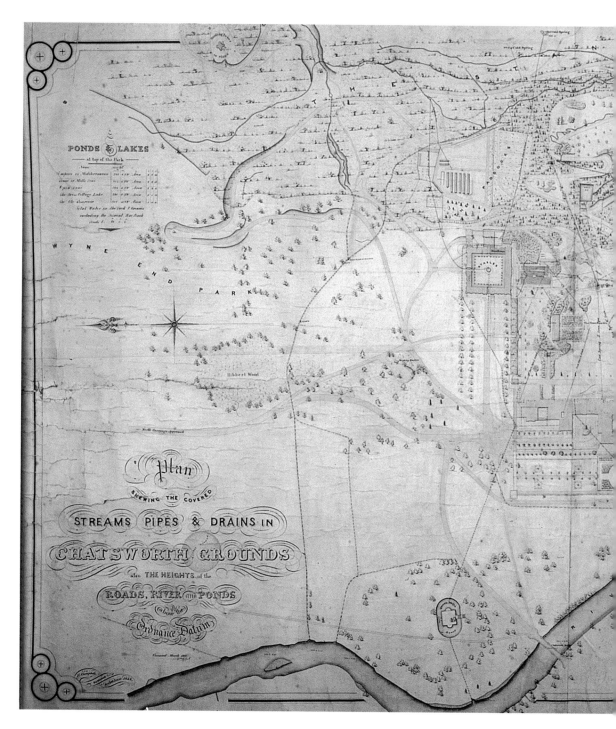

when the Midland Railway's line was extended to Manchester in 1863).[92] The Duke, and Paxton, appear to have been perfectly sanguine about the development, although controlling the visitors brought problems. Undated printed notices from the middle decades of the century instructed that:

FIGURE 67.
Campbell's fine plan, drawn up in 1858, shows the vast and elaborate nature of the gardens created by Wyatville, Paxton and the Sixth Duke; but it also indicates the continuing importance within them of many much earlier features, including the Cascade and the Canal Pond. It was drawn to show the complex series of pipes and drains necessary for the water features. © THE DEVONSHIRE COLLECTION, CHATSWORTH. REPRODUCED BY PERMISSION OF THE CHATSWORTH SETTLEMENT TRUSTEES.

Public carriages having brought parties to see the house and grounds will not be allowed to stand or loiter in the Park on the East side of the River Derwent, but they must arrange to return to the Lodge Gates to fetch the parties away at a fixed time … It is particularly requested that parties … will abstain from injuring the trees and shrubs, and from gathering ferns and flowers … Parties bringing their refreshment into the Park, are desired not to leave straw, paper, or other litter strewed about the ground.[93]

By this time Chatsworth had become the most famous garden in England. It was in many ways the quintessential Victorian garden, where glass, rockwork, and waterworks epitomised not only Paxton's particular synthesis of horticulture and engineering, but more generally the application of technical ingenuity to the garden in this age of Industrial Revolution.

And Paxton was himself now a household name. In 1831 he had launched a new journal, *The Horticultural Register and General Magazine*; this was followed from 1834 by *Paxton's Magazine of Botany and Register of Flowering Plants* and, most successfully of all, by *The Gardener's Chronicle*, launched in 1841. He was increasingly asked to advise on projects well beyond Chatsworth, ultimately developing a career which ran in tandem with his work here. In 1842 he was asked to design a new public park at Liverpool, the Princes Park; and the following year, to design one at nearby Birkenhead. In 1850 he designed the great Crystal Palace for the Great Exhibition in Hyde Park, for which he received a knighthood; he designed the Crystal Palace Park and the People's Park at Halifax. He became Director of the Midland Railway and MP for Coventry. He was the classic example of Victorian upward mobility, a man of phenomenal energy and confidence.[94]

But Chatsworth continued to absorb his attention, and Paxton's success simply redounded to the greater glory of the estate and its owner. It was one of the key gardens in England, not least because it acted, in effect, as a horticultural training school. Some of the greatest gardeners of the age began their careers there: Edward Milner and Edward Kemp, both of whom became leading writers on landscape design; and John Scott, who went on to become curator of the Calcutta botanic garden and carried out experiments for Charles Darwin.

Although the gardens at Chatsworth were largely completed by 1850, some further modifications were made later, principally in the Arboretum. Much trenching took place here between 1853 and 1855; stone was brought to the site, some trees cut down and stubbed up, and much 'earthwork' made here.[95] All this seems to have been associated with the construction of the sinuous, sunken tracks in the area between the Azalea Dell, the Ravine and the Conservatory, which do not seem to figure in visitors' accounts of the 1840s. They were in place by 1858, when a map of Chatsworth shows that all the main features of the Paxton gardens were now in existence (Figure 67).[96] But the 6th Duke died on 18 January 1858, and Paxton left the estate.

CHAPTER SIX

The Park in the Nineteenth Century

Introduction

So far as the evidence goes, the 5th Duke's activities in the park were largely limited to seeing through to completion the great schemes initiated by his father. The intense activity of the 1760s continued into the early 1780s, with much levelling and further modifications to the river banks.[1] But there were also some new developments (Figure 52). At least two properties, the parsonage and the Devonshire Arms, were demolished at the eastern end of Edensor village in the late 1770s. The former was in view of the house and a replacement was erected close to the site of the old inn; the latter, in contrast, was rebuilt at the other end of the village, on the public road to Baslow, as the New Inn (now the estate offices).[2] This was not a direct replacement for the village public house but was primarily intended as a place where 'polite' visitors to Chatsworth could stay. In addition, immediately to the north of this, the 5th Duke's most enigmatic contribution to the landscape was erected in c. 1780. This is an entrance lodge, which originally comprised rooms to either side of a central arch (infilled at a later date, probably sometime between 1836 and 1855 to judge from the map evidence).[3] It is an elegant structure. But it does not, nor apparently did it ever, provide access to a drive leading to the house. It may have been intended as a private entrance only for those on foot or horseback who wanted to take a short cut and avoid travelling through the village – especially, perhaps, visitors staying in the adjacent Inn. A second lodge, shown on an estate map of 1780–85[4] and later named as 'Wynne's Lodge' on the first edition one inch Ordnance Survey map (surveyed in 1839), was placed on the private drive to the house from the north to control access from the turnpike road leading from Baslow to Chesterfield (this latter lodge was demolished in the nineteenth century).

Some new work was thus carried out in the park in the 5th Duke's early years, but it was on a relatively limited scale. And from the mid 1780s the documents record little more than routine maintenance. The park was kept free of molehills and rushes, dunged and limed, and rubbish cleared away following floods, especially in 1799 and 1806.[5] The river bank was reinforced, and some changes made to the gardens around Queen Mary's Bower (in 1798 there were payments for 'lime for Rookery garden'[6] and in 1800 for 'work at gravel above Rookery Garden');[7] and the plantations around the park were regularly thinned.

In fact the most important changes under the 5th Duke concerned not the park, but rather the Old Park. This had continued to exist, still apparently stocked with deer, while the new park was being laid out. Its western edges – that is, the areas of ancient trees on the escarpment, to both north and south of the house and pleasure grounds – were brought fully into the new aesthetic landscape in the 1760s. But the main area of level rough ground, out of sight of the house and bleak and unappealing to contemporary taste, had now lost much of its *raison d'être*. The deer seem to have been moved out of this area in the 1770s, and new uses were soon found for it. As work began on the new park the old park was again investigated for its mineral wealth, in the form of coal (pp. 84–5), and mining went into full production later in the 1760s.

From medieval times onwards mines on the East Moors had exploited a number of relatively thin coal seams.[8] While never as productive as the seams further east in the Coal Measure foothills, they were conveniently sited for local markets to the west: the coal was used for lead smelting and lime burning, and also for domestic fires. The Baslow Seam, a good quality but thin bed of house coal, was worked locally in three areas; at the Baslow Colliery at Robin Hood; further south at Chatsworth Old Park Colliery; and on the moorland beyond at Beeley Moor Colliery. Baslow Colliery was the largest of the three and its southern half lay under fields now owned by Chatsworth Estate, on the gritstone shelf a little to the north-east of the park. There are still the remains here of about 85 small open-cast pits and closely-spaced, shallow but now backfilled shafts with associated waste hillocks. There are also a further 25 to 29 hillocks associated with deeper shafts, which were sunk to extract the coal as it dipped under the rising slope of the shelf to the south and south-east. It is uncertain when mining first took place here, although the shallower workings may have medieval origins. A mine is first documented in 1764–5, when it was being operated by one Edward Boler, on land owned by the Duke of Rutland.[9] In this year a long underground drainage level or sough reached the boundary of Chatsworth Old Park, then the estate boundary, and an agreement was reached with the 6th Duke of Devonshire and his officials to extend it southwards and create Chatsworth Old Park Colliery. Farey, in 1811, noted that the Baslow Colliery was still in use,[10] and it continued to be worked until at least the early 1830s.[11] Local tradition holds that it was reopened briefly in the 1914–18 war and the coal used to heat the Great Conservatory in the gardens.

Working for coal within the old deer park itself is recorded in the estate accounts for 1759–60 under the heading 'Trying for Cole on ye top of Chatsworth Park'.[12] Whether the estate was anticipating the extension of the sough, or simply capitalising on its resources, is unclear. About 10 trial 'pits' (shafts) were sunk, including one that had to be abandoned because it was too wet to pump. In one location the seam was described as being 'three quarters of a yard thick'. However, mining did not reach full production until after the

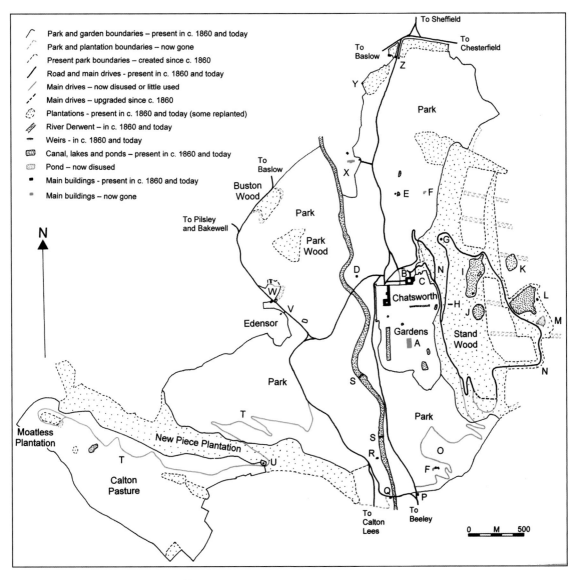

Legend:

- Park and garden boundaries – present in c. 1860 and today
- Park and plantation boundaries – now gone
- Present park boundaries – created since c. 1860
- Road and main drives - present in c. 1860 and today
- Main drives – now disused or little used
- Main drives – upgraded since c. 1860
- Plantations - present in c. 1860 and today (some replanted)
- River Derwent – in c. 1860 and today
- Weirs - in c. 1860 and today
- Canal, lakes and ponds – present in c. 1860 and today
- Pond – now disused
- Main buildings - present in c. 1860 and today
- Main buildings – now gone

Map labels: To Sheffield; To Chesterfield; To Baslow; Z; Y; Park; To Baslow; X; Buston Wood; To Pilsley and Bakewell; Park; Park Wood; E; F; G; D; B; C; N; I; K; Chatsworth; H; L; M; W; V; Edensor; Gardens; A; Stand Wood; N; Park; S; Park; N; Moatless Plantation; New Piece Plantation; T; T; S; O; Calton Pasture; U; R; F; Q; P; To Calton Lees; To Beeley; 0 M 500

FIGURE 68.

The area covered by the park and gardens in c. 1860 (A: The Great Stove; B: The Stables; C: the new kitchen gardens; D: Queen Mary's Bower; E: the ice house; F: deer barns; G: The Stand; H: The Aqueduct; I: Emperor Lake; J: Round Pond; K: Open Pond; L: Swiss Lake and Swiss Cottage; M: Old Pond; N: Paxton's new woodland drives; O: the south-east serpentine drive; P: Beeley Lodge; Q: Blue Moors Lodge; R: Paine's Mill; S: weirs; T: the south-west serpentine drive; U: Russian Cottage; V: Castle Lodge; W: The Lodge, Tudor Lodge and old lodge; X: Barbrook House, White Lodge, the kitchen gardens and nursery, and Crimea Farm; Y: Barbrook Lodge; Z: The Baslow Lodges and Park Lodge).

sough reached the park boundary some five years later. What became known as Chatsworth Old Park Colliery is first documented in 1764–5, when a proposal to work 'Parkgate Cole Mine' was drawn up.[13] The sough from Baslow Colliery was to be driven a further 30 yards (27 m) to reach the 'Coal Mine or Delph' in 'Chatsworth Park on the northside thereof', with the aim of dewatering all coal deposits updip of the sough. The proposed agreement allowed for the sinking of new shafts and levels as and when they became necessary, but stipulated that no more than four miners should work the coal underground unless the rent was increased – surviving estate accounts for the 1770s all record an annual rent of 40 shillings per year.[14] The mine was, in effect, an extension of Baslow Colliery, worked by the same miners under Edward Boler, but being under the Duke of Devonshire's land it was given a separate name, reflecting the different ownership of mineral rights. The coal was to be brought up shafts in the old park and removed using the existing 'Old Park Gate' (the road beyond the park to the north at the present Parkgate Farm); the miners 'must not be at liberty to make a road down the hill through the plantation [Stand Wood]'. A mine plan of 1832 shows that by this date the sough had been driven some 350 m southwards into the Park, with four ventilation shafts.[15] From the southernmost of these a drift ran to a shaft close to the later Emperor Stream; all the coal to the north of the drift, up-dip of the sough to the surface, had by now been removed. It may be that the seam thinned further south and extraction here was uneconomic. The plan gives no indication of when this part of the Colliery had last been mined but it may well be that the workings were already long disused. Farey commented in 1811 that the Colliery was worked 'formerly'.[16] One or two surviving shaft mounds on the shelf behind the southern end of Stand Wood are the only obvious sign today of coal mining within the old park, and these lie well to the south of the area drained by the sough and were presumably either sunk during the 1760 trials or earlier. That no shaft mounds survive today further north is not surprising given later agricultural land use, and the fact that the 1765 agreement states that all shafts be filled when abandoned and that all waste stone be carted 'to the stone pit or any other convenient place set out by the Steward'.

More important in terms of its impact upon the landscape, perhaps, was the reclamation of large parts of the Old Park for agriculture, something fuelled by rising grain prices and an increasing enthusiasm for agricultural 'improvement'. It is possible that parts were already being improved as early as 1781,[17] but it was in the following decade, as prices rose fast during the Napoleonic Wars, that unequivocal references appear to 'ploughing, pulling up turnips &c in the Old Park' (1794) and to 'ploughing in the old park' (1795).[18] In the following years there were regular references to 'ploughing' here, and in 1798 labourers were paid for reaping oats 'at the south of the Old Park'.[19] In the same year work began on 'The building at the top of the Old Park' – presumably Park Farm, at the southern end of the new fields – and further areas of the park were 'pared and burnt'.[20] Over the following years paring and burning, and ploughing, continued, together with some draining and massive applications of lime.[21] By 1801 the new farm appears to have been largely completed, although some work on the outbuildings continued until 1804. By this time the work of reclamation appears to have been completed.[22] Unwin's 1831 map of Chatsworth shows that much of the area of the Old Park was divided into neat rectangular fields, mostly defined by walled belts of trees.[23] Only the steeper slopes above, leading up to Gibbet Moor, remained uncultivated; these had been woodland since before the 1760s and remain so to this day.

The 5th Duke did not, therefore, leave the landscape around Chatsworth House entirely untouched. But it was, nevertheless, only with the accession of the 6th Duke that a new phase of intense activity began in the park itself, which, because of the fame and magnificence of the Chatsworth *gardens*, has not always received the attention it deserves. The park was expanded to the north and west, and acquired a number of new lodges and drives (Figure 68). The village of Edensor was partially removed, and the surviving section completely rebuilt as one of the most flamboyant model villages in England. And the planting was augmented and considerably modified. Much of this activity – especially the destruction of Edensor, the expansion of the park to the north, and the principle alterations to the roads and drives in the park – occurred before Paxton's arrival at Chatsworth, and certainly before his rise to prominence there. It is thus very probable that the architect Jeffry Wyatville played a major role in the development of the wider landscape at this time.

All these changes could be paralleled elsewhere in England but, as usual, the sheer scale of developments at Chatsworth dwarfed those at most other estates. Although we tend to think of the nineteenth century primarily as the period in which gardens returned to prominence, parks also received much attention from owners and designers. The essential form of the landscape park as developed by Brown and his contemporaries remained but a whole series of innovations radically altered both its appearance and the ways in which it was experienced.[24]

The destruction of Edensor and the expansion of the park

Work began soon after the Duke's accession in 1811. The 1810s and 20s saw a sustained campaign of planting, both in and around the park, and important changes to the layout of the public roads within it. But the most significant development of these early years was the destruction of much of Edensor village.

Three main myths surround Edensor. One is that the village has been moved, from an old site within the park to a new one on its margins. In fact it was not moved wholesale but instead the houses at the eastern end of the settlement were demolished, while those at the western were retained and eventually rebuilt or remodelled, as can be seen by comparing the map of the village drawn in 1785 with one made after the changes had been completed (Figures 69, 70).[25] The second myth is that this change was effected in the

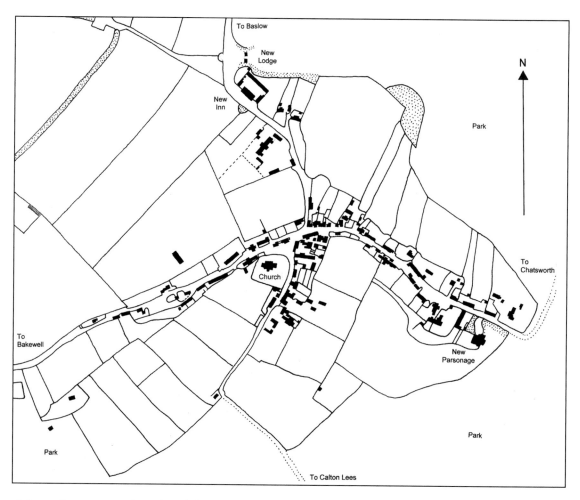

FIGURE 69.
The village of Edensor
as shown on estate
maps dating from
between 1780 and 1785,
before it was partially
cleared and extensively
reorganised in the early
nineteenth century.
The basic layout
probably had medieval
origins, although details
were undoubtedly the
subject of subsequent
alteration.

eighteenth century, when Capability Brown created the new park to the west of the river, whereas (as already noted) only the parsonage, the inn called the Devonshire Arms, and one or two other houses, all at the extreme eastern end of the village, were removed in the eighteenth century, probably because they were in view of the house. The rest of the village survived unscathed into the nineteenth century, hidden from view of Chatsworth House by a low hill. The third popular misconception is that the truncation of the village, and the reconstruction of the remainder in a new, 'model' form, were contemporary and co-ordinated activities. In fact, while the Duke may always have planned to rebuild the settlement, the two phases of activity were quite distinct.

The Cavendishes had been consolidating their hold on the settlement for decades, acquiring the remaining freeholds here. In 1798 they purchased the Courtenay family's holdings and in 1799 the property of John Hutchinson, at a cost of £600.[26] But it was another eighteen years before the first demolitions occurred, in 1817, when Mr Barker's house was removed.[27] In 1818 the accounts refer to 'pulling down houses at Edensor' and to the demolition of 'Mr

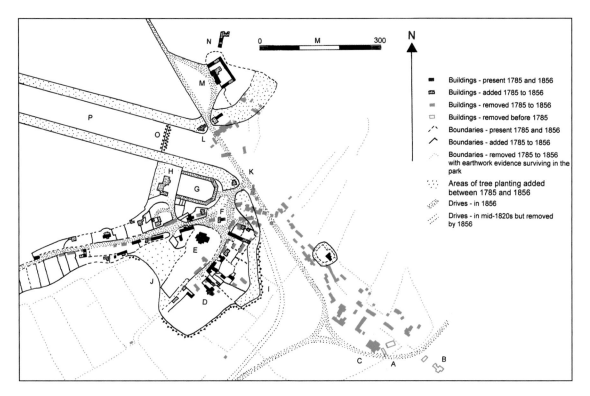

FIGURE 70.
The village of Edensor, as shown on an estate map of 1856, drawn after partial demolition and extensive remodelling under the 6th Duke were complete, compared with the sites of removed houses and field boundaries shown on a map of 1785 (A: Devonshire Arms – demolished late 1770s; B: Old Parsonage – demolished late 1770s; C: New Parsonage – built late 1770s; D: vicarage – after 1820s; E: church – now rebuilt; F: school – now demolished; G: model farm; H: farmhouse – later Edensor House; I: ha-ha; J: presumed ha-ha – later removed when churchyard enlarged; K: Castle Lodge; L: The Lodge and Tudor Lodge; M: The New Inn – built late 1770s; N: eighteenth-century lodge; O: ha-ha; P: the avenue – now removed).

Knowltons' house' here;[28] while in 1820 a cottage in Edensor 'late occupied by widow Bacon' was knocked down.[29] Systematic clearance of the eastern end of the settlement and the demolition of properties continued unabated through the 1820s and early 1830s.[30] The accounts record numerous payments for levelling ground at Edensor, both where buildings stood and where hedges ran;[31] and the houses, outbuildings and gardens do seem to have been levelled with particular thoroughness, making for some rather disappointing visible archaeology. The site of only one dwelling is indicated by slight earthworks, although the foundations of others sometimes appear as parch marks in the parkland turf during a dry summer, and the boundaries of several closes remain as lynchets. Rather surprisingly, one house was allowed to remain, and still stands somewhat incongruously, all by itself, within the park. There are a number of local stories which purport to explain this curious anomaly – that the house belonged to a freeholder who refused to sell, that it is still not owned by the estate, or that it was occupied by an elderly resident whom the Duke did not want to disturb, perhaps his former nanny – but none carry real conviction and the survival of 'Park House', as it came to be known, remains one of the mysteries of the Chatsworth landscape (Figure 71).

When Unwin surveyed his map of the Chatsworth estate in 1831 the destruction of the village had still not been completed.[32] Many of the houses on the north side of the main street remained (see Figure 57). The estate accounts for the following years record further removals: the demolition of 'Jonathan Littlewood's house' in 1832, several more buildings in 1833, cottages and a wheelwright's shop in 1834. More ground was levelled, Handley Old Lane hacked up, and stone carted away. By 1836 only the western end of the village survived and, while the estate accounts record some 'improvements' here, the houses were carefully screened from view of the park by new tree planting. A double row of limes was planted in the park to the south-east of the village, many of which still stand (Figure 72). These were probably planted in the 1820s (they are not shown on Unwin's 1831 map, presumably because they were still saplings). By 1836 a new all-encompassing tree screen had been established running round much of the village. Even after the remodelling of the village in an ornamental fashion that was to follow, these trees were retained for many years.

The removal of the village, it must be emphasised again, was not primarily motivated by any desire to improve the prospect from the house. Following the demolition and rebuilding of the parsonage in the late 1770s the settlement was already quite out of sight. The main concern seems to have been to improve the approach to the house. One account, written in 1838, explains how prior to destruction and rebuilding, the village 'presented a far different feature – unsightly houses and plenty of dirty, ragged-looking children generally appearing to open the gate on the passage of a carriage'.[33] As we shall see, changes to the settlement were accompanied by radical changes to the pattern of public roads and drives within the park. But the destruction of the eastern section of the village also served to make the park larger; and indeed, this was a period in which the park grew significantly in size towards both the north and the west.

The eighteenth-century park was bounded to the north of the village by the main road leading from Edensor to Baslow, which at this time ran some way to the east of its present line, just to the west of what is now Park Wood. On the eastern side of the Derwent, the kitchen garden established in the 1760s lay on the northern boundary: everything beyond to the north, both in Chatsworth and Baslow parishes, was still agricultural land. Between 1825 and 1831, however, substantial areas of ground to the west of the Derwent in Edensor parish, and east of the river in Chatsworth parish, were incorporated within a greatly expanded park. A new boundary east of the river was fixed in 1820, when Benjamin Staley was paid for 'surveying and setting out a give and take line as a proposed boundary at the North end of the park between His Grace and the Duke of Rutland', who owned the majority of Baslow parish; and for building a new boundary wall here.[34] But a short time later, in 1823, the area beyond this line was acquired through an important exchange of land between the two Dukes, and the park was expanded still further to the north.[35] This exchange allowed a significant area to be taken into the park and this was flanked at its western and northern edges by dense tree screens, as was normal at this period, cutting the park off from view from the world and creating a large exclusive space to be enjoyed only by those privileged few with access along the private drive to the house.

The expansion of the park to the north and west in the 1820s and 30s involved much work, which is described in some detail in the estate accounts. The line of the old Edensor – Baslow road (and that of the Edensor to Ashford turnpike, which joined it 700 m to the north of Edensor) was altered, following a Road Diversion Order in the late 1820s (Figure 38). The old road was systematically hacked up and its line covered with soil in 1831.[36] The replacement road, which formed the boundary of the newly expanded park on its north-eastern side, was bounded on the south by a 'sunk fence' all the way from Edensor to Buston Wood. A second main road, the 1759 turnpike that ran eastwards towards Chesterfield, through fields in what was to become the Baslow part of the park, was also closed to public traffic and diverted northwards by over 300 m in the mid to late 1820s. Again, this new road was placed immediately outside the new park but in this case behind a dense screen of trees.

These years (particularly from 1826 to 1834) saw a mass of activity in the 'Outer Park', the term used in the accounts to describe all the newly emparked areas. Walls and hedges were levelled, land drained, old stone quarries filled, trees planted and fenced: a range of activities which mirrored those carried out when the 'New Park' was initially laid out, in the 1760s.[37] And here, too, large numbers of hedgerow trees were retained, in the customary way, to provide ready-made parkland timber. The first edition Ordnance Survey six inch map of 1879 shows that a particularly high proportion of the trees in this part of the park stood in markedly straight lines, and a number of old oaks can still be seen here, growing on the earthwork remains of old field boundaries. Just as the creation of the new park in the 1750s and 60s served to preserve a whole range of archaeological features and earlier trees, so too did the expansion of the park northwards in the course of the 1820s and 30s (Figures 36, 73).

One other important change in the park occurred in the Duke's early years. As already noted, the estate accounts record payments for repairs to Queen Mary's Bower at the end of the eighteenth century, and in 1811 there was much movement of earth in this area. Palings were set around the Rookery Pond – i.e., the large 'moat' surrounding the Bower – and a bank raised and sloped to hide them from the river. Vast amounts – 1107 yards (1,012 m) – of soil were removed 'from the river Bank between the Rookery Garden and the bridge'; new turf was set here; and payments made for 'cleaning out sunk fence in the Rookery'.[38] But it was only in the early 1820s that the setting of the ancient building was radically altered. The estate accounts for 1822 record a flurry of activity here. The walls of the garden were taken down, the ha-ha

FIGURE 71. (*opposite*)
The 'Old House in the Park' was left behind when the other dwellings in the eastern section of Edensor village were removed in the early nineteenth century. Nobody knows for certain why this one house was allowed to remain, standing somewhat incongruously within the park. © PEAK DISTRICT NATIONAL PARK AUTHORITY.

FIGURE 72. (*opposite below*)
The screen of lime trees planted to hide the village of Edensor from the park in the 1820s, placed close to the new road from One Arch Bridge to Edensor (foreground and left), built in the mid 1820s, but abandoned a few years later when a new screen was placed around the village, planted between the ha-ha and the houses.

FIGURE 73.
This area, lying far to the north of the house in Baslow parish, was only brought into the park following the acquisition of land here from the Duke of Rutland in the 1820s. The photograph is taken looking down the old 1759 turnpike road from Baslow to Chesterfield, which was diverted northwards with the expansion of the park. Many of the trees in the background originally stood in hedgerows.

filled and levelled, 'soil and rubbish' were removed from the site and payments made for 'Taking down the stoves and hothouses, and levelling the Rookery garden previous to its being thrown into the park'.[39] The old square fish pond or moat around the feature was reduced in size at this time and given its present oval shape. The building was now to be made a feature of the park, rather than part of a separate area of enclosed gardens. Among Wyatville's architectural drawings in the Chatsworth archives is an illustration of the Bower, surmounted by an iron trelliswork superstructure (Figure 74).[40] The intention was to turn the structure into a kind of shrine to the Queen, the myth of her association with the Bower having firmly taken root in the mind of the Duke. A statue was to be placed here, a full-sized image of the queen. This was fashioned by the sculptor Westmacott at a cost of £350; however, by the mid 1830s the Duke seems to have lost interest in the project, later noting of the Queen:

> She is a false sign of the romance of history: she represents popular belief and tradition, in defiance of dates and facts.

The quality of the statue, moreover, made the Duke 'dread for it the open air, and the playful public'.[41] It was instead placed in the entrance hall at Hardwick, where it remains; the trelliswork superstructure was never erected. The stonework was, however, extensively repaired and added to in this period. Indeed, it is now hard to know quite what is original sixteenth-century work, and what is early nineteenth-century restoration. The stunted yews growing on the structure today may also date back to this brief flurry of interest in the early nineteenth century.

The rebuilding of Edensor

It is not entirely clear when the Duke decided to rebuild the remaining, western portion of Edensor as a 'model' village. But almost as soon as the last houses in the eastern section of the settlement had been removed, the first 'improvements' were made here. The accounts record payments for the creation of new gardens and for the erection of garden walls and gates in 1833; and, in the same year, for 'widening the road and improving the village of Edensor'. The following years saw unspecified 'improvements' to the church-yard,[42] and in 1836 the architect Decimus Burton was asked to design a new model farm a little to the north of the village. Two years later, John Robertson – an architect and draftsman who had been employed by the great garden designer and writer John Claudius Loudon (several of his drawings were published in Loudon's *Encyclopaedia of Cottage, Farm and Villa Architecture*) – supplied the Duke with ten designs for cottages.[43] Construction of the new houses began in 1839 and seems to have been largely completed by 1842. Edensor became an architectural showcase containing houses built in a bewildering assortment of styles (Figure 75). Whether the intention was always to create a settlement in this rather strange (not to say incongruous) amalgam of styles, or whether this evolved through experimentation, remains uncertain. The result, however, was one of the most striking estate villages in England.

The more ornamental of the buildings are in three main identifiable styles: Tudor, Italianate, and Norman. But these are mixed in with houses and cottages in no specific style, or with the simple gothic details typical of contemporary estate architecture (Figure 76). Most are of well-dressed sandstone, with sandstone or slate roofs, although Tudor Lodge is built of brick (it was used as an example in Loudon's *Encyclopaedia of Architecture*) (Figure 77). The majority were designed by Paxton, working in collaboration with John Robertson, who from 1841 until 1844 was permanently employed at Chatsworth. The more elaborate buildings which they designed include the 'Tudor' structures, Park View, the Post Office and adjoining cottage, and Church View; the 'Italianate' Italian Villa, Daisy Bank Cottage, and Top House; and the 'Norman' Norman villa. The 'Norman' Castle Lodge was designed by Robertson alone and the planned model farm to the north-east of the village, as already noted, was by Decimus Burton. Although at first sight the various styles of architecture seem to be jumbled up, with no apparent plan, on closer inspection it is evident that the more important, or the more prominently positioned, buildings were built in a defined style, while two properties in the same style were rarely placed side by side. This ensured that each could be appreciated as a piece of architecture in its own right – something assisted by the topography of the small valley along which much of the village is strung out.[44] It should be noted that, although we have talked so far about the 'rebuilding' of Edensor, it is evident that not all the houses were entirely new. Many of the existing buildings may have been remodelled, rather than swept away completely, as they occupy the same sites as dwellings here prior to the 1830s (Figure 70): 'Swiss Cottage', the Post Office and adjoining house, and parts of the vicarage are among these.[45]

The care and attention to detail apparent in the design of the houses in the village is matched in the linking walls, curtilage boundaries and other features. These include the ornamental drinking fountain, in Italianate style, designed by Robertson to the west of the Italian Villa, and the boundary flanking the main entrance to the village to the east, which is marked by a rustic stone wall. Boundary walls facing the main street and at the front of properties are of squared sandstone, sometimes mortared and often capped with flat coping stones; those to the rear, in contrast, are of rougher construction, simple drystone walls.

Although the reconstruction of the village was completed by 1843, a few buildings have been added subsequently. The Yews, a house in a restrained domestic gothic style, was added around 1860; while the building called Moor View at the western end of the village was built as late as 1912, in 'arts and crafts' mode, by the architect Romaine Walker. The most important later addition, however, is the parish church of St Peter, which was rebuilt to a design by the famous architect Gilbert Scott between 1867 and 1870, a project financed by the 7th Duke. It is huge building, its great spire dominating the

FIGURE 74.
This drawing, by Jeffry Wyatville, is a proposal for remodelling the sixteenth-century Queen Mary's Bower as a kind of shrine to the Queen, a plan which was never executed, although the stonework was restored. © THE DEVONSHIRE COLLECTION, CHATSWORTH. REPRODUCED BY PERMISSION OF THE CHATSWORTH SETTLEMENT TRUSTEES.

FIGURE 75.
Edensor, seen from the park, was rebuilt as an ornate 'model village' in the late 1830s and early 1840s. © THE DEVONSHIRE COLLECTION, CHATSWORTH. REPRODUCED BY PERMISSION OF THE CHATSWORTH SETTLEMENT TRUSTEES.

FIGURE 76.
The houses in the model village of Edensor are constructed in a bewildering variety of styles, with a broad range of architectural details.

FIGURE 77.
One of the two streets at Edensor, photographed several decades ago. Many of the buildings were entirely constructed in the 1830s and 40s but some are earlier structures, given a modish facelift at this time.

village and visible for miles around: it would, perhaps, look more at home in one of the nearby industrial towns (Figure 78). It may well be that the tree screens that originally hid Edensor from the main road and park were removed at the same time as the church was rebuilt, opening the view to the village for the first time to show off this grand new building (the map evidence shows that the screens had certainly been removed in the late 1860s or 1870s).[46]

Edensor is a quintessential example of a 'model estate village'. But what was it for, what did it *mean*? Model estate villages – settlements comprehensively rebuilt, either *in situ*, or in some new location, to an architect's plan – had first appeared in England in the late seventeenth century, but they increased in number in the middle decades of the eighteenth.[47] Early examples, like Houghton in Norfolk, were relatively plain and functional – they were often replacements for villages cleared away because they lay inconveniently close to a great house. But from the early nineteenth they became more flamboyant and picturesque in style, a trend perhaps first set by Blaise Hamlet near Bristol, built in 1810. And they were increasingly integrated with the landscape of the park, placed for example on approach roads or – as here at Chatsworth – at park entrances. From the 1830s, moreover, there was increasing concern on the part of the landed classes both for the physical and the moral welfare of estate workers, and estate villages – and other purpose-built estate housing – proliferated. It was widely believed that as old, rambling and ramshackle settlements were replaced with ones composed of aesthetically pleasing and well-built dwellings, the condition of the poor would similarly improve, particularly as alehouses were generally banished. At Edensor, each of the houses was supplied with good water, and a sound system of sewerage. But other aspects of the village were intended to foster the inhabitants' moral well-being. Llewellyn Jewitt, writing about Edensor in 1872, typically remarked that 'beside the Agent's house, there are in Edensor a good parsonage and a village school, but, luckily, there is neither a village ale-house, blacksmith's forge, wheelwright's shop, or other gossiping place; and unpleasant sights and discordant sounds are alike unknown'.[48] Prominently displayed at the entrance to the park, albeit initially kept separate by its tree screen, Edensor was a very public demonstration of the Cavendish's paternalism, but it was also a showpiece of architectural innovation – it advertised a range of ways in which the deserving poor might be housed in this age of moral improvement.

In the fields immediately west of Edensor and just north of the park edge, there is a remarkable collection of stone-built field barns, mostly now redundant and many in ruins (some examples have been removed altogether) (Figure 79). These lie in a series of small fields, which an estate map shows were laid out some time before 1785.[49] However, the barns were mostly added between the 1830s and 1850s and by the time the Ordnance Survey map of 1879 was surveyed, virtually every field had one. These fields were presumably allocated to smallholders living at Edensor, perhaps at the time the park was created on the east side of the river in the 1760s, as recompense for the loss of fields here. The addition of the field barns may have gone hand in hand with the remodelling of Edensor village, part of the wider scheme to improve the condition of the tenants.

The eclectic houses in the 'model village' at Edensor were not the only buildings to be constructed, or radically altered, within or around the park (Figure 68). In 1842 a new home was designed for Paxton by Robertson, an Italianate villa called Barbrook House, close to the kitchen garden: this was extended in the early 1850s into an even more substantial home, with a square tower, but has since been demolished. And three important ornamental buildings were erected, on the fringes of the park. The grand Park Lodge, just outside the park's northern end, east of the Baslow entrance lodges, was built between 1840 and 1842 as a home for the 6th Duke's physician, Mr Condell, to a design by John Robertson in Italianate style. The ornate structure called the Swiss Cottage, to the east of the main park beside the Swiss Lake, was built between 1839 and 1842: the estate accounts record payments for bringing materials to the site, for masons and carpenters' work, and for constructing the chimneys, in these years (Figure 80).[50] It was designed by either Paxton or Robertson as a focal point and ornament to the Swiss Lake. The Russian Cottage is also located just outside the park proper, on the high ground at the edge of Calton Pasture, overlooking not the park but the Calton valley to the south. Its design was taken from a model of a Russian village sent to the 6th Duke by his friend Tsar Nicholas. It is a single-storey building of cruciform plan, built mainly of timber beneath a steeply pitched slate roof; the northern arm, however, is of coursed sandstone. There are three chimney stacks and the gable ends have elaborate bargeboards. The logs are left with their natural finish. In 1855 the accounts record the construction of 'Russian cottage' at a cost of £346 15s 4½d, and payments for decorating it, at a cost of £46. The following year there are payments for removing soil and laying down turf here.[51] The building is interesting as one of several connections in the Chatsworth landscape between the Devonshires and the Russian royal family.

New drives and 'ha-has'

The alterations to the park and pleasure grounds taking place in the nineteenth century necessitated the construction of a number of new ha-has (Figures 38, 68). When the pleasure grounds were extended to the south in the 1830s, the accounts record the payments made for 'cutting out a length of the sunk fence for enlarging the Pleasure Grounds' and 'levelling ground, forming and soiling the slopes of the sunk fence'.[52] It is possible that the existing boundary between park and pleasure grounds to the south of the house was also realigned slightly at this time, and its associated ha-ha rebuilt, for the two lengths appear identical in construction. Both comprise a dry stone retaining wall of large, regular gritstone blocks, set in a ditch with a sloping side towards the park. Both are of conventional 'retaining wall' form, in that they comprise a ditch with one vertical and one sloping face. Yet at the same time they are slightly unusual in that the ditch is also flanked by a broad bank on the park side, which prevents

FIGURE 78.

The huge church at Edensor, built in the 1860s to replace the medieval church, was one of the few additions to the Chatsworth landscape made by the 7th Duke. It would perhaps look more at home in one of the nearby industrial towns, but its spire is one of the characteristic landmarks of the park. © THE DEVONSHIRE COLLECTION, CHATSWORTH. REPRODUCED BY PERMISSION OF THE CHATSWORTH SETTLEMENT TRUSTEES.

FIGURE 79. (*opposite top*)

The field barns in the area just to the north of the park, and west of Edensor, were mostly built between the 1830s and 50s for smallholders in the village.

FIGURE 80. (*opposite*)

The ornate structure called the Swiss Cottage, beside the Swiss Lake, was built between 1839 and 1842 and formed a focal point for the view from a new carriage drive running along the opposite shore.

the wall being seen from the park as well as from the gardens. A very similar arrangement is found on the boundary between the park and Edensor village; again, a broad, high bank is placed on the park side of a 'retaining wall' ha-ha of normal form, the vertical wall of which lies on the Edensor rather than the park side of the ditch. This feature again probably dates to the mid 1830s, when work on the model village was begun. To the south-west it is disrupted by a more typical ha-ha, formed by a simple deep, wide ditch containing a sunken wall. This flanks an extension to Edensor churchyard which was made in the late 1860s or 1870s, perhaps when the church was rebuilt in 1867–70.

Only one other ha-ha on the estate is, in fact, of 'conventional' form, without a masking bank. This runs along the edge of the Edensor – Baslow Road which, as we have seen, was created when the park was expanded in this direction in the 1820s. The ha-ha itself was built about 1830: its purpose was to disguise the boundary of the park when viewed from within, and to provide an uninterrupted view into the fields to the west, which could then be 'read' at a distance as an extension of the park itself. Elsewhere in the park, however, more idiosyncratic ha-ha-like features were again employed to hide walls or disguise boundaries – banks without any accompanying ditches, similar to those used in the previous century along parts of the boundary of Calton New Piece Plantation (see page 100). To the east of Crimea House, near the kitchen garden, a hedge is hidden from view by a broad bank raised on the side facing the park: the boundary here seems to have been altered some time between 1785 and 1831, but the bank itself may well be later, added in the late 1850s after the Crimea farmhouse was built just outside the park here. Along the eastern edge of Park Wood, a boundary was established (to judge from the map evidence)[53] between 1839 and 1855 and given a similar masking bank, perhaps the 'sunk fence for new plantation at Edensor' recorded in the accounts for 1860.[54] At the western edge of Stand Wood there is another example, almost identical in form, which was almost certainly constructed in 1847, as there is a reference in the estate accounts of that year to the construction of a 'sunk fence' 'under the Stand wood'.[55] The same principal was used to mask the boundary wall of the park, and a field boundary wall, in the area to the north of Edensor village.

More important by far were the changes made under the 6th Duke to the pattern of roads and drives within the park (Figure 38), changes which radically altered how the landscape was viewed and experienced, and which determine, to a large extent, how we see the park today. The first was relatively minor, and came quite soon after the Duke's accession. In 1818 the estate accounts record the payments made for diverting the 'park road' and for 'altering the park road from Beeley Bridge to Edensor',[56] work which continued into the following year and which included 'getting limestone for road by one arch bridge', as well as covering the old road with earth and sowing grass seeds on it.[57] In spite of such attention to detail its line is still clearly visible as an earthwork, a slight raised causeway in the parkland turf close to the river. As a result of this change, instead of turning to the right after crossing the One Arch Bridge, the drive now continued diagonally on uphill, and then curved more gently before following a line roughly parallel to the old drive for some 300 m, and then re-joining the old course of the road. All this was probably done for practical reasons: the alteration eliminated a particularly sharp bend immediately after the bridge. But it also meant that the drive no longer ran right past Paine's mill, but instead passed along the hillside some way above it. Clearly, the building was no longer considered a major feature of the park landscape.

A few years later a comprehensive and extensive reorganisation of drives and roads occurred, which is recorded as a separate item in the estate accounts for 1826, at the completion of the project. This included further alterations to the public road running from Beeley Bridge to Edensor.[58] This was again made to leave its old line 250 m north of the diversion made in 1818, sweeping westward in a shallow curve for c. 300 m before returning to the original course. Here, too, the old line survives as an earthwork, a raised causeway, around 10 m wide in total (but only 5 m carriage width). More importantly, as it approached Edensor the road was diverted to the north, so that instead of entering the village with an abrupt right-angle turn into the end of Jap Lane, it now ran some way to the east. Much of the village was still to be removed at this time but work on demolition was continuing and the eventual intention was clearly for the public road to pass the eastern end of the truncated settlement, as it does today, rather than run through the middle of it. The line of the road was altered yet again later in the nineteenth century but the route created in the mid 1820s is still visible as a carefully engineered terrace to the south-east of the present village. At the same time, a new private drive to the hall was laid out, leaving the public road some way to the south of the village and curving eastwards to meet the line of the existing drive built in the 1760s. These changes must clearly be considered alongside the alterations being made at around this time to Edensor: when both were completed, visitors would no longer need to pass through the village, and the house would stand in a more discrete and secluded landscape.

Yet all this formed only part of a wider package of alterations, which involved a major increase in the number of carriage drives leading through (and out of) the park. Few drives are shown on Barker's survey of 1773 (Figure 48).[59] Apart from the main drive to the hall, there were only two. One turned off the main drive at a point near Queen Mary's Bower and was probably only a service track to the new kitchen gardens. Another, leaving shortly before the stables, led northwards and then off the mapped area, to meet the turnpike road from Baslow to Chesterfield, created in 1759. That was all. The wider park landscape could be experienced on horse, or on foot, from innumerable vantage points. But the movement of carriages was evidently much more restricted; only a few set routes were available. It was from these, and in particular from the immediate vicinity of the house and pleasure grounds, that the principal vistas created by Brown and Millican could be enjoyed. But all this was changed by the programme of improvements effected in the mid 1820s.

Firstly, a new northern drive was laid out, a 'new line of road from Chatsworth House through the Park to Baslow', which ran closer to the river.[60] Like its predecessor to the east it continued as far as the turnpike road, but the latter had by now (as we have seen) been diverted further to the north by the recent expansion of the park. Secondly, the accounts record the making of a 'Green Drive' running from Edensor to Hacketts Plantation. This signifies the construction of the drive running down the centre of a new avenue, closely following the line of an earlier, eighteenth-century feature, on the hillside to the west of Edensor village. As already discussed, map and earthwork evidence suggests that the original intention was to create a drive, flanked by hedges, down its centre, but this was almost certainly never finished (above, pp. 79–80). The old avenue had disappeared entirely by this date: the new feature cut obliquely through a pattern of fields, bounded by thin strips of woodland, and the accounts duly note the payments made for 'walling the shaws connected with the same'.[61] Thirdly, another 'Green Drive' was made, leaving the public road at a point roughly halfway between One Arch Bridge and Edensor. This climbed the hill to the south and then headed west, up to Calton Pasture, before returning to the park via Calton Lees.[62] This is shown on the map surveyed by George Unwin in 1831 (Figure 57),[63] and can still be traced as an earthwork in the parkland turf. It evidently allowed, for the first time, carriage access to the 'outer park' on Calton Pasture, beyond the skyline plantations. The accounts for 1826 record a number of payments for new roads 'in New Piece Wood' and for 'improving the road at Calton Lees'.[64] Various other drives and carriage ways were made which encouraged movement beyond the park. The drive running along the avenue to the west of Edensor terminated at Handley Lane, and this was itself improved, to make it more fit for carriages; while, to the south of the park, a new road was made 'at Lindup Wood to communicate with a drive through Haddon Woods'.[65]

By 1831, when George Unwin produced his maps of the estate, a number of other drives were in place, the construction of which is less clearly signalled in the estate accounts. In particular, a long southern carriage drive ran from near the house towards Beeley, terminating at gates on the public road just to the east of the One Arch Bridge. There had been access here in the previous century, as Barker shows gates already standing at this point, although this was perhaps no more than a little-used track following the line of the redundant 1739 turnpike road from Bakewell to Chesterfield, which had been closed in 1759. Unwin's map also shows that the approach to the house from Three Arch Bridge had been given a more sinuous course than that shown by Barker in 1773; this change again probably took place in the 1820s, when the gardens around Queen Mary's Bower were being removed and the area incorporated within the park.

Far-reaching as these changes were, the following decades saw further additions to the pattern of roads and drives. The estate accounts show that some of the drives in Stand Wood were extensively altered in the early 1830s, and in

FIGURE 81. Campbell's plan of Chatsworth, revised in 1858, is not an entirely reliable representation: archaeological survey shows that some of the features it shows were proposed but never constructed, or were laid out on different lines, most notably the great serpentine drive in the south of the park (bottom-right), and the elaborate planting and other features in Beeley Warren (centre-right).

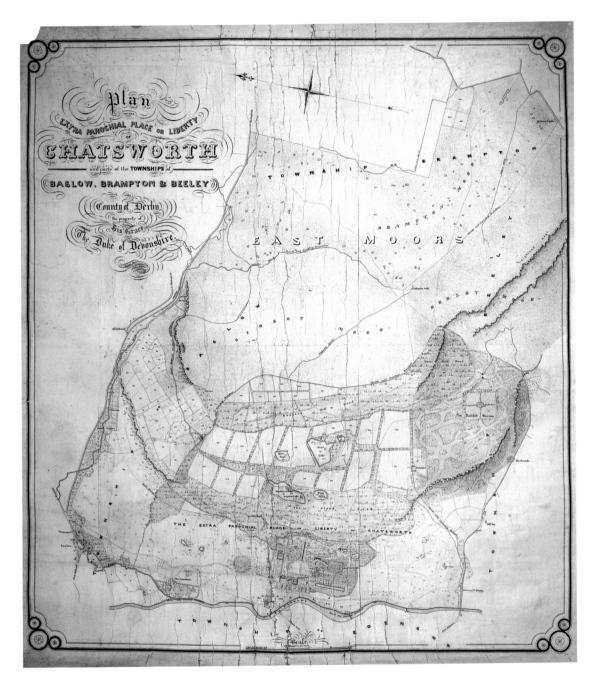

1836 payments were made for building a new road in the park. The latter probably refers to alterations made to the road network around the site of the recently-cleared eastern end of Edensor village, including the replacement of the old village street by the present road, running on higher ground a little to the south-west; and the abandonment of the route to the south of the village only recently created, in 1826, which was thereby rendered redundant.[66] Between 1837 and 1844 a new footpath was made from Edensor village to

Chatsworth Bridge.[67] This still exists: on the side facing towards the house the ground is raised in a bank in order to hide the gravel which would interrupt the panorama across the smooth turf. In 1838 a new drive was made, leading off the North Drive to the kitchen garden and Paxton's cottage, itself rebuilt four years later as Barbrook House.[68] In 1839 a new road was made in Stand Wood, presumably that running passing Swiss Lake (for this is not shown on the first edition one inch Ordnance Survey map, surveyed in 1839) (Figure 39). In 1842–3 the road from the Three Arch Bridge to the house was again realigned;[69] from the bridge it curved slightly more to the north and ran along a broad embankment that improved the view of the house and stable block as these were approached. In 1843 there are numerous references in the accounts to the making of new footpaths within the park, but also to the removal of 'walks' within it.[70] More importantly, in 1851 the accounts begin to record the construction of a new carriage drive in the park, and continue to record payments for a 'new road made in park', and associated levelling work, until 1858; a particularly ambitious project to which we will soon return.[71]

The results of all these changes are shown on two maps, produced by the surveyor E. Campbell, one depicting the land to the west of the river (1855), one the land to the east (1858) (Figure 81).[72] These confirm that there had, indeed, been a significant increase in the number of drives, especially in the area immediately to the north of the house. Here the western end of the eighteenth-century route from Three Arch Bridge to the stables remained in place, but the 1842–3 route, swinging northwards and then south, was now apparently the main formal drive. But there were a number of other drives, presenting a bewildering choice of routes between the stables, house forecourt, and the main western and northern drive. More importantly, a number of drives now ran through Stand Wood, one of which continued on past the Emperor Lake and then through the narrow belts of trees which had been planted around the new fields created when the Old Park, on the high shelf above the house, was destroyed around the start of the nineteenth century (Figure 39). There were, moreover, several drives and tracks branching off from this, one of which is shown followed a curving, serpentine route down the escarpment, through the south park, to join the south drive near Beeley gate.

To the west of the Derwent Campbell shows a rather similar drive, which also appears on the Ordnance Survey map of 1879 and, more importantly, survives today as a very prominent earthwork. This is the carriage drive whose construction is recorded in the estate accounts from 1851 onwards: but once again, archaeology can tell us things much less apparent, if apparent at all, from the documentary record. It is a broad, carefully engineered feature which zigzags up the steep slope and has three particularly sharp bends which are cut steeply back into the natural land surface. It was evidently intended to allow the passage, up this steep slope, of large coaches, and indeed to allow two coaches to pass each other (it is considerably wider, for example, than the public road leading through the park). It cuts boldly through ridge and furrow, lynchets, and all other earlier features, including the earthwork remains of the track or drive shown leading up this same slope towards Calton Pasture on Unwin's map of 1831 (Figure 82).[73]

What is particularly striking is that these remains are mirrored on the *eastern* side of the river, in the south park. Here, too, are the earthwork traces of a broad, carefully engineered drive which climbs the slope, with a series of hairpin bends, to join the earlier drives in Stand Wood. But this, somewhat confusingly, does *not* follow the line of the drive shown on Campbell's 1857 map,[74] instead making its first appearance on a map of 1867.[75] What is also striking is that a revised map by Campbell, dated 1858,[76] shows yet another route, although closer to that depicted on the 1867 map. The making of the 'new road in the park' was still being reported in the accounts in 1858 – but not in those for the following year. The new drive was thus still under construction when Campbell's maps were being produced. Indeed, Campbell's maps may show other features which were proposed at the time, rather than those completed or even under construction. In this context, it is noteworthy that within Beeley Warren, on the high shelf above the park, Campbell shows a complex series of ornamental paths and other features; no trace of these exists in the unimproved moorland, and there are numerous undisturbed prehistoric remains here, including barrows and stone circles.[77]

The proliferation, and continuous elaboration, of the network of drives within the park in the period between c. 1820 and the late 1850s – and in particular the carefully-engineered character, and evident expense, of some of the later examples – signals a major change in the way that the Chatsworth landscape was experienced. Brown's park had been enjoyed, primarily, as a series of relatively self-contained views from the area around the house and gardens. The higher ground was essentially a backdrop, either to the views towards the house from the west, or to the views towards the west from the house. Of course, the landscape *could* be enjoyed on horseback or on foot from other perspectives, and the tantalising evidence for the aestheticisation of Calton Pasture in the eighteenth century clearly indicates more extensive explorations. But the broad truth of this generalisation remains, and the contrast in particular with the pattern of drives laid out in the 1850s is striking. Careful engineering and attention to gradient allowed coaches to be taken up the steep slopes and views across the park and towards the house could now be enjoyed from a number of elevated view points. The drives were evidently designed with this in mind. The zigzag drive running through the south-east park, for example, makes a large detour to the north-east, up onto the shelf now occupied by Old Park Plantation, in order to take advantage of the fine view over the park from the shelf crest; while the course taken by the similar drive in the south-west of the park, climbing towards Calton Pasture, seems designed to maximise the views towards the house and gardens on the far side of the valley. But in addition, the carriage drives took privileged visitors out of the park altogether; one led into Stand Wood, the other into the Calton Pasture sheepwalk, so that visitors could enjoy extensive panoramas out across the surrounding countryside. In this context, it is

very striking how two of the principal ornamental buildings erected at Chatsworth in the nineteenth century were both positioned close to these new drives. The Swiss Cottage, built between 1839 and 42, thus formed the termination for a view over the Swiss Lake from the 1839 drive running along its western shore. The Russian Cottage, erected in 1855, lay beside the zigzag 1850s drive leading up to Calton Pasture. These buildings make little sense without the associated drives, which in both cases were built at around the same time.

These complex alterations and additions to the pattern of roads and drives in and around the Park were accompanied by the erection of a number of new entrance lodges (Figure 68). The two by Edensor village – 'Tudor Lodge' (as its name suggests, in Tudor style) and The Lodge (in Italianate style) – were both designed by Sir Jeffry Wyatville, but he died before they could be executed.[78] The designs were, however, taken up by Paxton and the buildings duly erected, as part of the general rebuilding and landscaping of the village in the late 1830s and early 1840s. The lodges in the new north park were also approximately of this date, in spite of the fact that the wider landscaping of this new part of the Chatsworth landscape seems to have been largely completed in the early 1830s. The Baslow Lodges were erected at the end of the new northern entrance drive between 1839 and 1842, although some work was continuing here, perhaps in the gardens, as late as 1847, when there were payments for building a wall 'at Baslow lodge'.[79] They were

FIGURE 82.
The great serpentine carriage drive in the south-west of the park, created in the 1850s, survives as a dramatic earthwork cutting through medieval strip lynchets as it climbs the slopes below New Piece Plantation.

designed by Wyatville but again only erected, under the aegis of Paxton, some time after his death. They are imposing structures that mirror the style of Chatsworth House itself. The £411 18s 3d spent in 1849 on 'Building Plantation Lodge'[80] probably refers to the small and plain Barbrook Lodge, erected just outside the park to the south-east of Baslow on a service lane. At a somewhat earlier but uncertain date, the small Blue Moors Lodge, named on the first edition Ordnance Survey map of 1839, was added to the farmhouse adjacent to One Arch Bridge at the southern end of the park. White Lodge was situated, not at a major entrance, but at the start of a service track leading to the kitchen gardens and Paxton's home at Barbrook House. It is a small cottage-style building, built of 'rustic' dressed gritstone in 1855 (Figure 83). In 1861 the accounts record the payment of £577 on the construction of 'New Lodge, Beeley' at the end of the south drive leading through the park on the eastern bank of the river Derwent.[81] This building is often said to have been designed by Wyatville but was, in fact, the work of Stokes, Paxton's son-in-law.

The large number of lodges appearing in the Chatsworth landscape at this time was typical. Although large landowners had been erecting lodges at their park gates since the early eighteenth century (and, as we have seen, Chatsworth acquired two in c. 1780), in the course of the nineteenth century – and particularly in the middle decades of the century – their numbers proliferated. Even the smallest estate usually acquired one; large parks like

FIGURE 83.
White Lodge, built in 1855, is one of several lodges erected at the entrances to Chatsworth Park in the middle decades of the nineteenth century.

Chatsworth often had many. They set the scene for visitors for what was to come and advertised to passers-by the presence of a great house, as well as providing a measure of security against poachers and other intruders.

The pattern of planting

Perhaps the most poorly documented aspect of Chatsworth's history in the nineteenth century relates to the development of the planting within the park: the estate accounts often simply record 'planting' or 'work in plantations' without providing any indication of where this was taking place. It is, however, clear that a sustained campaign of planting began soon after the Duke's accession: indeed, according to one source no less than 1,535,120 trees were planted on the estate in 1816 and 1817 alone.[82] Most of this activity was well beyond the boundaries of the park: the accounts for 1811 thus record that 13,500 holes for trees were dug in Cracknowls Plantation to the north-west of Bakewell, and a further 31,342 in 1818. Much planting also took place at Highlow, south-west of Hathersage, in 1818 and 1819.[83] But some at least of the unspecified planting noted in the accounts must have been in the park. Trees were certainly planted and fenced near the One Arch Bridge in 1818 at the same time as the road was diverted here, and in 1819 there were payments for 'fencing round trees in the park' and for 'planting in the park'.[84] In 1820 further holes for trees were dug in the park, and no less than 30,400 'in Chatsworth Plantations', perhaps augmenting the planting in Stand Wood.[85] Moreover, sporadic references in the estate accounts to 'planting in the park', especially in the mid 1840s, suggest further planting during the middle decades of the century. Barker's survey of 1773, and the 1785 estate map of Edensor, both suggest that the eighteenth-century park was fairly sparsely planted and that the majority of trees had been incorporated from earlier hedgerows.[86] Moreover, although the estate accounts for the 1760s contain many references to the establishment of plantations, there are relatively few entries which seem to relate to the planting of free-standing timber. The relatively open nature of the landscape is also suggested by a number of contemporary paintings and engravings. By the end of the nineteenth century, to judge from the present pattern of planting and the evidence of the Ordnance Survey six inch maps, the park was much more densely treed. Even areas which had already been fairly well-timbered, most notably the Old Park to the south of the house, were now augmented both with individual trees and small clumps.

In view of the limitations of the documentary record it would be helpful if we could confidently distinguish those trees in the park which were planted in the eighteenth century from those of nineteenth-century vintage. The problems involved in estimating the date of trees from their size has already been touched upon, but for the most part we can identify those added in the nineteenth century by comparing what exists on the ground today (Figure 3) with the trees shown on the 1785 map of Edensor (above, page 126). It is clear that planting carried out in the middle and later decades of the nineteenth century

was overwhelmingly dominated by the same kinds of species as had characterised Brown's park: lime, beech, elm and oak, with some sycamore and sweet
chestnut, together with cedar; while in the areas newly-emparked in the 1820s
and 30s, large numbers of hedgerow trees were retained in the usual fashion.
The main difference between the two periods seems to be the greater emphasis
placed on horse chestnut in the nineteenth century.

In keeping with contemporary fashions, some of the new planting was of a
formal, geometric nature. The parallel lines of lime trees running east–west to
the north of the house, towards the stables, were probably planted around
1820, to judge from Wyatville's drawings.[87] But more important was the
substantial avenue of closely-planted trees, aligned on the house, which George
Unwin's map shows running up the hill to the north-west of Edensor.[88] This
was apparently established as part of the comprehensive scheme of road and
drive construction in the mid 1820s and in 1827 labourers were paid for
'repairing the fences ... of the Avenue'.[89] But the archaeological evidence
strongly suggests that the drive running down its centre was never completed
(above, pages 79–80). By the later nineteenth century the avenue had again
disappeared, although a small number of beech and horse chestnut trees still
survive on its line. It was almost certainly destroyed around 1860, when the
estate accounts record the purchase of beer for labourers involved in 'stubbing
the avenue in Edensor' and the payments for 'stubbing and boughing trees,
trenching &c at ditto'.[90]

Conclusion: a new landscape

It is usual to discuss the landscape of Chatsworth Park largely in terms of
Capability Brown, and it is true that the essential structure of the park is,
indeed, much as he designed it in the middle decades of the eighteenth
century. But the overall 'feel' of the landscape which we see at Chatsworth
today owes just as much to the nineteenth century. Several of the main additions made in this period have, it is true, effectively disappeared from the
landscape, most notably the extraordinary zigzag drives climbing up the steep
slopes on the edges of the park, which now survive only as earthworks. But
much that the visitor enjoys today – the lodges, the model village of Edensor,
and above all much of the planting within the park – was created after 1800.
The influence of the 6th Duke, Wyatville and Paxton may not have been quite
as great in the wider landscape as it was in the gardens in the immediate
vicinity of the house, but it was nevertheless considerable. And what they
created in the park was, as in the pleasure grounds, typical of what could be
found in innumerable contemporary designed landscapes, yet on a scale that
was seldom matched elsewhere.

CHAPTER SEVEN

The Recent Past

After the death of the 6th Duke in 1858 the great days of Chatsworth were, at least for a while, over. In part, relative inactivity was a reflection of the character and interests of his successors. It was also, however, the consequence of wider social and economic changes. Additions and alterations were made to the grounds, some of considerable interest. But much that had been created previously was allowed to deteriorate or was removed, and few large-scale changes were carried out.

The 7th Duke inherited at the age of 50. He was, it need hardly be said, not the son of the Bachelor Duke. Indeed, he was only distantly related. William Cavendish was the grandson of Lord George Augustus Henry Cavendish, one of the younger sons of the 4th Duke. He was active in politics – first as MP for the University of Cambridge, latterly for Malton in Yorkshire and for North Derbyshire – and, following in the family's radical tradition, a fervent supporter of the first Reform Bill. But his heart was not really in public affairs. His great interest was scholarship, and in particular science and technology. At the age of 28 he was chosen as Chancellor of London University, and in 1861 became Chancellor of Cambridge University, presenting that institution with the Cavendish Laboratory and encouraging the study of scientific agriculture. He was also assiduous in developing his estates. Eastbourne in Sussex grew from little more than a holiday village to a major resort, the spa-town of Buxton was further developed, and – above all – the small settlement at Barrow in the Lake District was expanded into the great industrial town of Barrow-in-Furness through the development of a harbour and dockyard and, in particular, iron ore mines.[1]

Largely as a consequence of careful investments, and an active interest in the world of industry and commerce, the 7th Duke quite quickly completed the recovery of the family finances which had begun in the last years of his predecessor. While the 6th Duke had, by and large, spent money, the 7th was more adept at making it. Remarkably little was done to the Chatsworth landscape, or to the house, during his time: the great works of Paxton, Wyatville and the 6th Duke were maintained, but not embellished. The Duke's interests were commercial, philanthropic and evangelical, rather than artistic or horticultural: Edensor Church was rebuilt, and much energy was expended on improving the farmland on the estate.

The 7th Duke died in 1891 and was succeeded by his son, Spencer Compton Cavendish, then aged 58. He, too, did nothing major to the house, park or garden. Before inheriting, whilst still Lord Hartington, he had taken a keen interest in politics, entering Parliament in 1857 as the Liberal member for North Lancashire. He became Civil Lord of the Admiralty in 1863 and a Privy Councillor in 1866, and again followed the family tradition in staunchly supporting the second Reform Bill. He was made Postmaster-General, and eventually Irish Secretary under Gladstone, at a time when the Irish Question was a burning issue.[2] Eventually, following Gladstone's defeat in 1874 and the return to power of Disraeli, he was chosen as leader of the Liberal Party. He refused the office of Prime Minister on two occasions, served in the War Office, and was closely involved in opposing the introduction of the Irish Home Rule Bill. His involvement in politics continued after his accession to the dukedom, and he eventually joined Lord Salisbury's Conservative Cabinet. But political activity was not the only factor that kept him from making changes at Chatsworth. Away from public life, his main recreational interests was sport, and in particular horseracing.[3] Yet he did not neglect his estates, and the gardens and house at Chatsworth continued to be maintained, more or less, in the condition in which the 6th Duke had left them. Indeed, in 1900 no less than 80 people were employed in the garden. And visitors continued to come in their thousands: in 1906 alone 72,729 trooped through the gates.[4] It is said that the Duke was advised that the sheer bulk of day trippers was beginning to have a serious impact upon the fabric of the house but he was insistent that all should be welcome: 'I dare say they will bring down the floors some day, but I don't see how we can keep them out'.[5] The collections and the library were made available to scholars from across the world. He was a custodian, not a creator of new art. Nevertheless, some changes were made. A collection of eighteenth-century Herms – stone busts on tapering columns, based on ancient Greek models – was brought from Chiswick in 1893, where they had originally graced the exhedra designed by William Kent, and these were re-erected around the Ring Pond.[6] The monkey puzzles which originally flanked the Broad Walk to the east of the house were replaced, around 1900, with the yews which are now such a striking feature. The Duke was also responsible for the game larder, an octagonal building now used as a chicken house just to the north of the house: although it was only erected after his death in 1909, the earliest plans for the building are dated 1899.[7] It stands on the site of the ice house constructed in 1734. The Chatsworth landscape did not, therefore, remain entirely unchanged in the later nineteenth and early twentieth centuries. But compared with the period of Paxton and the 6th Duke, activity was at a relatively low level.

The relative stasis in the development of the Chatsworth landscape was part of a wider phenomenon. The great age of the country house landscape was passing. In the late nineteenth and early twentieth centuries major landowners were less keen to create vast parks around their homes, or indulge the fantastic schemes of their head gardeners. In part this was a consequence of economic factors. From the early 1880s agriculture was in a state of recession, and most landed estates relied on farm rents for their incomes. As rents fell, there was less and less money available to make 'improvements', and large estates were also now under threat from Death Duties. But not all great landowners were completely dependent on agricultural rents, and the Cavendish family, more than most, was able to draw on a range of urban and industrial rents and incomes. Indeed, the 8th Duke sold off much land in Derbyshire and Ireland in order to invest money in stocks and shares.[8] More important were wider cultural, political and social changes. As England became a more democratic country – as successive Reform Bills strengthened the power of the middle classes, and as institutions like County Councils came into existence and grew in power and competence – great landowners were no longer seen as the natural leaders of local society, and the country house and its grounds no longer served as a positive expression of their wealth and taste, and thus, of their fitness to rule. On the contrary: the steady growth of radical opinion made lavish embellishments to mansion, parks and gardens a potential embarrassment.

Around the turn of the twentieth century wealthy middle class residents in country areas – especially in the south of east of England – demanded new styles of architecture and garden design. Such people aspired not to a vast mansion with an extensive estate attached, but to a substantial country house with more manageable grounds. Leading designers and writers like Edward Lutyens and Gertrude Jekyll popularised 'arts and crafts' houses, executed in pseudo-vernacular styles and accompanied by relatively small, compartmentalised gardens. In these, an abundance of 'hard' landscaping (in the form of walls, paths and pergolas) was combined with informal, profuse planting, mostly of hardy species and mainly in wide borders. In addition, under the influence of writers like William Robinson, there was a fashion for 'wild gardens' and woodland gardens, in which paths meandered through areas of dense and irregular planting, featuring indigenous species or hardy perennials.[9] These new styles of gardening did not originate with the landed estates and only a few of their main elements – such as wild and woodland gardens – could be successfully adapted to the larger canvas of the country house.

The 8th Duke died in 1908 and was succeeded by the 9th Duke, Victor Cavendish, who was the elder son of the 8th Duke's younger brother, Lord Edward Cavendish. The need to modernise Chatsworth House (and in particular to install mains drainage for the first time), coupled with the impact of Death Duties, enforced some economies. Between 1907 and 1912 the number of under-gardeners at Chatsworth was reduced from 55 to 29, and fell even further during and after the First World War. The Great Stove was demolished in 1920. It had become derelict during the First World War, due to a lack of sufficient coal for heating or labour for routine maintenance.[10] It was eventually brought down by a series of controlled explosions: ironically, the work of demolition was supervised by Charles Markham, Paxton's grandson. The Duke's son described in a letter how:

> They had a great struggle with the Great House. The explosion was to have been on Saturday last at 4 but something went wrong and though

they were at it till midnight they had to leave it till Monday … they tried again and this time got the explosion all right, but the house still stood firm. They blew off well over 200 lbs [90 kg] of gelignite, so it must have been well built. They had another go of it on Tuesday and this time they did get more of it down … They fired 90 pounds [41 kg] in one charge under one corner and the house stood for about five minutes and then came down with a run. One piece of cast iron weighing over a pound was blown through one of the windows of the Book Gallery, but otherwise no damage was done.[11]

Other changes were more positive in character. In particular, the Duke's wife Evelyn – in collaboration with the head gardener, J. G. Weston – created the Ravine Garden and the Azalea Dell in the south of the garden, areas of planting which were clearly in the 'woodland garden' tradition. An article in the *Gardener's Chronicle* for 1933 described how

Having cleared, planted, and replanted, Mr Weston began to explore. One day he scrambled down a little ravine on the outskirts of the garden … On one side the descent is sharp, but the whole face is clothed with masses of Rhododendrons. On the other side of the ravine, less steep, were abundant trees and a dense thicket of Laurels and all manner of undergrowth. Commencing high up, a stream descends through the ravine, murmuring on its way to join the Derwent … The Duchess of Devonshire agreed that here was a great opportunity, and so the task of converting a wilderness into a charming ravine garden was commenced.[12]

Some trees were felled, undergrowth was cleared and planting commenced. Only six months had elapsed since the work began when the article was written, but the garden was 'already a delightful feature'. The stream was dammed at intervals to make pools and 'little waterfalls', various hardy primulas were established near the water, and ferns and meconopses planted all around. In addition:

Higher up, the drifts of Berberises, Diervillas, Viburnums, Buddleias, Pyruses, and the smaller Rhododendrons will presently present a charming picture under the thin canopy of trees.[13]

The article further described how the Rhododendrons on the cliff-like side of the ravine 'have been left severely alone except that a narrow path has been cut among them, and is reached by means of the rustic bridge which spans the upper part of the ravine'. Daffodils and other hardy bulbs had been planted beside the path.[14] The area was neglected during the 1939–45 War, but restored in the 1980s and some of the original planting remains, most notably the purple-flowered *Rhododendron ponticum*, a highly invasive species.

The 9th Duke died in 1938 and the 10th Duke, Edward Cavendish, inherited at the age of 43. Due to the establishment of the Chatsworth Estate Company in 1926, the impact of Death Duties was, on this occasion, limited.[15] Indeed,

soon after his accession modifications were made to the interior of the house (including the installation of a passenger lift in the north-east corner) while, outside, his wife Mary began to made further changes to the grounds, most notably redesigning the rose garden to the south of the 1st Duke's Greenhouse. But all this activity came to an abrupt end with the outbreak of War in 1939. A private boarding school, Penrhos College, was moved to Chatsworth from north Wales when its own premises were taken over by the Ministry of Food. The house was converted for use as dormitories and class-rooms, and four grass tennis courts were laid out before the South Front.[16] The lawns were left unmown and heather began to establish itself; the kitchen garden in the north park was effectively abandoned; and, by the time the War was over, the landscape was in a poor state.

The 11th Duke inherited in 1950 and, for a while, lived with his family at Edensor. The future of Chatsworth was uncertain. The estate faced massive death duties – no less than £4.72 million – and there were plans for the house to become an arts centre, attached to Manchester University.[17] But instead other properties were sold to cover the huge debt, including extensive lands in Scotland, while Hardwick Hall and its associated park and treasures passed to

FIGURE 84.
The Serpentine Hedges flanking the 'Rough Walk' were planted in 1953. Inspired by a 'crinkle-crankle' wall at Hopton Hall near Wirksworth, they are one of the most original and successful of the many twentieth-century additions to Chatsworth's gardens.

FIGURE 85.
The Maze was planted with 1,209 yews in 1962, on the site of Paxton's Great Stove.

the Nation, and thence immediately to the National Trust. Several important works of art from Chatsworth were also given to the Treasury but the house itself, and its garden and park, remained in the hands of the Duke. In 1959 he made the decision to move into the house, and soon afterwards, with the Duchess, began the first of a long series of improvements.

The last fifty years have seen many important programmes of conservation and restoration, including the repairs carried out on Flora's Temple in the 1990s and the ambitious works carried out on the rockworks in 2002–3. But of equal importance are the new additions which have been made to the gardens.[18] These began in 1952 with the planting of the pleached red-twigged limes (*Tilia platyphyllos* 'Rubra') on either side of the South Lawn, soon followed in 1953 by the creation of the 'Serpentine Hedges', flanking the path leading south from the Ring Pond (Figure 84). A path, the 'Rough Walk', had existed on this alignment since the 1820s but the flanking hedges, which are of beech, were entirely new. They were inspired by the 'crinkle-crankle' wall at Hopton Hall near Wirksworth. At the same time, the circle of beech hedging around the Ring Pond was planted.

In 1960 the new West Front garden was created, with the ground plan of Chiswick House picked out in golden box. Two years later the Maze was planted on the site of the Great Conservatory, designed by the house comptroller Dennis Fisher and comprising no less than 1,209 yews (Figure 85). A weeping willow-leafed pear marks its centre (*Pyrus salicifolia* 'Pendula') and the paths, originally of turf, were later replaced with gravel. The 1970s saw further changes, with the erection, close to the house and beside the 1st Duke's Greenhouse, of the Display Greenhouse. Designed by George Pearce in 1970, this contained separate sections for the cultivation of temperate, Mediterranean, and tropical species. In 1974, the Snake Terrace was constructed in the space between these two greenhouses. This, like the Maze, was designed by Dennis Fisher, using materials taken from Paxton's old Lily House, and with the serpent motif (the crest of the Cavendish family) picked out in pebbles taken from the beach at Eastbourne. The terrace was linked to Paxton's Conservative Wall by the Laburnum Tunnel. At the same time alterations were made to the First Duke's Greenhouse, involving the reopening of an original entrance.

Changes continued into the 1980s and 90s, with the creation of the 'Hundred Steps', a long, straight ascent carved out of the Arboretum, which runs uphill from the Conservatory Maze and is aligned on the Maze's centre: halfway along it is interrupted by a lone monkey puzzle, left as a dramatic incident in the view by the clearance of the surrounding vegetation. The Cottage Garden was created in 1989, with topiary 'rooms' and 'furniture' created out of box, privet and yew; in 1990 the 'human sundial' was laid out in the turf to the north of the Great Conservatory Garden; and in 1992 the overflow from the stream leaving the Grotto Pond was turned into a water feature, the 'Trough Waterfall', using a series of old stone drinking troughs gathered from the nearby fields. The kitchen gardens, immediately to the east of the stables, were revamped, elaborated and opened to visitors in 1994, and in 1998 the 'kitchen garden stream' was created, flowing through and across a number of features here. Beside it the 'Sensory Garden' was created in 2003, at the instigation of the 11th Duke's grandson, Lord Burlington, with plants chosen for their impact on the five senses – sight, smell, touch, hearing and taste. And, supplementing these major additions, innumerable minor changes in the details of planting have been made, and a number of important works of modern sculpture have been placed at key points in the gardens. These include the War Horse by Dame Elizabeth Frink, placed at the southern end of the Canal Pond in 1992, and Angela Conner's water sculpture, 'Revelation', at the centre of the Jack Pond.

There have also been changes in the wider landscape of the park although these have, for the most part, involved restoration and conservation, rather than the creation of entirely new features. Additions to such a large, public and naturalistic canvas are always more difficult, and potentially more controversial, than those in the gardens, where change, novelty and overtly man-made elements are to be expected. There has been much new planting, mirroring for the most part the existing mixture and disposition of species; many of the older trees are reaching the end of their lives and new planting is essential to retain the character of the park as inherited from the nineteenth century. Paine's mill was wrecked in the 1960s when a tree fell on it in a gale but, instead of being demolished or rebuilt, the structure has been stabilised as a picturesque ruin. In the late 1990s the vista created by Brown, southwards from the gardens to the mill, was restored through judicious felling of trees. On the rising ground to the west of Edensor the line of the avenue planted in the 1820s, and felled in 1860, has been re-established by cutting a gap through the woodland on the skyline west of Edensor. Some entirely new additions have also been made, including Maud's Plantation, planted in the 1950s, and the recent Tercentenary Avenue, planted all along the north drive from the house to the Golden Gates in celebration of the three hundredth anniversary of the creation of the dukedom.

Great landscapes like Chatsworth have always been changing, as we hope this book will have amply demonstrated, and it is hardly surprising that the present owners should wish to make alterations and additions of their own. What is particularly striking about Chatsworth, however, is that few of the twentieth-century elements sit uncomfortably within the inherited structure of the landscape (Figure 86). In part this is because their siting has tended to perpetuate the overall disposition of elements and spaces within the grounds. The Display Greenhouse, an uncompromisingly modern structure, might look out of place if it had been erected in the depths of the Arboretum. It seems entirely at home beside the 1st Duke's Greenhouse. Indeed, the placing of new elements has often served to bring additional emphasis to old features, and to forge new relationships between them. Frink's War Horse statue is clearly a product of the twentieth century but its position – at the end of the Canal Pond, continuing and emphasising the main axis towards the house – makes

it sit easily with these seventeenth- and eighteenth-century features. The Serpentine Hedges create a formal space perfectly in keeping with the surrounding nineteenth- and seventeenth-century features. The Hundred Steps, and the continuation of this alignment to the west of the Maze as far as the Serpentine Hedges, creates an entirely new way of experiencing the area of the Arboretum, and contrasts strongly with the original nineteenth-century pattern of paths and drives, which are all serpentine in character. But the new feature in no way detracts from these earlier elements, and instead serves, better perhaps than they do, to reveal the vast extent of Paxton's planting in the southern section of the gardens.

For the most part the recent additions thus blend in well with the existing fabric, adding to rather than detracting from what is, after all, a multi-period landscape. Many great gardens in England have not been so fortunate in the character of their twentieth-century additions. Only in the park have changes been made that perhaps do not always sit comfortably with the aesthetics of their surroundings. Two large perfect circles of trees were planted here several decades ago, to the north-east and south-west, which as they become mature

FIGURE 86.
An aerial view of the gardens as they are today: an amalgam of features spanning more than 400 years, which nevertheless have an overall integrity and coherence.

stand out rather sharply within the studied informality of the park. Similarly, the recently constructed walls in the north-west park, added to commemorate Queen Elizabeth's recent jubilee and spelling E^{II}R in large letters, are not to the authors' taste, at least.

Of course, not all the changes and additions to the landscape have been of an aesthetic nature. Some have been made to enhance the attractiveness of Chatsworth for visitors, or to ameliorate the impact of visitors upon the historic landscape. In these categories we should mention the car park at Calton Lees, carefully screened from the park by contours and planting; the caravan site completely hidden away within the walls of the old kitchen garden in the north of the park; the adventure playground constructed on the site of the old building yard to the north-east of the stables; the nearby farmyard; and the golf course in the north-west park. Paine's stables have become a restaurant; the Orangery in the north wing is a shop. These features dramatically signal Chatsworth's role as a paramount tourist attraction – and they are themselves a part of the history of the landscape. It would certainly be wrong to see them as a completely new departure, an aberration from past grandeurs. Chatsworth has always been far more than a private home and an artistically designed landscape: it has always been a place of display and entertainment. The waterworks which startled and amused seventeenth- and eighteenth-

FIGURE 87.
Chatsworth House from the west park: what appears to be a landscape of timeless grandeur has, in reality, a long and complex history. What we see today is a palimpsest of features, spanning many thousands of years.

century visitors – the Cascade House with its hidden jets of water, the Willow Tree that drenched the unwary – were about fun as much as art. And, when the long lines of coaches arrive each day in the summer, the visitors are following in a well-trodden path which, as we have seen, began with the arrival of the railway nearby in 1849. Chatsworth was once a magnet for visitors because it lay so close to nearby industrial conurbations and could be reached with relative ease by day trippers using the railway. It now draws on a much wider hinterland, privileged by its strategic position so close to the M1 and within a National Park whose economy is, more than ever before, geared towards tourism and leisure.

Yet Chatsworth is not tacky. It may be one of England's prime visitor attractions but it achieves its prominence without dumbing down or appealing to the lowest common denominator. There is no fun fair here, no extensive safari park. It remains, as it has long been, a spectacle – a place of wonders, horti-cultural, sculptural, and hydraulic. The estate is managed with care and restraint, in order to enhance the cultural and historical importance of this very special place (Figure 87).

CHAPTER EIGHT

Chatsworth Today:
A Tour Through History

Many of the individual features in the park and gardens have been discussed in the chapters above, but they often sit cheek by jowl with others from very different periods. It is impossible to do justice to this exciting historic and archaeological landscape without bringing them all together, exploring the rich complexity of each area in turn (Figure 88). This chapter, in effect, provides the visitor with a guided tour of Chatsworth's historic landscape. Cross-references are made to earlier chapters to enable the reader to place particular features in their historical context.

The house and gardens (Figure 89)

The gardens around the house [1] are a complex amalgam of features of very different periods, made more difficult to interpret by the fact that several have been altered or moved from their original positions over the centuries. The visitor enters the gardens beside Flora's Temple [2], the Bowling Green House of the 1680s, which Knyff's famous aerial view shows in its original position, on a level terrace below and to the south-west of the house (pp. 61–2 and 68). It was moved to its present site in the 1750s. A few steps further to the south-east stands another peripatetic building, the 1st Duke's Greenhouse [3]. This was built in the 1690s and originally stood a little to the south of the site now occupied by Flora's Temple: but it, too, was relocated in the 1750s (pp. 64 and 68–9). Although the basic structure of this building is late seventeenth-century, it has also been altered and modified on a number of occasions.

Of the other features of the great gardens shown by Kip and Knyff there are less obvious remains. Slight earthworks nearby and running across the Salisbury Lawn appear to preserve the lines of two of the great terraces, which were swept away in the course of the eighteenth century [4]. Indeed, only the two lower terraces – that on which the house stands, and that immediately to the east of the house, beside the Broad Walk – now remain of the once impressive series, and even these have been much rebuilt in later centuries. Some of the ponds shown on the engraving still survive, however. The Ring Pond [5] once stood at the centre of the great circular wilderness, with the Willow Tree Fountain at its centre; while the Jack Pond [6], now home to the Revelation water sculpture, was then a supply pond for the waterworks, and lay on the

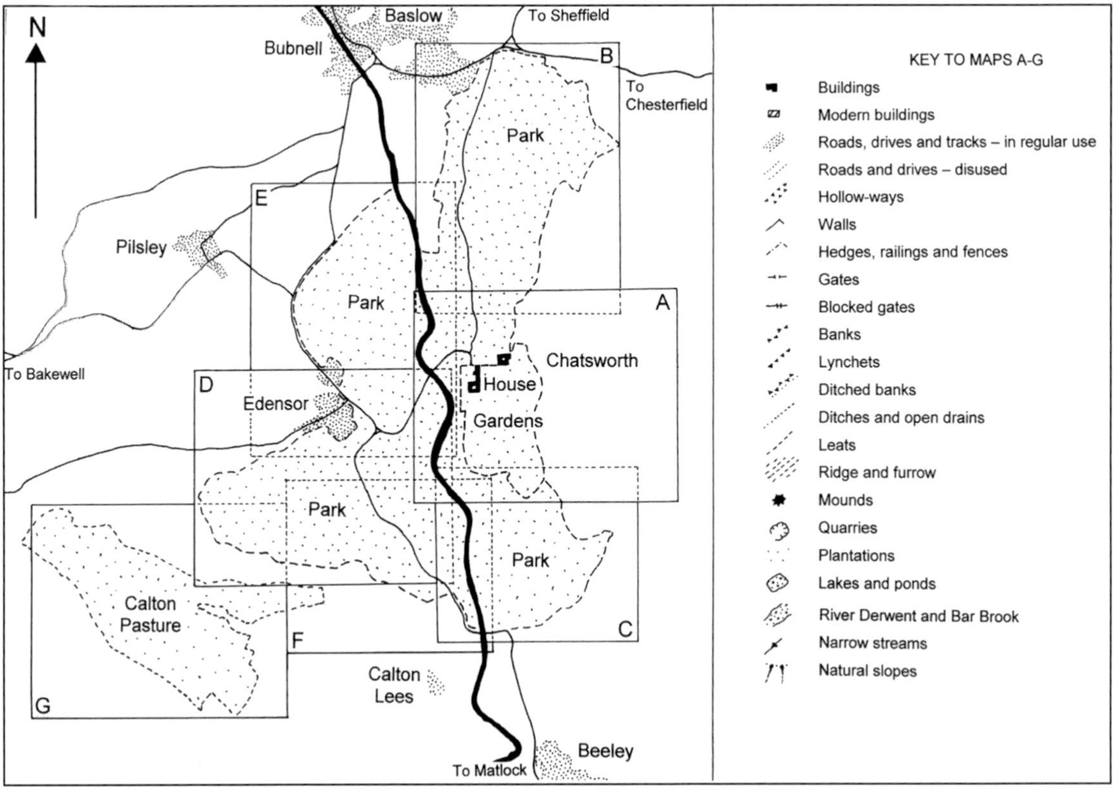
N
Baslow
To Sheffield
Bubnell
B
To
Chesterfield
Park
E
Pilsley
Park
A
Chatsworth
To Bakewell
D
House
Edensor
Gardens
Park
Park
Calton
Pasture
F
C
Calton
Lees
G
Beeley
To Matlock
KEY TO MAPS A-G
Buildings
Modern buildings
Roads, drives and tracks – in regular use
Roads and drives – disused
Hollow-ways
Walls
Hedges, railings and fences
Gates
Blocked gates
Banks
Lynchets
Ditched banks
Ditches and open drains
Leats
Ridge and furrow
Mounds
Quarries
Plantations
Lakes and ponds
River Derwent and Bar Brook
Narrow streams
Natural slopes

FIGURE 88.
The parts of the park and gardens illustrated in Maps A-G, used in Chapter 8 to describe the complex historic and archaeological landscape that survives at Chatsworth.

edge of the gardens (pp. 64 and 68). While there is now no visible trace (save occasional parch marks in summer, best seen from above) of the great parterre shown by Kip and Knyff to the south of the house, which was laid out in 1694 by London and Wise, the great Triton and Sea Horses fountain, created by Cibber, still remains in place [7], now surrounded by an expanse of neat lawn (pp. 60–1).

More obvious and striking are the survivals from the next phase of the garden's history: the features created by the 1st Duke in the years immediately following the production of Knyff's famous view. The Cascade [8] in its present form was built between 1702 and 1703, replacing the more diminutive feature shown by Knyff. It is, perhaps, the most famous of Chatsworth's water-works. At its summit stands Thomas Archer's Cascade House, erected between 1703 and 1711 (pp. 72–3). And to the south of the house, the Canal Pond [9] extends southwards across the area earlier occupied by Flora's Garden. Much earth-moving and terracing was carried out in the first decades of the eighteenth century in order to create the level terrace on which this magnificent mirror of water lies (pp. 69–72). It is best appreciated from the southern end, from where the house appears to rise directly from the water, a trick of perspective which serves to remove the intervening area of lawn. Also at the southern end of the Canal Pond, beneath a low dome of earth, is the ice house, built in 1728 [10], but later superseded by those to the north of the

FIGURE 89.
(opposite)
Map A: The main historical and archaeological features in the area around Chatsworth House and Stand Wood (numbers refer to the main text).

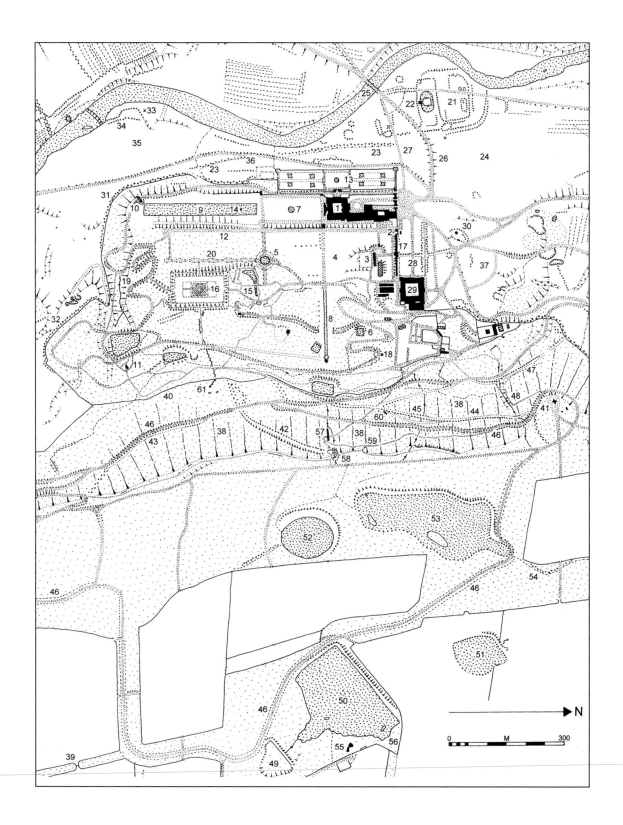

house. A number of trees scattered around the grounds, such as the massive sweet chestnuts growing beside the Ring Pond, probably date back to these late seventeenth- and early eighteenth-century phases of the gardens.

Although many features survive from the great Baroque gardens created by the 1st Duke, they do so as disconnected elements, fragments within a very different design. Most of the terraces and other formal features shown by Knyff were removed during the 1730s by the 3rd Duke, possibly on the advice of William Kent. Others went when the new park was created by Capability Brown, in the years around 1760. These successive changes created a more 'naturalistic', less formal garden in which paths wound through areas of woodland and shrubbery (the former in part the outgrown remnants of the earlier 'wildernesses') and past the various surviving ponds and water features. Some planting from this period remains, including a number of large beeches, such as those in the vicinity of the Jack Pond. But there is, on the whole, little trace of this phase of the garden's history. In part this is because the design, like others of its time, was based on grass lawns and ornamental shrubs and trees, which were relatively ephemeral in character, and did not feature the elaborate 'hard landscaping' of terraces, waterworks and rock features which characterised previous and subsequent phases. The only exceptions are the Grotto [11], created by Duchess Georgiana in the 1790s but extensively remodelled in the 1820s by the 6th Duke, which stands in the depths of the Arboretum beside the Grotto Pond (pp. 127 and 130) and, perhaps, the ha-ha which forms the south-western boundary of the gardens, south of the house and immediately below the Canal Pond [31] (but see p. 117).

The main reason why the eighteenth-century pleasure grounds have left relatively little trace, however, is the sheer scale of subsequent developments carried out from 1811 by the 6th Duke, Wyatville and Paxton. It is these changes which give the modern gardens their dominant atmosphere – that of a Victorian extravaganza. To the period before Paxton's arrival in 1826 we owe the great gravel walk – the Broad Walk [12] – which runs north–south immediately to the east of the house and Canal Pond. This begins at Flora's Temple and terminates at the Urn dedicated to Blanche Howard, the 6th Duke's niece, who died aged twenty-eight. Many of the other straight walks in the grounds originated at this time, including the Rough Walk [20] leading south from the Ring Pond, and the gravel path aligned on the South Front of the house, leading up to the Cascade. In this period the essential layout of the Rose Garden beside the 1st Duke's Greenhouse (although this was extensively remodelled in the 1930s) was created and Wyatville's great architectural terraces immediately to the west of the house were built [13]. The walls of these terraces incorporate the great stone pedestals, carved by Cibber, which had originally formed part of the western forecourt to the 1st Duke's house, but which had been left by Brown's improvements marooned, somewhat incongruously, in the parkland below the house (p. 54).

The period after 1826, when Paxton was in charge of the gardens, has left a greater mark. The basic pattern of serpentine paths which articulates the southern and eastern parts of the grounds was developed in this period, along with the great Arboretum which occupies so much of this area, planted with a bewildering variety of exotic trees. Paxton improved the waterworks, adding the Emperor Fountain in the Canal Pond [14], which replaced a more diminutive water spout; and he created the impressive rockworks [15], including the Wellington Rock and the ornamental torrent known as 'The Strid', which occupy the central area of the grounds (pp. 143–5). His finest work, the Great Stove or Conservatory, was demolished in the 1920s but its site, with massive surrounding earthwork banks and stone base, remains impressive [16]. So too does his Conservative Wall, which runs up the slope to the east of the house [17] (p. 142). Other nineteenth-century features include the Summer House or Lutterell's Seat [18], built of sandstone in 'Saracenic' style in 1839 to designs by either Paxton or Robertson, which stands beside the path to the north-east of the Jack Pond; and the Willow Tree (a copy of the original feature), which stands – still delighting visitors – on the northern edge of the rockworks.

The gardens had attained their essential form when the 6th Duke died in 1858 and remained largely unchanged during the late nineteenth and early twentieth centuries; one of the few additions of significance was the Ravine Garden in the far south of the pleasure grounds, laid out in the early 1930s [19]. With the accession of the 11th Duke and Duchess a new phase of activity commenced (pp. 186–9). Of note are the lines of pleached limes flanking the lawn (the former south parterre) below the South Front; the Serpentine Hedges beside the Rough Walk [20] together with plain beech hedges, in a circle, around the Ring Pond; the Maze, established on the site of the Great Stove; and the new Display Greenhouse, erected near the 1st Duke's Greenhouse.

A designed landscape which appears at first sight to be a coherent whole is thus, in reality, complex and many-layered. Its coherence, however, is more than superficial. Features from certain periods were retained in subsequent phases not simply through inertia or accident, but because they were valued by later generations. They were accordingly respected, or reinterpreted, as new features were laid out. This is true of many large designed landscapes, but is strikingly evident at Chatsworth.

The archaeological landscape of the park

As previous chapters have shown, Chatsworth Park represents one of the richest fossilised archaeological landscapes in Britain, containing a complex palimpsest of features built up over a period of more than 4,000 years. The range of these features is wide; it includes prehistoric barrows, extensive agricultural earthworks dating from the medieval period to the nineteenth century, and the impressive drives and buildings associated with the park's ornamental landscape. Generations of ordinary people have left behind traces of their lives, of the places where they lived, farmed and carried out a range of industrial activities – a legacy no less important than the great works created by the Cavendish family. Every earthwork and building has a tale to tell, and these tales interweave in a fascinating and complex landscape. Some archaeological features are obvious, but many are only slight earthworks and there is a need to train the eyes to recognise and interpret their subtle contours.

Features immediately beyond the house and gardens (Figure 89)
The areas of the park lying immediately to the north and west of the house and gardens, and to the west between the garden terrace and river, have been parkland since Brown and Millican transformed the setting of the mansion in the years around 1760. Here there are a number of important earthworks [21] surrounding Queen Mary's Bower [22], all that survives of the impressive sixteenth-century formal gardens that once surrounded Chatsworth House (pp. 40–3). These remained in use, albeit much modified, into the 1820s, long after the wider formal landscape laid out in the sixteenth, seventeenth and early eighteenth centuries had been swept away (pp. 116–7 and 161–4). Although these earthworks are now only low banks and hollows, smoothed and covered in grass, the rectangular plan of this part of the gardens can still be traced. Raised walkways are clear around rectangular areas that once contained ponds and decorative orchards, later transformed into formal gardens with hothouses. Queen Mary's Bower itself was extensively 'restored' by Wyatville in the 1820s; at the same time the stone-lined pond in which it stands was reduced in size to its present dimensions (pp. 41–2 and 161–4). In contrast, a low linear earthwork [23] near the river is relatively modern, marking the line of a large buried pipe that was laid here in the first decade of the twentieth century by the Derwent Valley Water Board. This still takes water from the Derwent and Howden Reservoirs north of Bamford to Derby, Nottingham and Leicester. The remarkably level and featureless area of parkland [24] immediately to the east of Queen Mary's Bower and its associated earthworks is a testament to the extent of the levelling and earth-moving undertaken by Brown and Millican around 1760. Before this work, an impressive canal and several large ponds existed here, together with further areas of formal gardens (p. 113). No hint of any of this now survives in the parkland turf.

The present drive to the house crosses the elegant Three Arch Bridge [25], built by Paine when the landscape park was first created (pp. 107–8 and 124). This drive sits on a large embankment [26], created in 1842–43 (p. 176); the original drive took a more direct route, now fossilised as a track [27]. Several lime trees [28] survive from a double avenue which flanked a central drive leading to the grand stable block [29] built by Paine during the first phase of the landscape park (pp. 107–8). The limes themselves are a later feature, added in the early nineteenth century (p. 181). Today much of the original impact has been lost; many of the trees have been removed, the southernmost line being completely grubbed out in the 1830s when the garden immediately adjacent was restructured (pp. 141–2). The surviving limes have recently been pollarded and are intermixed with more modern planting. To the north of the stables and avenue there is a small Game Larder for pheasants which was built in 1909 [30] and is now used as a chicken house (p. 183). This building occupies the site of an earlier ice-house, almost certainly built in 1734 (p. 101).

To the south, another notable feature is the large ha-ha bank [31] that flanks the sunken wall of the present gardens and masks them from view as the house is approached along the southern drive. This was probably remodelled in the mid 1830s, an interpretation supported by the fact that it is identical in construction to the ha-ha and associated bank which form the boundary of the Arboretum [32], which certainly date from 1836 (pp. 136–7 and 169–72). However, a ha-ha had existed around the boundary of the garden since the 1760s (p. 117).

The sites of several pre-park features in this area are worthy of note. Adjacent to the river was a corn mill that was demolished around 1760 [33]. A mill at Chatsworth is first documented in the 1330s and was possibly located on this site (p. 32). Breaks of slope nearby [34] mark the modified riverbank, created when the site of the mill was dug away by Brown and Millican to create a narrow, sinuous lake (p. 116); the river has subsequently silted and a mound has been added here in the twentieth century. To the east of the mill Brailsford's map of 1751 shows a large rectangular pond, with a central wooded island, called the Cana Deerpond [35].[1] This was an early eighteenth-century creation and was removed in about 1760; it is also referred to as the 'Canadier' in the records and may have been a duck-trapping pond. Some distance to the north of the site of the mill are two slight lynchets [36]. The westernmost one marks the boundary between a riverside road leading from the old Chatsworth Bridge to the house and an area occupied in the late seventeenth century by an orchard, and in the early eighteenth century by the kitchen gardens. The eastern lynchet marks the boundary between this area and that occupied, in the late seventeenth and early eighteenth centuries, by the ornamental gardens (pp. 77–8).

This whole area of parkland contains very little that dates from the medieval period, largely due to the creation of the sixteenth-century formal gardens and their subsequent destruction in the eighteenth century. An important exception is the group of ancient oaks [37] in the area to the north-east of the Game Larder. Oaks have probably grown here, within the lower part of the old deer park, since medieval times (pp. 33 and 35). This area was incorporated into the new landscape park in the mid eighteenth century, while the bulk of Stand Wood was excluded by the building of a boundary further up the hillside (see p. 143).

Features in Stand Wood (Figure 89)

A number of public walks running through Stand Wood allow the inspection of a variety of important features. Until the mid eighteenth century this whole area lay within the old deer park (pp. 31 and 44–6) and parts of Stand Wood lying along the steep scarp slope have probably been wooded since at least medieval times. The trees now growing within the wood are, however, more recent; among the oldest, at the scarp crest, are several mature beech trees of eighteenth- or early nineteenth-century date. Senior's plan of 1617[2] and Knyff's drawing of 1699 suggests that much of the woodland directly upslope from the house had been removed [38], and extensive replanting seems to have taken place here from the eighteenth century (pp. 78, 99–100 and 109). The woodlands on the high shelf above the escarpment were mostly created in the decades either side of 1800, when much of the old deer park was enclosed and turned over to agriculture. The new fields here were each surrounded by shelterbelts laid out in an ambitious rectangular grid design (pp. 156–7). The integrity of this pattern was lost later in the nineteenth century, although elements still survive to the south-east [39], often planted with more recent trees.

The seventeenth-century formal gardens around the house were divided from the deer park by a boundary wall, but this was removed in the mid eighteenth century when the landscape was transformed by Brown and Millican (p. 117). A new boundary wall [40] was built in the late 1830s, clearly separating the two areas again. However, Stand Wood was still evidently seen as part of the pleasure grounds, as it was extensively ornamented by Paxton at this time (pp. 143–5).

The most impressive survival at Chatsworth from the days of 'Bess of Hardwick' is the Hunting Tower or Stand [41], built in the 1570s. This high prospect tower is sited on the crest of the scarp, ideally placed to provide extensive views of the 'wild' deer park, both for locating deer and for observing the chase. It was also no doubt used as a place of resort, for banquets and other activities. Guests would have enjoyed the contrasting views to the west, with its 'tamed' landscape, including the house and formal gardens below and fields beyond. Although the views eastwards are now obscured by trees, there is still a fine vista westwards (pp. 46–8).

On the steep slopes within Stand Wood there are several hollow-ways, roads, drives and woodland paths. Some are still in use, while others are abandoned and overgrown; several of these have been identified, while some doubtless remain to be found. A complex history of re-routing can be unravelled (Figure 39). Senior's map of 1617[3] shows a road – Holmes Lane – running eastwards from the old Chatsworth Bridge to the base of the steep escarpment. As this entered the deer park it forked. One branch led towards Chesterfield and can still be traced as a deep hollow-way running diagonally up the slope [42] (pp. 86–8). The other headed south-eastwards towards Ashover and one part of its line is fossilised by the disused terrace of a coach road built in 1710–11 [43], when the gardens around Chatsworth House were extended. This route is not shown on Barker's map of 1773.[4] By this time it had presumably been superseded as a coach road by the Bakewell to Chesterfield turnpike, built in 1739, which ran southwards from Chatsworth Bridge along the western bank of the Derwent, before rising onto the moors to the south of the park. The old coach road however continued in use for other traffic until 1759 when, now described as a 'drift way', it was closed by Chancery writ and all travellers were diverted over One Arch Bridge at the southern end of the park (pp. 86–8 and 105).

Senior also shows a 'road' running to the Stand (p. 87) and it is possible that a short section of this survives in earthwork form [44], although this feature was remodelled when the slope was replanted in the eighteenth century. Part of it was straightened in the late eighteenth or early nineteenth century [45], and it was abandoned in the late 1830s when the present drive network was created [46] (p. 176). Another redundant route visible on the slope [47] dates from a short-lived re-routing of the drives on the lower slopes in the early nineteenth century, possibly in the early 1830s. In 1815 a new 'gravel walk' and steps between the Stand and park were created, and one of the steps is inscribed with this date [48].

Out of sight of the house and gardens, the shelf above Stand Wood has four impressive reservoirs and the site of a fifth, created at various dates to provide a reliable water supply for the ponds, fountains and other features within the gardens. They also provided habitat for wildfowl, presumably for shooting. Old Pond, the smallest and earliest, remained in use into the twentieth century but is now dry, although its overgrown earthworks survive [49]. This was probably constructed in the 1690s to supply the Great Cascade, but may have had earlier origins. The next to be built was the much larger Swiss Lake [50], first known as the Great Pond, begun in 1710 and finished in 1717. This is supplied by Umberley Brook Leat, which runs across the moorland to the east. This leat was not created until 1719, but a second leat from Harland Sick to the south-east (which now supplies the Ring Pond) may well have been Swiss Lake's (and perhaps the Old Pond's) original source of water (pp. 73–6).

In the nineteenth century further lakes were added. Open Pond [51] was constructed some time between 1824 and 1831, while Ring Pond [52] dates to 1830–32. The impressive Emperor Lake [53], initially also known as the Mediterranean Pond, was started in 1845 and enlarged in 1849; this fed Paxton's great Emperor Fountain in the gardens. The lake is supplied from the north-east by a long open leat dug across the moors in 1847–48, which has come to be known as the Emperor Stream [54] (pp. 145–8).

Swiss Lake acquired its current name from Swiss Cottage [55], built between 1839 and 1842. This was designed to be viewed from the woodland drive [46] on the other side of the lake, which forms part of a scenic carriage route created by Paxton in the late 1830s (pp. 169, 176 and 177–8). At this time a private zoo or 'menagerie' may have existed immediately to the north, judging by the first Ordnance Survey map (surveyed in 1839) [56]. This appears to have been a short-lived feature: no documentation relating to it has so far come to light and no trace remains on the ground today. In fact, it is possible that features here may have been misinterpreted by the Ordnance Survey.

Below the summit of the steep scarp stands the impressive folly known as The Aqueduct: four immense arches with a waterfall falling from the end [57]. Immediately above there is a second, much smaller, waterfall falling over and amongst boulders; that at the scarp crest is traditionally known as the Sowter Stone [58]. Both waterfalls are fed by the Ring Pond. The upper falls once had a footbridge immediately below them, of which only an abutment, and slots for timbers, now survive. The bridge was part of a revetted path [59] that followed a scenic route up through Stand Wood to The Stand itself, taking in The Aqueduct and Sowter Stone waterfall and featuring a stone staircase between cliffs linking an upper and lower route. All these features were again created as part of the ornamentalisation of the Stand Wood area carried out by Paxton in the late 1830s and early 1840s (pp. 143–5).

Other noteworthy features in this area include the Cold Spring, apparently used as a bathing place in the eighteenth century but now remodelled as water tank [60]; and, to the south, the chimney [61] for the boilers serving Paxton's Great Stove, built between 1836 and 1840 and carefully hidden away in the woodland just above the then new upper wall of the gardens (pp. 137–41).

The park north of the house (Figure 90)

This extensive area has a complex history. The higher ground to the east, as far as the parish boundary with Baslow [1], formed part of the original deer park, probably dating back to the late medieval period (see Figure 7); this was incorporated into the landscape park on its creation in the years around 1760. There are large numbers of ancient oaks [2] within this area, many clearly of medieval origins; they comprise one of the finest collections of 'veteran trees' in Britain, although many are now, inevitably, approaching the end of their life (pp. 33 and 45). Low earthworks of field boundaries suggest that the flatter areas of land here were divided into fields at some time in the seventeenth or early eighteenth century; evidently the park either contracted from the boundaries shown by Senior in 1617, or the earthworks represent enclosures created within the park to grow fodder, such as turnips, for the deer (pp. 81–3). The lower ground closer to the river, to the west, both within Chatsworth and Baslow parishes, was occupied by fields until incorporated within the landscape park in the eighteenth and nineteenth centuries. The land between the house and the walled kitchen garden was emparked around 1760 [3]; the area to the north [4], however, not until the 1820s and 30s. These areas contain many low earthworks which fossilise the pre-park agricultural land-scape, especially banks marking the course of old hedge lines. There is a great deal of ridge and furrow here and some of the broader examples are probably medieval in date. Numerous mature trees, mainly oaks, grow on the old boundary lines, which were retained as features in the new parkland landscape (pp. 9–11, 109, 121 and 161).

On the sloping ground above the kitchen gardens [28] the low footings of stone buildings and yards indicate the site of a farmstead (or possibly two) that stood here in the eighteenth century [5], approached by a lane from the north [6]. The name of this settlement has not survived, but it is possible that it stood at or near the same site as the lost medieval hamlet of Langley. If so, occupation was not continuous as no buildings are shown on Senior's survey

FIGURE 90.
Map B: The main historical and archaeological features in the north-eastern park (numbers refer to the main text).

of 1617 (pp. 25, 32 and 81): at this time the surrounding area lay in large closes used for pasture.[5] The pattern of rectilinear fields around the farmstead [7], which survives in earthwork form and is shown on a map of 1780–5,[6] must have been laid out in the course of the seventeenth or eighteenth centuries. The broad ridge and furrow here indicates that in the medieval period at least some of this area was arable land [8] (pp. 28, 29–30 and 81–3).

Further areas of probable medieval ridge and furrow occur to the south [9], within the areas emparked in the 1760s, but whether the land here was farmed from Langley or Chatsworth in this period is uncertain. In the parts of the park lying well to the north of the house there are indications that the land was again divided into small fields sometime in the seventeenth or early eighteenth centuries; here some or all of the ridge and furrow may date from this period. Immediately to the south of the walled kitchen gardens one curved lynchet with a few surviving mature trees growing on it marks the site of an old riverbank [10]. Here the Derwent once made a sharp loop eastwards, as shown on Senior's map of 1617.[7] Shortly after emparkment in the 1760s, in contrast, the river ran in a loop bending westwards, suggesting that the course of the river had changed naturally and was subsequently straightened to its present line in the late eighteenth or early nineteenth century. It is not known if the flat area east of the river [11] was landscaped in the 1760s by Brown and Millican, or whether this is a more recent levelling associated with the cricket pitch created in the late nineteenth century.

In the far north of the park, across the parish boundary in Baslow, there are further areas of fossilised fields [12], many of which were still extant in the early nineteenth century when this area was taken into the park. Some of the fields contain ridge and furrow, most of which is narrow and of post-medieval date. However, three examples of medieval-type broad rig also survive [13]. Large numbers of hedgerow trees were retained, in the usual fashion, and many of these still survive (pp. 9–11 and 161).

The areas of parkland lying to the north of the house also contain the earthwork traces of a number of old roads (pp. 85–6, 106 and 161). Running sinuously up the escarpment is a fine example of a braided hollow-way [14]. This is particularly deep as it winds up the steeper part of the slope, where water run-off has caused much erosion (Figure 91). It represents part of a major route with probable medieval origins that led from Baslow to Chesterfield. This was superseded in 1759 by the Chesterfield to Hernstone Lane Head turn-pike, the straight course of which can also still be traced [15]. This in turn was diverted northwards when the park was expanded in the 1820s, although the original course continued to be used for estate traffic. Another curious old road, abandoned in the 1820s, can be traced as an overgrown linear hollow [16] in the tree screen to the east of the Golden Gates. While this may have been nothing more than a field track, and is indeed shown as such on maps from 1799 onwards,[8] its straightness suggests it was perhaps part of an aborted eighteenth-century road improvement scheme. At its eastern end it joins a sinuous and presumably older field-access lane winding up the slope [17].

Another interesting survival of the pre-park landscape is the collection of quarries cut into the Dobb Edge scarp at the top end of the park to the east [18]. These were dug primarily to produce domed millstones, several unfinished examples of which can still be seen lying on the ground. It is unclear when the quarrying began, for while millstone production in the Baslow area is documented from the fourteenth century onwards, the scale of these particular quarries in their final form suggests activity some time in the period between the seventeenth to early nineteenth century (pp. 83–4). Later, in the 1840s, they were used again, to provide the great stones for Paxton's rockworks in the gardens (pp. 143–5).

The parkland north of the house also contains a variety of interesting features created since emparkment. Two main drives run northwards. That nearest the river [19] was created in the mid 1820s, when the landscape park was expanded into Baslow Parish, as a grand approach to the house from the newly-diverted turnpike road to the north (p. 174). The entrance to the park, flanked by dense tree screens of the 1820s, was embellished two decades later by the erection of the wrought-iron Golden Gates, flanked by lodges designed by Wyatville but built only after his death [20]; the grand gates themselves originally gave access to the forecourt immediately to the west of the house, shown on Knyff's engraving, and are of late seventeenth-century date (pp. 54 and 78–9).

The drive further to the east [21], now only a parkland track, is earlier. This was the eighteenth-century route to the house from the north, created in about 1760 when the landscape park was first laid out (p. 205). A small lodge house, Wynne's Lodge, [22] stood close to the old entrance to the park, with the drive continuing northwards as a fenced lane as far as the 1759 turnpike road. The lodge was apparently built in the late 1770s or early 1780s, as it is not shown on Barker's map of 1773, but does appear on an estate map of 1780–85;[9] it is named for the first time on the 1839 Ordnance Survey map. It was demolished in the mid nineteenth century after the creation of the lower drive in the 1820s made it redundant, and there is now little trace of it, on the surface at least (p. 153). Another building that has disappeared, apart from slight footings, is a deer barn [23], sited high on the slope above the drive. This was built in the 1760s or early 1770s and was demolished in the twentieth century (p. 116).

The wall that divides the park from Stand Wood has a ha-ha bank masking it from view [24]. Parts of the sinuous park edge here had probably been created in the late 1820s, as part of a decorative scheme to make the previous, straighter boundary less formal by expanding Stand Wood slightly downhill to the north-east of the stables. Documents in the estate archives make it clear that the ha-ha bank itself was not added until 1847 (p. 172).

Running through the upper part of the park there is a narrow leat, covered with stone slabs, once known as The Trout Stream [25]. This was dug in 1835–36 and supplied water to a meandering ornamental stream in the upper part of the gardens, created when the Arboretum was planted by

Paxton (p. 137); it is now largely dry, and was apparently disused by the late 1870s, although the stream in the gardens still runs, now fed from elsewhere.

Below the eastern drive are two features that stood just within the original 1760s boundary of the park. One is an underground ice house [26] with a reservoir pond above and a distinctive long and shallow ice-pond running south, where water could be frozen in winter. These were presumably constructed at the time the landscape park was created around 1760, and the pond was certainly here by 1773, when it was mapped by Barker (see p. 109).[10] The ice house remained in use until at least the 1920s. The 1773 map also shows Brick Kiln Pond [27]. This may be the place where clay was extracted to make the bricks used to build the kitchen garden in the 1760s, and possibly those used in the construction of the New Inn at Edensor (now the estate office) in the 1770s (pp. 108–9 and 153). The pond has been turned into an ornamental feature and there are no traces of an associated kiln; the sites of further possible backfilled pits are faintly visible nearby.

FIGURE 91.
This sinuous hollow-way at the north-eastern edge of the park, once the main road from Baslow to Chesterfield, probably has medieval origins: it was superseded in 1759 by a nearby turnpike road, which in turn has now also been abandoned.

Close to the river, immediately beyond the original northern limit of the 1760s park, the high brick walls of the kitchen gardens survive [28]. These were created at the same time as the park and were finished in 1765 (p. 109). In the 1950s they were abandoned; the interior of the gardens has now been mostly cleared and is used as a caravan park. To the north is the site of Barbrook House. Paxton lived here from 1826, when he first arrived at Chatsworth. He rebuilt and enlarged what was originally a gardener's cottage in two stages (1842 and 1851–52), to create a grand gentleman's house; unfortunately after a long period of neglect this had to be demolished in 1963 (p. 169). The farmhouse of Crimea Farm [29], built between 1856 and 1860, still stands, as does White Lodge [30]. The latter was built in 1855 to create a grand entrance to Paxton's house, offices and grounds (p. 179). North of this the hedge marking the park edge has a ha-ha bank [31] presumably also constructed some time in the 1850s (p. 172).

The park south of the house (Figure 92)

This part of the park again contains a range of valuable historic features, but is strictly private. Fortunately, equally good examples of the principal features can be seen elsewhere, in the public areas of the park.

As in the area to the north of the house, the flat ground near the river comprised enclosed fields until it was emparked in the 1760s by Brown; some ridge and furrow of medieval or later date exists here [1]. The parkland on the slopes above, in contrast, once lay within the old deer park and contains large numbers of magnificent old oak trees (pp. 33 and 45). A number of low banks indicate that the lowest parts were converted to agricultural fields, or enclosures for growing deer fodder, in the seventeenth or early eighteenth century [2] (pp. 81–3). In one area the ancient trees are growing on top of cultivation strips, defined by lynchets, which are almost certainly of medieval date [3]; not all of this area has always been woodland or wood pasture (see p. 33).

Parts of a deer barn and associated courtyard still stand hidden away near the southern end of the park [4]. They were erected in the 1760s or early 1770s, soon after the landscape park was created (p. 116). Nearby is the start of a wide and carefully engineered serpentine drive [5], constructed in the late 1850s, which runs up the slope into the southern end of Stand Wood in a series of extremely sinuous loops. Beeley Lodge [6], in Tudor style, was constructed in 1861, shortly after the drive was finished (pp. 176–7 and 179). Today's straight carriage drive [7] from here to the house is earlier. For much of its life it may have only been used for estate traffic and as a private entrance to the park; surprisingly, it is not shown on Barker's map of 1773,[11] as it probably follows the route of the 1739 turnpike road from Bakewell to Chesterfield, diverted west of the river in 1759–60 (pp. 88, 105–6 and 174). The road may have medieval origins, as it is the only logical route from Beeley to Chatsworth and Edensor before Paine's bridge was constructed.

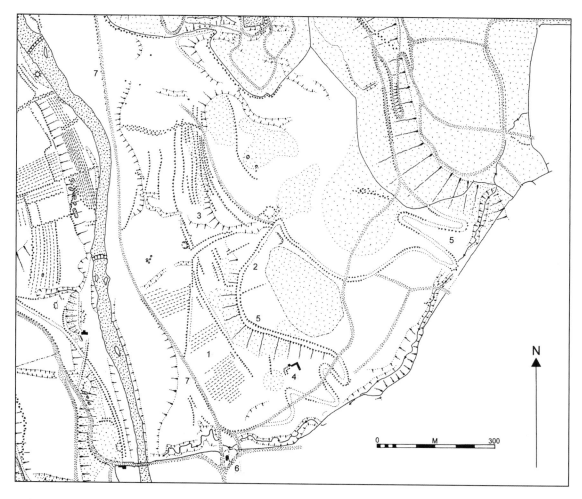

The western park south of Edensor (Figure 93)

This area contains many well-preserved earthworks which indicate very clearly the successive and radical changes in land-use which occurred in the long centuries before the park was laid out.

When Senior mapped Edensor, in 1617, the ground to the south of the village formed part of the demesne's open sheepwalk (p. 29).[12] By the mid eighteenth century, however, this was divided into hedged fields (pp. 81–3). Emparkment followed in *c.* 1760, with the exception of areas adjacent to Edensor village, where fields remained until the 1820s and 1830s.

This area contains the earliest archaeological sites surviving within the park: two or possibly three prehistoric round barrows, probably built in the late Neolithic or early Bronze Age, about 4,000 years ago – remarkable survivals considering the intensity of later land use in the locality (p. 24). The best-preserved example is an obvious mound [1], about 20 m across and 1 m high, on a flat shelf overlooking Edensor village and the river. Hollows in its top probably indicate investigation by early antiquarians but no record of what was found survives. A second, smaller, barrow exists on higher ground to the

FIGURE 92.
Map C: The main historical and archaeological features in the south-eastern park (numbers refer to the main text).

208

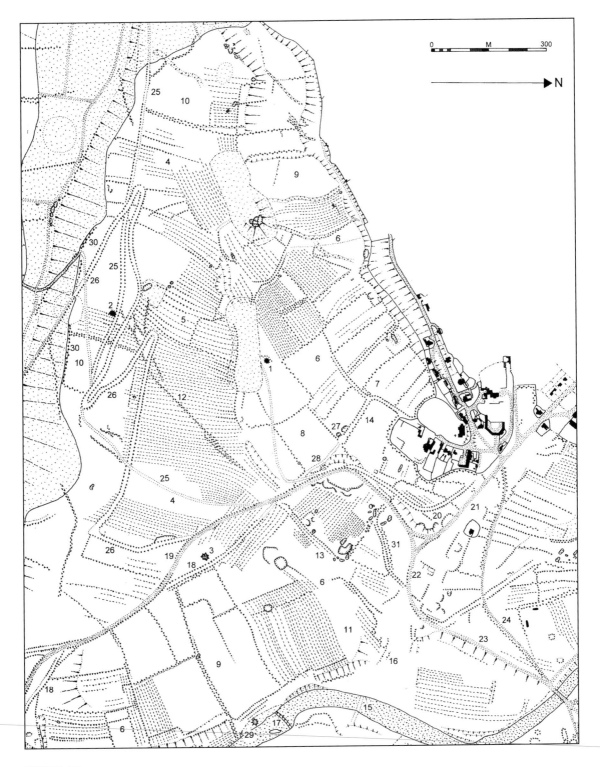

FIGURE 93.
Map D: The main historical and archaeological features in the western park, south of Edensor (numbers refer to the main text).

south [2]; this has been badly truncated by medieval cultivation. The third example is less certain [3]; it lies to the east on a tree-covered knoll called Lindup Low overlooking the river and lower land nearby. It has been badly mutilated, but a roughly circular rim of about 25 m diameter can still be made out.

One of the highlights of this part of the parkland landscape are the great swathes of ridge and furrow, together with strip lynchets on sloping ground, which represent in part the remains of the medieval open fields of Edensor (pp. 28–9) (Figure 94). On the higher land south of the village there are numerous well-defined cultivation ridges and lynchets defining narrow parcels of land [4]. These have been little modified by later agriculture because the area was used as unenclosed grazing from the later Middle Ages. Examples to the south-east of Mauds Plantation are particularly impressive [5]. On lower ground, areas of low ridge and furrow survive amongst later field banks [6]. The date of these earthworks is less certain, for here farmers continued to plough their arable land in ridges into the eighteenth century; while the overall pattern of strips has medieval origins, the orientation and width were periodically modified to suit changing farming practices.

Much of the pattern of late-medieval and post-medieval hedged fields can still be traced as low banks. These are particularly clear in the area to the south of the village, which remained farmland until the early nineteenth century [7]: the small rectangular fields, created by early piecemeal enclosure, fossilise the general layout of the medieval furlongs. Senior's map of 1617 [13] shows a pattern of rather larger enclosures in this area, which were subdivided in the course of the seventeenth and eighteenth centuries. Fields of identical form can be traced on the adjacent land [8], already enclosed by Senior's time and taken into the park in about 1760 (p. 81).

Further south and west, within the area that in the early seventeenth century formed part of the demesne's open sheepwalk, there are again clear indications that prior to emparking the land had been divided into fields. Throughout this area numerous hedgerow trees were retained, as elsewhere, when the park was laid out. Some of the enclosures are similar in size and shape to those just described [9], but on higher ground they are larger [10]. The excellent state of preservation of medieval cultivation earthworks in these upper fields suggests that they were predominantly used for pasture (pp. 9–11, 81–3, 109 and 121). Exactly when all these fields were created is uncertain, though the complexity of the earthworks here suggests they were in use for some time. Paintings of Chatsworth made by Tillemans in the mid 1720s and by Smith in around 1743 both show the area immediately south-west of the old Chatsworth Bridge [11] as one large horse pasture. Unless both used a considerable degree of artistic licence and omitted several field boundaries, this may suggest that well-established seventeenth-century boundaries had been removed prior to the execution of the paintings. Smith's painting in fact shows gentlemen and ladies inspecting thoroughbred horses, as well as an ornamental gate into the pasture from the old main road to Chatsworth Bridge. This development was part of

FIGURE 94.
A fine series of strip lynchets on the rising ground to the west of the Derwent. Chatsworth Park contains some of the most extensive earthwork remains of the medieval landscape in the Peak District.

FIGURE 95.
This 'hollow-way' to the south-west of Edensor village marks the course of Jap Lane, the main way into the village from this direction until the mid 1820s. Soon afterwards it was brought into the park.
© FRAN HALSALL.

the wider ornamentalisation of the landscape to the west of the river which was going on at this time (see pp. 98–100).

The pre-park earthworks also include a number of old roads and tracks (see pp. 85–88). A braided hollow-way [12] cuts through the ridge and furrow and probably dates from the period when this area was open sheepwalk. Further east it is visible today as the earthworks of a slightly sunken lane [13] running between closes to the north, which were present when Senior drew his map in 1617,[14] and fields to the south later taken in from the sheepwalk. This route ran from the old Chatsworth Bridge, bypassing Edensor village, to Haddon (with a branch to Bakewell), and the relative shallowness of the visible braids on the old sheepwalk suggests it was either short-lived or little-used compared with the main road to Bakewell, which passed through Edensor. Signs of cultivation within the sunken lane indicate that it had gone completely out of use prior to the creation of the park. Another old, sunken route [14], Jap Lane, provided the main southern access from the village to its fields, and to the demesne's open sheepwalk beyond, before continuing on to the hamlet of Calton Lees (Figure 95). It was retained by Brown as the point of entry into Edensor from the newly-built public carriage road leading from One Arch Bridge and Beeley (pp. 105–7). This new road, except at its southernmost end, followed the line of the earlier route from Calton Lees. Jap Lane lost its importance for through-traffic with the construction, in the mid 1820s, of a new public drive running somewhat further to the east, and it was subsequently closed. Some of the sycamores growing on its flanking hedgebanks were retained upon emparkment: these still survive, their contorted form showing that the hedge had once been 'plashed', or laid (Figure 96).

Nothing remains of the old Chatsworth Bridge, rebuilt in 1688 but of medieval origin [15]: its five stone arches were demolished in the early 1760s after Paine's bridge upstream had been completed. Similarly, the old road leading from it to Edensor village has gone, leaving only slight earthworks at one point along its course [16]. As on the opposite side of the river, the land surface here was evidently extensively modified by Brown and Millican (see p. 113). The removal of the old bridge was part of Brown's grand design to widen the river in order to create a lake-like expanse of water in front of the house, a project which also involved digging away the eastern bank of the Derwent, around the site of the mill, and the construction of a weir, slightly further downstream, to raise the water level [17]. The weir first clearly appears in the records in 1772, but this reference is probably to the construction of a replacement for an earlier feature, built around 1760. The desired effect, a broad expanse of water below the house, is not as striking today as it would have been in the eighteenth century, due to the silting and infilling of the river on its eastern side (pp. 113–6).

Various new roads and drives in this part of the park were created from the mid eighteenth century (see pp. 105–7). The road running in from the south was laid out when the new park was first established, although its line was subsequently altered. The initial route can still be traced for much of its course as a relatively narrow raised causeway or terrace of single carriage width [18]. The new, slightly more sinuous, course was created in the mid 1820s as part of a grand scheme to alter the roads and drives around Chatsworth [19] (p. 173). Close to Edensor [20], this wider road was in turn abandoned in the 1830s after the demolition of the eastern half of the village; a new route was put in midway between it and the old village street. Thus a single road [21] replaced two, with the added advantage that the new arrangement avoided an awkward turn into the drive leading to the house from the bottom end of the old village street. A drive branching off the road from the south was also part of the extensive reorganisation of roads and approaches which took place in the 1820s [22]. The straight section of drive [23] running beyond the line of the old village street (pp. 174–5), towards Paine's bridge, was however created much earlier, in the 1760s, and was carefully contrived to provide a fine approach to the house. A footpath from Edensor to the bridge was created between the years 1837 to 1844 [24], and provides a classic example of attention to detail, for it is purposely hidden from the drive and house by a low bank on its downslope side (pp. 175–6). Two other drives survive in earthwork form in this part of the park, one of which superseded the other. The earliest is a relatively modest affair [25]. It can be traced as a narrow causeway, in parts terraced into the slope, and was built in the mid 1820s, again as part of the scheme to embellish the park with a new pattern of drives. It continued beyond the park to Moatless Plantation on Calton Pasture. In the 1850s this drive was replaced by a spectacular broad carriageway following a more serpentine course [26], carefully engineered with a terraced causeway and several sharp bends. This too extended beyond the park boundary (pp. 86, 174 and 176–7).

Three eighteenth-century features in the park near Edensor have now all but disappeared. By the road to One Arch Bridge, hidden from view from across the river by an adjacent field corner, a small 'Deer Barn' was built in the 1760s or early 1770s. This appears to have been demolished by the mid 1780s and the site was subsequently disturbed by small-scale quarrying [27]. A short distance to the south-east, again adjacent to the road, a 'Venison House' is shown on Barker's map of 1773 (p. 116).[15] Following its removal in the 1830s, all that survives today is a small platform [28]. The 1773 map also shows a small stable by the river bank a little to the south of the weir [29]. This pre-dates the park (it is shown on Smith's painting of Chatsworth of c. 1743) and has now disappeared.

High in the park, to the south-west, several stretches of substantial ha-ha bank hide short adjacent sections of the boundary wall of New Piece Plantation [30]. These are significantly earlier in date than the other ha-has in the park, for they are shown on an estate map of 1785[16] and may have been created as early as the 1730s, when the series of clumps was planted on the ridge here, possibly under the direction of William Kent (see p. 100).

One curious feature is a well-defined ditch [31] which originally lay at the

FIGURE 96.
The unusual growth
pattern of this
sycamore, on the edge
of the hollow way
marking the course of
Jap Lane, shows that it
originally formed part
of a managed hedge.

© FRAN HALSALL.

boundary between the fields adjacent to Edensor and the new parkland created around 1760. It is not a ha-ha, as one edge is surmounted by a hedge bank, and it is not in a visually strategic position from the house or its eighteenth-century drives; it may have been designed to prevent deer leaping out of the park. It became redundant in the 1820s or 1830s with the remodelling of the village and the emparkment of the fields between the ditch and the village.

Edensor and the north-western park (Figure 97)

The north-eastern part of this area currently has no public access, while the western section is a private golf course. Both were mostly added to the park in the 1820s and 30s. Visitors are only allowed to roam at will in the south-eastern part, which was emparked around 1760. With the exception of a small number of fields lying immediately to the north-west of Edensor, Senior's map of 1617 shows this whole area as a large open 'cunigre', or rabbit warren, bounded only at its perimeter.[17] Today the area boasts eight 'pillow mounds' [1], low oval mounds built to accommodate the rabbits and to facilitate their

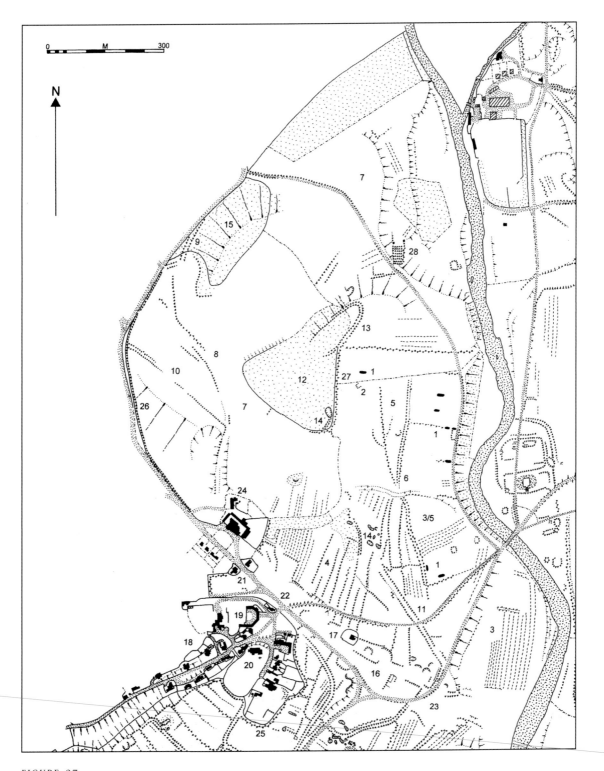

FIGURE 97.
Map E: The main historical and archaeological features at Edensor and in the north-western park (numbers refer to the main text).

trapping. The warren, which may have had medieval origins, survived until 1757–58 (pp. 48, 101 and 105). Barker's estate map of 1773[18] shows a building in this area named as a 'Lodge' [2] – presumably the warrener's lodge, first documented in the estate accounts for 1601. Why it was retained after the park had been laid out remains unclear, but it was removed soon after 1773 and its site is now marked by a small, level platform (p. 116).

Within the southern areas of the warren there are well-preserved medieval strip lynchets and ridge and furrow [3], showing that this area was part of Edensor's medieval open fields before it was incorporated into the warren. In the area to the north-east of Edensor [4], clearly-defined lynchets ascend the slope, running north from the sites of demolished houses in the part of the village which was removed. These are again of medieval date and mark the sites of narrow closes behind individual properties (pp. 28 and 29).

Nearby, but within what was once the warren, there are also traces of a number of hedge banks (pp. 81–3). They are post-medieval in character [5] and must date from the first half of the eighteenth century, since this area is depicted as still unenclosed on the Ombersley Court painting of Chatsworth, dated between 1707 and 1711. These enclosures may have been created to regulate the grazing of cattle and horses which are documented as being kept within the warren in the eighteenth century, keeping them off crops grown to feed the rabbits. One of the most ambiguous earthworks in the park is a double bank/lynchet forming what appears to be a narrow hedged lane [6]. This seems to have been a late medieval or post-medieval feature, as it does not conform with strip lynchets to the west. It went out of use some time prior to the creation of the park, as it is clearly cut by one of the relict field boundaries.

There is only sporadic earthwork evidence of medieval and later cultivation within those parts of the warren to the north and east, which were not emparked until the 1820s and 30s [7]: this stands in marked contrast to the situation in other parts of the park, indicating a different history of land use. Relatively regular late eighteenth- or early nineteenth-century arable production may have taken place in the large fields which are shown here on estate maps pre-dating the 1820s, and it is known there was ploughing for arable in this part of the park in the 1939–45 war.

At the western edge of the park the sites of two roads can be traced as degraded earthworks running across the golf course (pp. 106, 160 and 161). One [8] was the traditional road from Edensor to Baslow, which formed in part the boundary of the 1760s park. The road was upgraded in or shortly after 1759 as part of the wider reorganisation of routes in and around the newly emparked area. One section of this new road survives as a carefully-made terraceway in Buston Wood [9]. The other road [10] was a branch road to Pilsley, upgraded in 1812 to form part of the Ashford to Edensor turnpike. Both were diverted when the park was expanded to the north and north-west in the late 1820s, and were systematically levelled in 1831. Another lost lane [11] survives in earthwork form on the slope above the drive to the Three Arch

Bridge, and runs to the ridgetop. This lane skirted the northern edge of Edensor village, heading towards Pilsley and Baslow, and is shown on the Ombersley Court painting of 1707–11; like several of the other roads, it was closed early in 1759, immediately before the creation of the landscape park (pp. 88–9 and 105–6).

Two plantations in this part of the park are of eighteenth- and nineteenth-century date (pp. 100 and 180). One of them, Park Wood [12], was extensively modified over these two centuries, only taking on its present form in the 1840s or early 1850s. At its north-eastern end there are twin lynchets [13] marking the edge of a small oval plantation on the ridgetop. This may have been part of Brown's design; alternatively, it may have been planted in the 1730s as part of the scheme, possibly associated with William Kent, for improving the view westwards from the house. In 1773 two smaller plantations also lay a short distance to the south west, presumably created as part of the same decorative scheme. Their position is still marked by lengths of boundary ditch [14], in each case defining the side that would have faced the house. In the late eighteenth or early nineteenth century the two northernmost plantations were linked by an area of a new planting between them, subsequently named 'The Shoulder of Mutton'; this was later subsumed into the present Park Wood. The shape of the southernmost plantation had been altered by the 1830s and its eastern ditch is likely to be earlier. The other well-established plantation, Buston Wood [15], has also been here since at least 1785, as it is shown on a map of this date.[19] It originally lay outside the park, perhaps indicating that it was another part of the earlier, 1730s scheme of ornamentation. The two other plantations in this part of the park, nearer to the river, are modern.

Little survives of the eastern half of Edensor village [16], which was removed between the late 1810s and early 1830s (pp. 157–60). One house, for reasons unknown, escaped demolition [17], and its vernacular style sits incongruously both with the surrounding parkland and with the architect-designed houses nearby in the western part of Edensor. The sites of the demolished buildings appear as parch marks in the parkland turf in dry summers, but there are few other surface traces. The western half of the village [18] was retained, and between 1835 and 1842 it was transformed into the picturesque model village we see today, with its eclectic mixture of architectural styles (pp. 164–8). Many of the dwellings appear to have been kept, but were remodelled, with new exteriors designed mostly by Paxton and Robertson. Others are entirely new, the most important being the model farm by Burton [19]. The church [20], which dominates the village, was rebuilt between 1867 and 1870 by Sir George Gilbert Scott. Its saving grace is its spire; while at close quarters this appears too large, from a distance it forms an eye-catching reference point, visible throughout the park. When first remodelled, Edensor was largely hidden by tree screens but these were removed at around the same time as the church was built, radically changing the visual impact of the village upon those passing along the road (pp. 160 and 168).

Outside the curtilage of the model village, lodges flank the main road where it enters the park [21]. These were designed by Wyatville in contrasting styles and were built in the years 1837 to 1839. A third lodge [22], at the entrance to the model village, was added in 1842 (pp. 165 and 178). The impressive brick building just outside the park [22], now the estate office, is earlier; it was built by Pickford as a coaching inn in the late 1770s, replacing an earlier inn sited at the eastern end of the village (p. 153). The site of the first inn was reused for a new parsonage, as the old parsonage standing a short distance further east [23] was demolished because it lay in full view of the house. A fourth lodge [24], on the north-western outskirts of Edensor behind the estate office, was built somewhat earlier than the others, around 1780, and continued in use until the early 1830s, when the park was enlarged; the building was then remodelled and the central arch filled in. No drive ever ran into the park from here and the entrance was presumably used by people on horseback or on foot, providing a shortcut across the park that avoided the village (p. 153).

This part of the park also has its share of ha-has (pp. 169–72). The one forming the boundary of Edensor village was created in the 1830s as part of the remodelling, and consists of a ditch with a vertical retaining wall on one side and a low bank on the other [25]. Another example, following the boundary of the expanded park of the 1820s–30s [26], serves to open up the view over the fields west of Edensor, where there is a further series of (somewhat later) field boundary ha-has. The masking bank following the east side of Park Wood [27] was presumably added when the wood was remodelled in the 1840s or early 1850s.

A final feature worthy of note in this part of the park is a set of target platforms for a rifle range [28]. This was mapped by the Ordnance Survey in 1879, when the other end of the range was several hundred metres to the north, adjacent to the river; it may well have been built shortly before this date.

The south-western park (Figure 98)
Many of the features shown on Figure 98 have already been described in the discussion above linked to Figure 93. Here we are concerned only with the far south-western section of the park. This formed part of the original eighteenth-century landscape park, and contains a number of old trees which, in the usual fashion, were retained when hedges were stubbed (pp. 9–11, 109 and 121). The slopes around Paine's Mill have been woodland since at least 1617, when Senior mapped the area,[20] but all the trees here date from a later period. At the southern end of the park is the elegant One Arch Bridge [1], designed by James Paine and erected in 1759–60 to carry the new public road from Edensor to Beeley across the Derwent (pp. 106–7 and 108). On the west side of the bridge, attached to a farmhouse, there is a gatekeeper's lodge [2]. This small building was named 'Blue Moor Lodge' on the Ordnance Survey map of 1839 and was probably built shortly before that date (p. 179). The original line of the new road can still be traced as a low causeway [3] running northwards from the

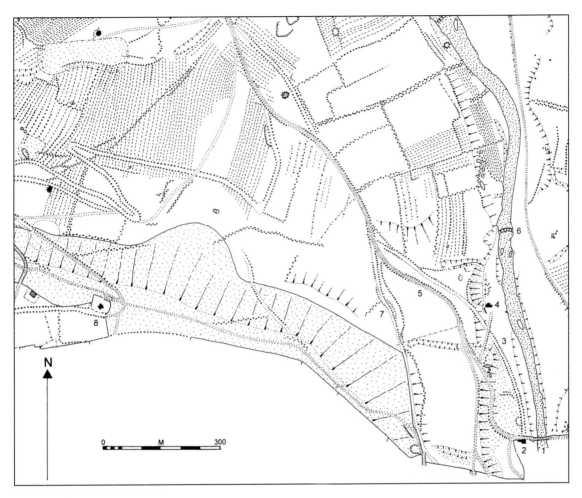

FIGURE 98.
Map F: The main historical and archaeological features in the south-western park (numbers refer to the main text).

bridge and passing close to the shell of Paine's Mill [4]. This was built in the early 1760s as a replacement for Chatsworth Mill, which was situated too near to the house. Not merely a utilitarian structure, the mill was also intended to be a decorative feature of the approach and of the view southwards from the pleasure grounds beside the house (pp. 108–124). The road was diverted to its present course [5] in 1818–19, unfortunately lessening the impact of the mill, but removing the need for an awkward sharp turn after the bridge (pp. 172–3). A little upstream from the mill there is an imposing weir [6] which fed water to the millwheel via a covered leat. There has been a weir here since 1761–62 but the present structure was built in 1838 (p. 108).

A second road, probably created in the 1820s, branched southwards from the main road and led to the hamlet of Calton Lees. Its straight causeway [7] overlies an earlier and more sinuous lane, pre-dating the park, traces of which can also be seen (pp. 89 and 174).

Calton Pasture (Figure 99)

This extensive area of unenclosed pasture, lying beyond New Piece Plantation, was probably created in the 1760s as a sheepwalk and 'outer park'. It is crossed by a number of public footpaths, but it is still used for sheep rearing and there is no general public access. Although it has suffered from some twentieth-century ploughing the area still contains many important earthworks. These include four or five prehistoric round barrows in the area to the south of the brook, all somewhat mutilated but some nevertheless still impressive monuments. A further three possible examples exist to the north, albeit these are small and very denuded [1] (pp. 24–5). Four of these mounds were excavated by the antiquarian Thomas Bateman – on one day, 2 May 1850.

Senior's map of 1617 shows this whole area as an open sheepwalk, but two small areas with lynchets and banks [2] indicate that parts were used for arable in earlier times (p. 30). Close to the easternmost of these areas are the earthworks of a deserted farmstead or hamlet, consisting of between three and five dwellings and outbuildings together with yards, garden plots and a trackway [3]. This may be the site of the lost settlement of Calton, documented from the late twelfth to late thirteenth centuries, and probably abandoned in the fourteenth century (p. 28).

One of the great surprises of the archaeological survey carried out in the late 1990s was the discovery that Calton Pasture had once been enclosed into a pattern of rectangular fields. Their remains, in the form of denuded hedge-banks, survive across much of the area [4]. These were created in the seventeenth or early eighteenth century but were swept away again later in the eighteenth century when the area was made into an 'outer park' (see pp. 81–3). There had also been earlier ornamentation here. Prior to the creation of New Piece Plantation in around 1760 [5], the ridgetop had been crowned by a number of circular clumps of trees, perhaps planted in the 1730s (pp. 98–100). These are now largely subsumed within the later plantation, but the perimeter of part of one is still just recognizable, protruding into Calton Pasture, in the form of three sycamores [6]; these are not old enough to be part of the original planting, but must date to the mid nineteenth century, shortly before this clump was removed sometime between 1831 and 1855.

On Calton Pasture itself there were a further five small decorative plantations, only one of which still contains some of its original beech trees [7]. The one on Moatless Plantation is a modern replanting, although the ruins of a surrounding wall of uncertain date remain [8]: the boundary bank of a second is just visible [9] and Beech Plantation [10] has now been replanted and subsumed within the edge of the Lees Moor woodlands. Four of these plantations appear on the first available estate map, dating to 1785,[21] and may have been created in the 1760s when the area was opened up (p. 120); a fifth, filling the gap in the middle of the line, had been added by 1831. The pond [11], again in existence by 1780–85, may also have been decorative in purpose. The clearest signs of the area's aesthetic role, however, are the remains of an

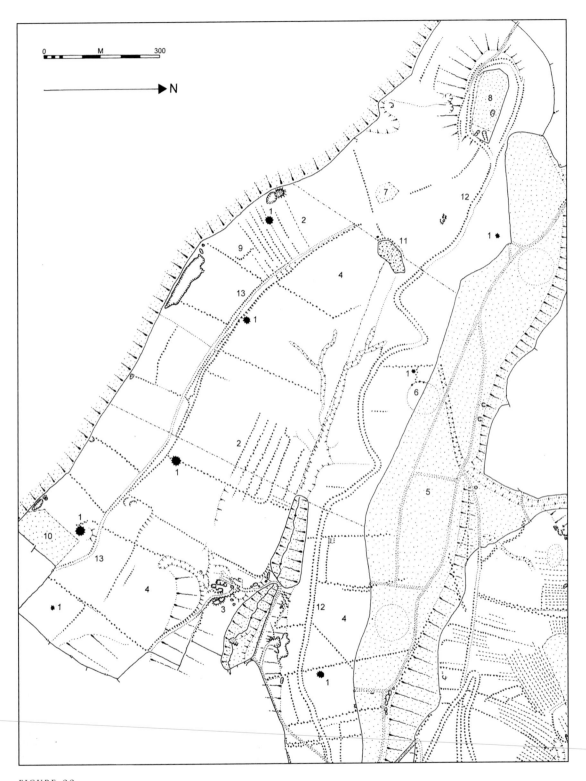

FIGURE 99.
Map G: The main historical and archaeological features in Calton Pasture (numbers refer to the main text).

impressively-engineered serpentine drive [12], created in the 1850s, which runs from the park up to and around Moatless Plantation, from where there are striking views across Calton Pasture and the landscape beyond (pp. 176–8). *En route* from the park the drive passes close to the Russian Cottage [Figure 98: 8], a chocolate-box creation of 1855, based on a model of a Russian farm sent to the 6th Duke by Tsar Nicholas I (pp. 169–78). There are also traces of a mid 1820s scenic drive, which again came up from the park through New Piece Wood, but ran on to Calton Lees before re-entering the park at its southern end [13] (p. 174).

This brings us to the end of our 'tour through history', which has embraced features as diverse as Bronze Age barrows and twentieth-century greenhouses. Chatsworth is one of the most important and fascinating landscapes in England. We hope that our account, which has sought to marry together the evidence of historical documents and field archaeology, has managed to convey something of its rich complexity.

CHAPTER NINE

Postscript

We are often asked how important the landscape of Chatsworth really is. How does it compare with other great gardens and parks in Britain, or with those further afield? In official terms, certainly, Chatsworth is accorded high marks. The house is a Grade 1 Listed Building, and many of the buildings and structures in the gardens and park are also listed. The landscape as a whole is accorded a similar grade in English Heritage's *Register of Parks and Gardens of Special Historic Significance*. Such accolades do not, however, quite capture the full importance of the place – for Chatsworth is unquestionably one of the greatest designed landscapes in Britain. It ranks with places like Blenheim, Stowe and Castle Howard, and arguably with such European sites as The Boboli Gardens in Florence, or even Versailles.

Some parks and gardens are considered significant because they are the work of important designers, something which is certainly true of Chatsworth. George London and Henry Wise, William Kent, Lancelot 'Capability' Brown, and Joseph Paxton all worked here. However, such associations count for little if the work of the designers in question survives only in damaged, truncated, or residual form. And while nothing remains of the parterres created by London and Wise and the true nature of Kent's contribution is uncertain, the work of Brown and Paxton still dominates, respectively, the park and the gardens.

It is true, as we have seen, that much of the planting in the park, together with the present network of paths and drives, was established in the nineteenth and twentieth centuries. The overall structure of the landscape, however, is much as Brown left it, with the Derwent visible in the foreground, and the vast area of open grassland beyond, scattered with trees, climbing to the distant ridge-top plantations. The carefully-contrived views which Brown created are also still largely intact: southwards from the gardens towards Paine's mill, west over Paine's three-arched bridge, and back from the bridge to the house itself. Paradoxically, the later additions to the landscape have in some ways served to preserve the visual impact of Brown's design, for the large numbers of relatively young trees give his parkland a fresh, healthy feel. In comparison, many of his other creations now seem tired, their planting terminally over-mature. Chatsworth is a classic Capability Brown landscape to which, in terms of overall condition as much as brilliance of original conception, few of his other surviving works can compare.

In the gardens around the house the work of Joseph Paxton is even better represented. The great rockworks, the Strid, the Emperor Fountain, the pattern of paths and the planting in the Arboretum all survive in excellent condition. While his most impressive achievement, the Great Conservatory, has been demolished, enough survives to appreciate something of its vast scale. Nor should Paxton's contribution to the wider landscape be forgotten. Edensor village, as we see it today, is largely his creation and is probably the most remarkable nineteenth-century 'model' village in the country. Paxton designed other gardens, but these were public spaces rather than private landscapes, such as Birkenhead in Liverpool and the People's Park in Halifax, and they have not fared well over the decades. Chatsworth is the best-preserved creation of this important, influential, and quintessentially Victorian figure.

A host of other designers and architects of national or international importance have left their mark on Chatsworth, including William Talman, Jeffry Wyatville, and James Paine. Indeed, no other park contains four structures designed by the last architect; his mill, two bridges and stable block all function in the landscape much as originally intended. In contrast, other, earlier, features have been reappropriated and reinterpreted by later generations: thus the relics of Chatsworth's Elizabethan greatness – the Stand, and Queen Mary's Bower – now stand in settings very different from those they originally graced, and the same is true of surviving elements of the Baroque gardens, such as Thomas Archer's Cascade House and the Cascade itself, which together form the most important early eighteenth-century formal water feature now remaining in England.

Yet this complex, many-layered landscape *works* in both aesthetic and visual terms. Little seems out of place. Successive designers, guided by successive generations of the Cavendish family, utilised and exploited what they inherited from previous generations with sensitivity and flair, just as they took maximum advantage of the remarkable and diverse terrain of the Derwent valley, the hydraulic possibilities of the landforms, the strong and symbolic contrasts between the bleak and rugged moorland and the more gentle terrain on lower ground. The result is an almost unparalleled collection of features and layouts from which, as we have seen, one could almost tell the whole story of English, if not of European, garden design.

That we can even attempt such a task is also the consequence of another key aspect of Chatsworth. Some great landscapes are very imperfectly documented. But Chatsworth has been illustrated and described by many visitors, and its estate archives are probably unparalleled in their size and detail. We can think of no other great country house where so much of the landscape's development over the last 500 years is documented in such detail. We can often appreciate the significance of even the most disjointed relics of past phases of Chatsworth's designed landscape because we know so much about the whole of which they originally formed a part.

But Chatsworth is particularly important for another reason, one largely unrelated to the history of garden design – the rich and complex archaeology preserved in the parkland turf. There are, it is true, many other great parks in

England which contain earthwork traces of the landscapes they replaced, and of earlier phases of their own design history. But few if any can boast the extent, or the variety, of the remains which survive here, ranging as they do from Bronze Age barrows through medieval field systems and post-medieval settlements to abandoned drives created in the eighteenth and nineteenth centuries. Some of these remains allow us to fill gaps in the documentary record relating to the evolution of the landscape – for even at Chatsworth there are some radical changes to the landscape which maps and documents fail to tell us about, or fail to tell us about with sufficient clarity or certainty. But equally important is the light they throw on the wider history of this part of England. The park contains earthworks which, in the surrounding countryside, have been largely obliterated by subsequent phases of farming and settlement. Few Bronze Age barrows thus remain in the Peak District in the kind of relatively low-altitude locations seen at Chatsworth, and it is rare that we can we find such extensive earthworks of medieval field systems. Similarly, we get here a unique glimpse of the evolving enclosed landscapes of the seventeenth and eighteenth centuries, the remains of which have usually been extensively modified in the Peak District by later farming. Another vital feature of Chatsworth Park is the enormous number of ancient oak pollards which remain: hundreds of important *living* relics of the medieval and early post-medieval landscape, concentrated especially in the area to the east of the Derwent. This is, indeed, one of the most important groups of 'veteran trees' in England, rivalling those which exist at places like Moccas Park in Herefordshire.

What makes this rich legacy particularly important is that almost all of it is accessible to the public – and in the case of the parkland, free of charge. Virtually everything we have discussed in this book can be experienced at first hand: observed, touched, even walked over. It is, perhaps, a curious paradox that a landscape created for the enjoyment and glory of a private family should now serve as an unparalleled educational resource for the public as a whole.

Notes to the Chapters

Chapter 1: Studying Chatsworth

1. Bannister, D. E. and Bannister, N. R. (1997) *Chatsworth Buildings Survey 1996–1997*, unpublished report for the Trustees of the Chatsworth Settlement and English Heritage; Bannister, N. R. (1997) *The Chatsworth Estate: Fields, Boundaries and Woodland Survey 1996–7*, unpublished report for the Trustees of the Chatsworth Settlement and English Heritage; Bannister, N. R. (1998) *The Chatsworth Estate: Fields, Boundaries & Woodland Survey 1997–1998*, unpublished report for the Trustees of the Chatsworth Settlement and English Heritage; Bannister, N. R. (1998) *Chatsworth Buildings Survey 1997–1998*, Addendum 1 volume, unpublished report for the Trustees of the Chatsworth Settlement and English Heritage; Bannister, N. R. (1999) *The Chatsworth Estate: Fields, Boundaries & Woodland Survey 1998–1999*, 2 volumes, unpublished report for the Trustees of the Chatsworth Settlement and English Heritage; Barnatt, J. (1997) *Chatsworth Park: Archaeological Survey 1996–7*, 2 volumes, unpublished report for the Trustees of the Chatsworth Settlement and English Heritage; Barnatt, J. (1998) *Chatsworth Moorlands: Archaeological Survey 1997–8*, 2 volumes, unpublished report for the Trustees of the Chatsworth Settlement and English Heritage; Barnatt, J. (2000) *Chatsworth Inbye Land: Archaeological Survey 1999–2000*, 2 volumes, unpublished report for the Trustees of the Chatsworth Settlement and English Heritage; Barnatt, J. and Bannister, N. J. (2002) *Vestiges of a Rich and Varied Past: An Archaeological Assessment of the Earthworks, Field Boundaries and Buildings of the Chatsworth Landscape 1996–2000*, Unpublished report for the Trustees of the Chatsworth Settlement and English Heritage; Percifull, E. and Thomas, S. (1998) *Chatsworth Historic Landscape Survey, the Park and Gardens*, unpublished report for Chatsworth Estate; Percifull, E. and Thomas, S. (1998) *Chatsworth Historic Landscape Survey, the Park and Gardens:*
A Notebook, unpublished report for Chatsworth Estate; Williamson, T. (1998) *Chatsworth Historic Landscape Survey, The Park and Gardens: A Brief History*, unpublished report for Chatsworth Estate.

2. Thompson, F. (1949) *A History of Chatsworth: Being a supplement to the Sixth Duke of Devonshire's Handbook*, London.

3. William Cavendish (6th Duke of Devonshire) (1845) *Handbook of Chatsworth and Hardwick*, London.

4. The Duchess of Devonshire (1982) *The House: A portrait of Chatsworth*, London; and (1987) *The Garden at Chatsworth*, Derby.

5. Barker, George (1773) *A plan of Chatsworth Park and pleasure ground belonging to His Grace the Duke of Devonshire*, Chatsworth archives, map 3330.

6. Campbell, E. (1857) *Plan of the Extra Parochial Place or Liberty of Chatsworth and parts of the Townships of Baslow and Brampton in the County of Derby*, Chatsworth archives, map 2656S; Campbell, E. (revised 1858) *Plan of the Extra Parochial Place or Liberty of Chatsworth and parts of the Townships of Baslow and Brampton in the County of Derby*, Chatsworth archives, uncalendared map.

7. Barnatt, *Chatsworth Park*; Barnatt, *Chatsworth Moorlands*; Barnatt, *Chatsworth Inbye Land*; Barnatt and Bannister, *Rich and Varied Past*.

8. Bannister and Bannister, *Chatsworth Buildings Survey 1996–1997*; Bannister, *Fields, Boundaries and Woodland Survey 1996–7*; Bannister, *Fields, Boundaries and Woodland Survey 1997–8*; Bannister, *Chatsworth Buildings Survey 1997–1998*; Bannister, *Fields, Boundaries and Woodland Survey 1998–9*; Barnatt and Bannister, *Rich and Varied Past*.

9. Percifull and Thomas, *The Park and Gardens* and *A Notebook*; Williamson, *Brief History*.

10. Mitchell, A. (1974) *A Field Guide to the Trees of Britain and Northern Europe*, London, pp. 25–7; Whyte, I. (1994) 'Estimating the Age of Veteran Trees

from Girth Measurements', Forestry Commission technical paper.

11. Crossley, D. and Kiernan, D. (1992) 'The Lead Smelting Mills of Derbyshire', *Derbyshire Archaeological Journal* **112**, pp. 6–47; Barnatt, J. with Rieuwerts, J. H. and Roberts, J. G. (1996) *The Lead Mine Related Landscape of the Peak District: Part 1 – Smelting Sites, Fuel Sources and Communications*, unpublished report for English Heritage.

12. Barnatt, J. and Smith, K. (2004) *The Peak District: Landscapes Through Time*, 2nd edn, Bollington.

13. Barnatt and Smith, *The Peak District*; Cooper, B. (1991) *Transformation of a Valley: The Derbyshire Derwent*, Cromford; Heath, J. (1993) *An Illustrated History of Derbyshire*, Derby.

14. Barnatt, J. (1990) *The Henges, Stone Circles and Ringcairns of the Peak District*, Sheffield; Barnatt, J. (1996) 'Moving Between the Monuments: Neolithic Land Use in the Peak District', in *Neolithic Studies in No-Man's Land: Papers on the Neolithic of northern England, from the Trent to the Tweed*, ed. P. Frodsham, *Northern Archaeology* **13/14**, pp. 45–62; Barnatt, J. (1996) 'Barrows in the Peak District: A Review and Interpretation of Extant Sites and Past Excavations', in *Barrows in the Peak District: Recent Research*, eds J. Barnatt and J. Collis, Sheffield.

15. Ainsworth, S. and Barnatt, J. (1998) 'A Scarp-Edge Enclosure at Gardom's Edge, Baslow, Derbyshire', *Derbyshire Archaeological Journal* **118**, pp. 5–23; Barnatt, J., Bevan, B. and Edmonds, M. (2001) 'A Time and Place for Enclosure: Gardom's Edge, Derbyshire', in *Neolithic Enclosures in Atlantic Northwest Europe*, eds T. Darvill and J. Thomas, Oxford; Barnatt, J., Bevan, B. and Edmonds, M. (2002) 'Gardom's Edge: A Landscape Through Time', *Antiquity* **76**, pp. 50–56.

16. Barnatt, J. (1999) 'Taming the Land: Peak District Farming and Ritual in the Bronze Age', *Derbyshire Archaeological Journal* **119**, pp. 19–78; Barnatt, J. (2000) 'To Each Their Own: Later Prehistoric Farming Communities and Their Monuments in the Peak', *Derbyshire Archaeological Journal* **120**, pp. 1–86.

17. Barnatt, *Henges, Stone Circles and Ringcairns*; Barnatt, *Barrows in the Peak District*; Barnatt, J. (1996) 'Recent Research in Peak District Stone Circles, Including Restoration Work at Barbrook II and Hordron Edge, and New Fieldwork Elsewhere', *Derbyshire Archaeological Journal* **116**, pp. 27–48.

18. Stetka, J. (2001) *From Fort to Field: The Shaping of the Landscape of Bakewell in the 10th Century*, Bakewell.

19. Barnatt and Smith, *The Peak District*, pp. 64–9.

20. Ford, T. D. and Rieuwerts, J. H. eds (2000) *Lead Mining in the Peak District*, 4th edn, Ashbourne; Barnatt, J. and Penny, R. (2004) *The Lead Legacy: The Prospects for the Peak District's Lead Mining Heritage*, Bakewell.

Chapter 2: The Early History of the Chatsworth Landscape

1. Barnatt, 'Barrows in the Peak District'; Barnatt, 'Taming the Land'; Barnatt, 'To Each Their Own'.

2. Bateman, T. (1861) 'Ten Years Diggings in Celtic and Saxon Grave Hills in the Counties of Derby, Stafford and York', London and Derby, pp. 64–5.

3. Pegge, S. (1792) 'Derbeiesseira Romana', *Archaeologia* **10**, pp. 17–36; Bateman, T. (1848) *Vestiges of the Antiquities of Derbyshire*, London, p. 22.

4. Williams, A. and Martin, G. H. eds (1992) *Domesday Book: A complete translation*, London.

5. Senior, W. (1617) *The Manor of Chatsworth Belonging to the Right Honnrable William Lord Cavendish*, bound volume of early seventeenth-century surveys by William Senior, Chatsworth House.

6. Senior, W. (1617) *Lees and Edensore*, bound volume of early seventeenth-century surveys by William Senior, Chatsworth House.

7. Cameron, K. (1959) *The Place-Names of Derbyshire*, 3 volumes, Cambridge, Vol. 1, p. 74.

8. Barnatt and Smith, *The Peak District*, p. 74.

9. Cameron, *Place Names of Derbyshire*, p. 91.

10. Fowkes, D. V. and Potter, G. R. eds (1988) *William Senior's Survey of the Estates of the First and Second Earls of Devonshire c. 1600–28*, Derbyshire Record Society Volume 13, Chesterfield.

11. Jackson, J. C. (1962) 'Open Field Cultivation in Derbyshire', *Derbyshire Archaeological Journal* **82**, pp. 54–72; Carr, J. P. (1963) 'Open Field Agriculture in mid-Derbyshire', *Derbyshire Archaeological Journal* **83**, pp. 66–76.

12. Barnatt and Smith, *The Peak District*; Hart, C. R. (1981) *The North Derbyshire Archaeological Survey*, Chesterfield.

13. Senior, *The Manor of Chatsworth*.

14. Kerry, Rev. C. (1901) 'The Court Rolls of Baslow, Derbyshire (continued)', *Derbyshire Archaeological Journal* **23**, pp. 1–39; p. 38.

15. Kerry, 'The Court Rolls of Baslow (continued)', p. 33.

16. Brighton, T. (1996) 'In Search of Medieval Chatsworth', *Bakewell and District Historical Society Journal* **23**, pp. 21–35; p. 22.

17. Brighton, 'In Search of Medieval Chatsworth', p. 30.

18. Thompson, *History of Chatsworth*, p. 23.

19. Craven, M. and Stanley, M. (2001) *The Derbyshire Country House: Volume 1*, Ashbourne.

20. Craven and Stanley, *The Derbyshire Country House*, p. 22.

21. Fowkes and Potter, *William Senior's Survey*.

22. Senior, *The Mannor of Chatsworth*; Senior, *Lees and Edensore*.

23. Bickley, F. (1911) *The Cavendish Family*, London, pp. 1–10; Brown, P. D. and Schweitzer, K. W. (1982) *The Devonshire Diary 1759–62*, Camden Fourth Series Vol. 27, London, pp. 1–2; Pearson, J. (2002) *Stags and Serpents: a history of the Cavendish family and the Dukes of Devonshire*, revised edn, Bakewell, p. 11.

24. Pearson, *Stags and Serpents*, pp. 11–14.

25. Pearson, *Stags and Serpents*, pp. 11–14.

26. Girouard, M. (1983) *Robert Smythson and the Elizabethan Country House*, New Haven and London, pp. 115–18.

27. Girouard, *Robert Smythson*, p. 115; Thompson, *History of Chatsworth*, pp. 23–6.

28. Buxton, J. ed. (1958) *The Poems of Charles Cotton*, London, p. 88.

29. Girouard, *Robert Smythson*, p. 116.

30. Senior, *The Mannor of Chatsworth*: the discussion that follows owes much to the important research by Trevor Brighton; Brighton, T. (1995) 'Chatsworth's Sixteenth-Century Park and Gardens', *Garden History* **23.1**, pp. 29–55.

31. Pearman, M. (nd, 1994?) 'Chatsworth Garden History: some notes', Chatsworth archives, p. 1.

32. Buxton, *Poems of Charles Cotton*, p. 89.

33. Everson, P. (1998) '"Delightfully Surrounded with Woods and Ponds": Field Evidence for Medieval Gardens in England', in *There by Design: Field Archaeology in Parks and Gardens*, ed. P. Pattison, Swindon.

34. Buxton, *Poems of Charles Cotton*, p. 88.

35. Buxton, *Poems of Charles Cotton*, p. 88.

36. Chatsworth archives, Ms IV, 117.

37. Thompson, *History of Chatsworth*, p. 29.

38. Brighton, 'Chatsworth's Gardens', pp. 31.

39. Brighton, 'Chatsworth's Gardens', pp. 33–35.

40. Chatsworth archives, Ms IV, 106.

41. Hobbes, Thomas (1678) *De Mirabilis Pecci, being the wonders of the Peak in Darby-shire ... in English and Latin*, London, pp. 8–9.

42. Senior, *The Mannor of Chatsworth*.

43. Rackham, O. (1986) *The History of the Countryside*, London, pp. 122–9.

44. Kiernan, D. (1989) *The Derbyshire Lead Industry in the Sixteenth Century*, Chesterfield, pp. 170–2.

45. Browne, E. 'Notes Taken in a Tour through the West of England in 1662', British Museum Sloane MS 1900, fols 59–63.

46. Buxton, *Poems of Charles Cotton*, pp. 88–9.

47. Senior, *Lees and Edensore*.

48. Sheail, J. (1971) *Rabbits and their History*, Newton Abbot.

49. Loveday, R. and Williamson, T. (1988) 'Rabbits or Ritual? Artificial Warrens and the Neolithic Long Mound Tradition', *Archaeological Journal* **145**, pp. 290–313.

50. Bickley, *Cavendish Family*, pp. 34–40; Brown and Schweitzer, *Devonshire Diary*, pp. 2–3.

51. Brown and Schweitzer, *Devonshire Diary*, pp. 2–3.

52. Pearson, *Stags and Serpents*, pp. 49–61.

53. Senior, *The Mannor of Chatsworth*.

54. Quoted in Thompson, *History of Chatsworth*, p. 79.

Chapter 3: A Baroque Landscape: Chatsworth under the First and Second Dukes

1. Bickley, *Cavendish Family*, pp. 147–181; Brown and Schweitzer, *Devonshire Diary*, pp. 3–4; Pearson, *Stags and Serpents*, pp. 62–84.

2. Pearson, *Stags and Serpents*, pp. 62–84.

3. The following description of the building of the 1st Duke's house draws heavily on Thompson's monumental account *A History of Chatsworth*.

4. Kennet, W. (1708) *A Sermon Preach'd at the Funeral of the Right Noble William Duke of Devonshire ... with some memoirs of the family of Cavendish*, London.

5. Defoe, D. (1724) *A Tour through the Whole Island of Great Britain*, Vol. 3, London, p. 582.

6. Cruickshank, D. (1985) *A Guide to the Georgian Buildings of Britain and Ireland*, London.

7. Thompson, *History of Chatsworth*, p. 36.

8. Thompson, *History of Chatsworth*.

9. Thompson, *History of Chatsworth*, pp. 39–48.

10. Kennet, *Sermon Preach'd*, p. 139.

11. Thompson, *History of Chatsworth*, pp. 46, 48.

12. Chatsworth Archives, First Series, 70.6.

13. Thompson, *History of Chatsworth*, pp. 60–61.

14. Kennet, *Sermon Preach'd*, p. 140.

15. Thompson, *History of Chatsworth*, p. 68.

16. Chatsworth archives, First Series, 18.4.

17. MacDougall, E. B. and Hamilton Hazelhurst, E. eds (1979) *The French Formal Garden*, Washington.

18. Hopper, E. (1982) 'The Dutch Classical Garden and André Mollet', *Journal of Garden History* **2,1**, pp. 25–40.

19. Dixon Hunt, J. (1988) 'Reckoning with Dutch

Gardens', in *The Anglo-Dutch Garden in the Age of William and Mary*, eds J. Dixon Hunt and Erik de Jong, published as *Journal of Garden History* **8,2** and **8,3**, pp. 41–60; p. 46.

20. Turner, T. (1986) *English Garden Design: history and styles since 1660*, Woodbridge, p. 57.

21. Williamson, T. (1995) *Polite Landscapes: gardens and society in eighteenth-century England*, Stroud, p. 25.

22. Dixon Hunt and de Jong, *The Anglo-Dutch Garden*, p. 144.

23. Dixon Hunt and de Jong, *The Anglo-Dutch Garden*, pp. 137, 141.

24. Freemantle, K. (1970) 'A Visit to the United Provinces and Cleeves in the time of William III. Described in Edward Southwell's Journal', *Nederlands Kunsthistoriche Jaarboek* **21**, pp. 39–69; pp. 53–4.

25. de Jong, Eric (1988) '"Nederlandish Hesperides": Garden Art in the period of William and Mary, 1650–1702', in *The Anglo-Dutch Garden*, eds Dixon Hunt and de Jong, pp. 15–40; p. 35.

26. Chatsworth Building Accounts, I.

27. Senior, *The Mannor of Chatsworth*, Chatsworth archives, AS/396.

28. Chatsworth archives, gardens file, '1ˢᵗ Duke', no reference number: 'Changes to the Canall'.

29. Chatsworth archives, First Series, 70.0.

30. Green, H. (1956) *Gardener to Queen Anne: Henry Wise (1635–1738) and the formal garden*, Oxford.

31. Switzer, S. (1718) *Ichnographia Rustica*, London, p. 81.

32. Chatsworth archives, First Series, 70.0.

33. Chatsworth archives, First Series, 70.1.

34. Chatsworth archives, First Series, 70.12.

35. Chatsworth Building Accounts I, p. 23.

36. Chatsworth archives, First Series, 70.13.

37. Chatsworth Building Accounts I, pp. 26, 29, 35, 39.

38. Chatsworth Building Accounts I, p. 26.

39. Chatsworth Building Accounts I, p. 39.

40. Chatsworth Building Accounts I, pp. 198–112; III, pp. 6, 18.

41. Chatsworth Buildings Accounts III, pp. 6, 12, 16, 20.

42. Morris, C. ed. (1995) *The Illustrated Journeys of Celia Fiennes*, Stroud, p. 105.

43. Chatsworth Building Accounts IV, *passim*.

44. Chatsworth Buildings Accounts I, p. 135.

45. Chatsworth Building Accounts I, p. 88.

46. Morris, *Celia Fiennes* p. 105.

47. 'A Tour from Cambridge to Halifax and Wakefield', 1725: Bath Reference Library ms 914.238b. Accn No. 38.34, fols 3–5.

48. Chatsworth archives, First Series 70.12; Chatsworth Building Accounts I, p. 23.

49. Chatsworth Building Accounts I, pp. 26, 50, 98, 98; III, pp. 12, 43, 49, 55.

50. Chatsworth Building Accounts III, *passim*. For the 'perspective walls', p. 51.

51. Chatsworth Building Accounts III, pp. 107, 109.

52. Morris, *Celia Fiennes*.

53. Anon, 'Iter boreal, or a Journey into the Peaks': no. 27 of *The Manuscripts of Evelyn Philip Shirley Esq. of Ettington Hall, Co. Warwick*, Historic Manuscripts Commission, Report Vol. 5, p. 366.

54. Chatsworth Building Accounts, II-VIII, *passim*.

55. Chatsworth archives, C21, p. 37.

56. Chatsworth archives, C17.

57. Senior, *The Mannor of Chatsworth*.

58. Chatsworth Building Accounts VI, p. 67.

59. Chatsworth Building Accounts VI, p. 99.

60. Chatsworth Building Accounts VI, pp. 85, 86.

61. Chatsworth Building Accounts VI, p. 25.

62. Chatsworth archives, C17, unpaginated.

63. Chatsworth archives, First Series 70.19.

64. Defoe, *Tour*, p. 582.

65. Morris, *Celia Fiennes*, p. 105.

66. Chatsworth archives, C21, pp. 1–3.

67. Chatsworth archives, C17, unpaginated.

68. Chatsworth archives, C17, unpaginated.

69. 'A Tour from Cambridge to Halifax and Wakefield'.

70. Chatsworth archives, First Series, 70.19.

71. Chatsworth archives, C17, unpaginated.

72. All these references are in Chatsworth archives, C17, unpaginated.

73. Chatsworth archives, C17, unpaginated.

74. Chatsworth archives, C21, *passim*.

75. Defoe, *Tour*, p. 583.

76. Chatsworth archives, C17, unpaginated.

77. Chatsworth archives, First Series, 70.26.

78. Chatsworth archives, C17.

79. Chatsworth archives, First Series, 70.18; C17.

80. Chatsworth archives, First Series, 70.18.

81. Chatsworth archives, First Series, 70.18; Chatsworth Building Accounts VI, p. 72.

82. Chatsworth archives, C17.

83. Chatsworth archives, C17.

84. Chatsworth archives, C17.

85. Chatsworth archives, C17, unpaginated.

86. Chatsworth archives, C17, unpaginated, 1716 and 1722; A/439.

87. Chatsworth archives, A/439.

88. Chatsworth archives, A/439.

89. Chatsworth archives, C15.

90. Chatsworth archives, C17, unpaginated.

91. Barker, *A Plan of Chatsworth Park*.

92. Chatsworth archives, AS/439.

93. Chatsworth Building Accounts VI, pp. 103, 122, 150.

94. All these references are in Chatsworth Archives, C17, unpaginated.

95. Untitled survey of Edensor and Pilsley (1785), Chatsworth archives, map 258I; Unwin, G. (1831) untitled map of Devonshire holdings between Chatsworth and Buxton, Chatsworth archives, map 266IS.

96. Untitled survey of Edensor and Pilsley.

97. Untitled map, possibly by George Unwin (c. 1825–1830), Chatsworth archives, map 2719.

98. *The Liberty of Baslow, Derby* (1799): Haddon Hall, bound volume of estate maps.

99. Senior, *Lees and Edensor*.

100. Chatsworth archives, C/107.

101. Chatsworth archives, AS/1408.

102. Senior, *The Manor of Chatsworth*.

103. Polak, J. P. (1987) 'The Production and Distribution of Peak Millstones from the Sixteenth to the Eighteenth Centuries', *Derbyshire Archaeological Journal* **107**, pp. 55–72; Radley, J. (1963–4) 'Peak Millstones and Hallamshire Grindstones', *Transactions of the Newcomen Society* **36**, pp. 165–173; Tucker, G. (1985) 'Millstone Making in the Peak District of Derbyshire: The Quarries and the Technology', *Industrial Archaeology Review* **8.1**, pp. 42–58.

104. Kerry, Rev. C. (1900) 'The Court Rolls of Baslow, Derbyshire, Commencing Anno 13 Ed. II (1319–20)',

Derbyshire Archaeological Journal **22**, pp. 52–90; Kerry, 'The Court Rolls of Baslow (continued)', pp. 1–39.

105. Chatsworth archives, L91/1/1.

106. Polak, 'Peak Millstones'.

107. Chatsworth archives, AS/948.

108. Chatsworth archives, Hardwick Manuscripts 27.

109. Chatsworth Archives, Hardwick Manuscripts, book of disbursements 1656–1668.

110. Dodd, E. M. and A. E. (1980) *Peakland Roads and Trackways*, 2nd edn, Ashbourne; Radley, J. (1963) 'Peak District Roads Prior to the Turnpike Era', *Derbyshire Archaeological Journal* **83**, pp. 39–50; Hey, D. (1980) *Packmen, Carriers and Packhorse Roads*, Leicester; Barnatt and Smith, *The Peak District*, pp. 103–111.

111. Senior, *The Manor of Chatsworth*.

112. Dixon Hunt and de Jong, *The Anglo-Dutch Garden*, p. 216.

113. Buxton, *Poems of Charles Cotton*, pp. 88–89.

114. Nichols, J. ed. (1780–90) *Bibliotheca Topographica Britannica*, 8 volumes, London, Vol. 3, p. 76.

115. Dodd, J. 'Journal of a Tour through England 1735', British Museum Add MS 5957.

116. de Jong, 'Netherlandish Hesperides', pp. 29–31.

Chapter 4: Kent, Brown, and the Making of the New Park

1. Hill, B. (1976) *The Growth of Parliamentary Parties, 1689–1742*, London; Clark, J. C. D. (1985) *English Society 1688–1742: ideology, social structure, and political practice during the Ancien Regim*, Cambridge; Clark, J. C. D. (1980) *Revolution and Rebellion: state and society in the seventeenth and eighteenth centuries*, Cambridge.

2. Pearson, *Stags and Serpents*, pp. 84–108; Bickley, *Cavendish Family*, pp. 181–88; Brown and Schweitzer, *Devonshire Diary*, pp. 4–6.

3. Pearson, *Stags and Serpents*, pp. 74–108.

4. Pearson, *Stags and Serpents*, pp. 109–118; Brown and Schweitzer, *Devonshire Diary*, pp. 6–8.

5. Brown and Schweitzer, *Devonshire Diary*, pp. 6–8.

6. Pearson, *Stags and Serpents*, pp. 109–120.

7. Williamson, T. (1998) *The Archaeology of the Landscape Park*, British Archaeological Reports, Oxford, p. 49; Williamson, *Polite Landscapes*, pp. 42–5; Cruickshank, *Georgian Buildings*, pp. 20–3.

8. Williamson, *Polite Landscapes*, pp. 35–45.

9. Dixon Hunt, J. (1987) *William Kent: Landscape Garden Designer*, London.

10. Pope, A. (1967) 'Epistle to Burlington', in *Poetical Works*, ed. H. Davies, Oxford, p. 318.

11. Thompson, *History of Chatsworth*, p. 88.

12. Stukeley, W. (1776) *Itinerarium Curiosum*, 2 volumes, London, Vol. 1, pp. 55–6.

13. All in Chatsworth archives, C17, unpaginated.

14. Chatsworth archives, C17A; C17B; C8; AS/1060.

15. Chatsworth archives, C8.

16. Chatsworth archives, C8; see also L91/1/2 and C13.

17. Chatsworth archives, C13; L/95/6.

18. Chatsworth archives, C13, Vol 3.

19. Chatsworth Album 26A, items 3, 4, 7, and 8.

20. Chatsworth Album 26A, item 4.

21. Dixon Hunt, J. (1986) *Garden and Grove: the Italian Renaissance garden in the English imagination, 1600–1750*, London, p. 206.

22. Chatsworth Album 26A, items 2 and 3.

23. Chatsworth Album 26A, item 8.

24. Chatsworth Album 26A, item 7.

25. In particular, 21 and 43 may be proposals for 'deformalising' and planting up the canals and fish ponds to the west of the House, while 70, usually thought to be a Chiswick design, could be a proposal for a temple beside the Ring Pond.

26. Wyatville, J. (c. 1770) redrawn sketch plan, Chatsworth archives, uncalendered; Barker, *A plan of Chatsworth Park*.

27. Chatsworth archives, C8.

28. Chatsworth archives, AS/1060.

29. Chatsworth archives, C17.

30. Chatsworth archives, C13.

31. Untitled survey of Edensor and Pilsley; Barker, *A plan of Chatsworth Park*.

32. Walpole, H. (1982) *The History of the Modern taste in Gardening*, Garland Edn, New York, p. 46; Williamson, *Archaeology of the Landscape Park*, pp. 69–70.

33. Chatsworth archives, C17, unpaginated; L91/1/1.

34. Chatsworth archives, 70.28; C 17.

35. Chatsworth archives, 163.31, 33.

36. Chatsworth archives, C13; C17A; AS/439; AS/1060; AS/1061; AS/1083.

37. Chatsworth archives, C15; C17A; L91/1/1; AS/439; AS/1060; AS/1061; AS/1080; AS/1082; AS/1083.

38. Chatsworth archives, AS 1061; AS/1083.

39. Chatsworth archives, C13 Vol. 4; C17A; AS/80; AS/1083.

40. Chatsworth archives, C15; AS/80; AS/439; AS/1061.

41. Chatsworth archives, C17, unpaginated.

42. Brailsford, S. (1751) *Plan of the house and part of the garden*, Chatsworth archives, uncalendared.

43. Chatsworth archives, AS/1061.

44. For the development of the landscape park, see: Turner, T. (1986) *English Garden Design: landscape and style since 1660*, Woodbridge; Hussey, C. (1967) *English Gardens and Landscapes 1700–1750*, London; and above all Jacques, D. (1983) *Georgian Gardens: the reign of nature*, London. For a contemporary view, see Walpole, *The History of the Modern taste in Gardening*.

45. For the relationship between the landscape park and the deer park see Williamson, *Polite Landscapes*, pp. 94–6; Williams, R. (1987) 'Rural Economy and the Antique in the English Landscape Garden', *Journal of Garden History* 7,1, pp. 73–96, especially p. 86; and Rackham, *History of the Countryside*, pp. 126–9.

46. Langford, P. (1992) *A Polite and Commercial People*, Oxford, pp. 59–124; Girouard, M. (1978) *Life in the English Country House*, Yale, pp. 188–93.

47. Williamson, *Polite Landscapes*, pp. 100–118.

48. For Brown and his career see: Stroud, D. (1965) *Capability Brown*, London; and Turner, R. (1983) *Capability Brown and the Eighteenth-Century English Landscape*, London.

49. Brailsford, *Plan of the house*.

50. Barnatt, J. (2002) 'The Development of Deep Ecton Mine, Staffordshire, 1723–1760', *Mining History* **15.1**, pp. 10–23; Porter, L. and Robey, J. (2000) *The Copper and Lead Mines around the Manifold Valley, North Staffordshire*, Ashbourne.

51. Chatsworth archives, AS/1062 and 1063.

52. Chatsworth archives, L/25/31.

53. Williamson, *Polite Landscapes*, pp. 104–5.

54. Chatsworth archives, L/25/31.

55. Dodd and Dodd, *Peakland Roads and Trackways*.

56. Chatsworth archives, AS/1062.

57. Harley, J. B., Fowkes, D. V. and Harvey, J. C. (1975) *Burdett's Map of Derbyshire 1791*, Derbyshire Archaeological Society.

58. Chatsworth archives, C21, pp. 109, 113, 140, 175; AS/1063.

59. Chatsworth archives, AS/1063.

60. Chatsworth archives, AS/1063.

61. Chatsworth archives, AS/1063; AS /1064; C21, pp. 151, 194.

62. Chatsworth archives, AS/1064; C21, p. 197.

63. Chatsworth archives, AS/1064; C21, pp. 109, 113, 197, 211, 213.

64. Leach, P. (1988) *James Paine*, London.

65. Summerson, J. (1993) *Architecture in Britain 1530–1830*, 6th edn, Newhaven, pp. 342–5.

66. Summerson, *Architecture in Britain*, p. 344.

67. Leach, *Paine*, pp. 39–48.

68. Leach, *Paine*, p. 27.

69. Leach, *Paine*, pp. 178–9; Thompson, *History of Chatsworth*, pp. 109–112.

70. Leach, *Paine*, p. 117.

71. Leach, *Paine*, pp. 117–120.

72. Leach, *Paine*, p. 134.

73. Chatsworth archives, AS/1064, 1065; Leach, *Paine*, p. 120.

74. Chatsworth archives, AS/1064; estate accounts, 1838, no catalogue number.

75. Chatsworth archives, AS/1063 and 1064; C21, pp. 108–118, 151, 199.

76. Chatsworth archives, AS/1064; C21, p. 199.

77. Barker, *A plan of Chatsworth Park*.

78. Chatsworth archives, AS/1064 and 1065; C21, pp. 179–186.

79. Chatsworth archives, AS/1064 and 1065; C21, pp. 214–239, *passim*.

80. Chatsworth archives, C21, *passim*.

81. Chatsworth archives, C21, pp. 115, 197, 211.

82. Chatsworth archives, AS/1062, AS /1063, AS /1064, AS /1065; C21, *passim*.

83. Chatsworth archives, AS/1063, AS/1064; C21, pp. 161, 199.

84. Chatsworth archives, C21, pp. 224–225, 239, 241; C22, unpaginated.

85. Chatsworth archives, AS/1062.

86. Chatsworth archives, C21, pp. 194–195.

87. Chatsworth archives, C21, pp. 224–225.

88. Chatsworth archives, C22, unpaginated; C21, pp. 46–7, 211–215.

89. Chatsworth archives, C21, pp. 46–7, 211–215.

90. Toynbee, P. ed. (1928) *Horace Walpole's Journal of Visits to Country Seats &c.*, Walpole Society Volume XVI, pp. 28–9.

91. Stroud, *Capability Brown*, pp. 126–8, 206. Information from David Brown, who has extensively researched the subject. This fact, coupled with the complete absence of references to Millican in the estate archives prior to 1760, throws some doubt on Stroud's suggestion that Millican was employed at Chatsworth prior to Brown's involvement here, and that his connection with Brown only dates from this time.

92. Copy of marriage certificate, November 25 1764, Royal Botanical gardens, Kew; letter, 2 January 1765. Lancelot Brown to Millican at Chatsworth: in possession of his descendant, Michael Millican. We are grateful to David Brown for providing us with these references.

93. Brailsford, *Plan of the house*.

94. Senior, *Lees and Edensore*.

95. Toynbee, *Horace Walpole's Journal of Visits*, pp. 28–9.

96. Chatsworth archives, C22, unpaginated.

97. Barker, *A plan of Chatsworth Park*.

98. Brighton, 'Chatsworth's Gardens', pp. 29–55.

99. Chatsworth archives, estate accounts 1822, p. 76.

100. Chatsworth archives, estate accounts 1811; C21, p. 115.

101. Chatsworth archives, estate accounts 1822, p. 76.

102. Chatsworth archives, C21, p. 115.

103. Cavendish, *Handbook of Chatsworth and Hardwick*, p. 160.

104. Wyatville, redrawn sketch plan; Barker, *A plan of Chatsworth Park*.

105. Chatsworth archives, Green Cabinet, Draw 3.

106. Chatsworth archives, L/95/8.

107. Chatsworth archives, gardens file, no catalogue number.

108. Chatsworth archives, C21, *passim*.

109. Toynbee, *Horace Walpole's Journal of Visits*, p. 65.

110. Chatsworth archives, L/95/8; C21, *passim*; AS/1063, AS/1064, AS/1065.

111. Climenson, E. ed. (1899) *Passages from the Diary of Mrs Lybbe Powys*, London, p. 29.

112. Untitled Survey of Edensor and Pilsley.

113. Barker, *A plan of Chatsworth Park*.

114. Barker, *A plan of Chatsworth Park*.

115. Untitled survey of Edensor and Pilsley.

Chapter 5: The Sixth Duke's Garden

1. Thompson, History of Chatsworth, p. 221.

2. Chatsworth archives, estate accounts, 1800, p. 45.

3. Chatsworth archives, estate accounts 1800, p. 66.

4. Bruyn Andrews, C. ed. (1935) *The Torrington Diaries*, 4 volumes, London, Vol. 2, p. 37.

5. Quoted in Thompson, *History of Chatsworth*, p. 100.

6. Cavendish, *Handbook of Chatsworth and Hardwick*, p. 17.

7. Chatsworth archives, estate accounts 1798, pp. 10, 15; 1799, p. 59.

8. Chatsworth archives, estate accounts 1798, p. 18.

9. Chatsworth archives, estate accounts 1798, p. 8.

10. Chatsworth archives, estate accounts 1800, p. 42.

11. Bickley, *Cavendish Family*, pp. 269–73.

12. Cannadine, D. (1977) 'The Landowner as Millionaire: The Finances of the Dukes of Devonshire c. 1800-c. 1926', *Agricultural History Review* 25, pp. 77–97, 80; Pearson, *Stags and Serpents*, pp. 162–8.

13. Pearson, *Stags and Serpents*, pp. 80–1.

14. Pearson, *Stags and Serpents*, pp. 81–2

15. Thompson, *History of Chatsworth*, pp. 191–200.

16. Thompson, *History of Chatsworth*, pp. 191–200.

17. Linstrum, D. (1972) *Sir Geoffrey Wyatville*, Oxford.

18. Cavendish, *Handbook of Chatsworth and Hardwick*, p. 238.

19. Linstrum, D. (2000) 'Remembering Vanbrugh', in *Sir John Vanbrugh and Landscape Architecture in Baroque England 1690–1730*, eds C. Ridgeway and R. Williams, London, pp. 190–214, 204.

20. Cavendish, *Handbook of Chatsworth and Hardwick*, pp. 162–163.

21. Chatsworth archives, estate accounts 1815, pp. 59, 64.

22. Chatsworth archives, estate accounts 1820, pp. 74, pp. 76–77.

23. Cavendish, *Handbook of Chatsworth and Hardwick*, p. 171.

24. Cavendish, *Handbook of Chatsworth and Hardwick*, pp. 181–2.

25. Chatsworth archives, estate accounts 1818, p. 9.

26. Bickley, *Cavendish Family*, pp. 271–2.

27. Cavendish, *Handbook of Chatsworth and Hardwick*, p. 163.

28. Chatsworth archives, L/108/27.

29. Chatsworth archives, estate accounts 1820, p. 78.

30. Unwin, map of Devonshire holdings.

31. Cavendish, *Handbook of Chatsworth and Hardwick*, p. 166–7.

32. For the life of Joseph Paxton, see Colquhoun, Kate (2003) *A Thing in Disguise: the visionary life of Joseph Paxton*, London.

33. Colquhoun, *Thing in Disguise*, pp. 28–9; Cavendish, *Handbook of Chatsworth and Hardwick*, pp. 110–11.

34. The best account of the development of gardens in the Victorian period remains Elliott, B. (1986) *Victorian Gardens*, London.

35. Quoted in Cavendish, *Handbook of Chatsworth and Hardwick*, pp. 111–12.

36. Chatsworth archives, estate accounts 1828, p. 76.

37. Chatsworth archives, estate accounts 1828, p. 77.

38. Chatsworth archives, estate accounts 1828, pp. 79–80.

39. 'The Industrial Palace in the Park, Mr Paxton's Lecture at the Society of Arts': *Illustrated London News*, 10 Nov. 1850.

40. Chatsworth archives, C165a; C165c.

41. Chatsworth archives, estate accounts 1830–35.

42. Chatsworth archives, estate accounts 1830, p. 79; 1831, p. 73; 1832, p. 73; 1833, p. 75; 1834, p. 78; 1835, p. 75.

43. Chatsworth archives, estate accounts 1830, p. 85; *Magazine of Botany* I, (1834) pp. 46–8; *Leicester Journal*, 26 Feb. 1836.

44. Cavendish, *Handbook of Chatsworth and Hardwick*, pp. 170–1; Chatsworth archives, estate accounts 1830, p. 85; 1831, pp. 86–7; 1832, p. 73.

45. *Magazine of Botany* 9 (1841).

46. Pearman, 'Chatsworth Garden History', pp. 10–12; Chatsworth archives estate accounts 1830, p. 87; 1831, p. 87; 1832, pp. 73–4; 1833, pp. 76–7; 1834, pp. 79–80; 1835, pp. 76–77; 1838, p. 38.

47. *Magazine of Botany* 2 (1835), pp. 105ff; *Horticultural Register* 4 (1835), pp. 57ff.

48. *Magazine of Botany* 2 (1835), p. 80.

49. Cannadine, 'Landowner as Millionaire', pp. 81–2.

50. Cavendish, *Handbook of Chatsworth and Hardwick*, p. 113.

51. Coloquhoun, *Thing in Disguise*, p. 75–9.

52. Chatsworth archives, estate accounts 1836, p. 57; 1839, p. 53.

53. Chatsworth archives, First Series, 3.285; estate accounts, 1835; Coloquhoun, *Thing in Disguise*, pp. 62–3.

54. Chatsworth archives, estate accounts 1835, pp. 84–9.

55. Chatsworth archives, estate accounts 1836, pp. 86–8.

56. Cavendish, *Handbook of Chatsworth and Hardwick*, p. 172.

57. Barker, *A plan of Chatsworth Park*; Unwin, map of Devonshire holdings.

58. *Gardener's Magazine* (August 1835), pp. 395–391.

59. Chatsworth archives, estate accounts 1836; Chadwick, G. (1961) 'Paxton and the Great Stove at Chatsworth', *Architectural History* 4, pp. 75–91.

60. *Magazine of Botany* 8 (1841), pp. 183, 255.

61. Chadwick, 'Great Stove', pp. 77–7; Cavendish, *Handbook of Chatsworth and Hardwick*, p. 179.

62. Chatsworth archives, estate accounts 1841, p. 48; 1842, pp. 47–9; 1843, pp. 49–52.

63. Chatsworth archives, estate accounts, 1836–41; Chatsworth archives, Edward Swaine, 'Measurement of interior of Conservatory, Chatsworth', gardens file, no catalogue number; Chadwick, 'Great Stove'; *Journal of Horticulture and Cottage Gardener* (December 1870), p. 433; Colquhoun, *Thing in Disguise*, pp. 104–6.

64. Granville, A. B. (1841) *The Spas of England and Principal Sea-Bathing Places*, Vol. 1, London, pp. 66–8.

65. Chatsworth archives, estate accounts 1838 and 1840.

66. Colquhoun, *Thing in Disguise*, pp. 104–5.

67. Chatsworth archives, estate accounts 1841, p. 48; 1842, pp. 47–9.

68. Burkhardt, F. and Smith, S. (1985) *The Correspondence of Charles Darwin*, Vol. 3, 1844–6, Cambridge, pp. 259–60.

69. *Illustrated London News*, 8 Dec. 1843.

70. *Magazine of Botany* 12 (1845), pp. 62–3, pp. 180–4.

71. Chatsworth archives, estate accounts 1836–40.

72. Chatsworth archives, garden file, no catalogue number.

73. Cavendish, *Handbook of Chatsworth and Hardwick*, p. 172.

74. Cavendish, *Handbook of Chatsworth and Hardwick*, p. 174.

75. *Magazine of Botany* 5 (1838), p. 227; 8 (1841) pp. 135–7.

76. Chatsworth archives, estate accounts 1844, pp. 49–53.

77. Chatsworth archives, estate accounts 1844, p. 49.

78. Chatsworth archives, estate accounts 1847, p. 54.

79. Chatsworth archives, estate accounts 1848, p. 52.

80. Chatsworth archives, estate accounts 1847, p. 54.

81. Chatsworth archives, Edward Swaine, 'Measurement of interior of Conservatory, Chatsworth'.

82. Toynbee, *Horace Walpole's Journal of Visits*, p. 65.

83. Chatsworth archives, estate accounts 1844–1849; *Magazine of Botany* 11 (1844).

84. Chatsworth archives, Edward Swaine, 'Measurement of interior of Conservatory, Chatsworth'.

85. Cannadine, 'Landowner as Millionaire', p. 82.

86. Bruyn Andrews, *The Torrington Diaries*, Vol. 2, p. 37.

87. Tinniswood, A. (1989) *A History of Country House Visiting*, Oxford, p. 140.

88. Loudon, J. C. (1831) *Gardener's Magazine* 7, p. 397.

89. Chatsworth archives, garden file, no catalogue number.

90. 'Excursion to Chatsworth by Rail from Derby, June 1849', quoted in *The House: A portrait of Chatsworth*, the Duchess of Devonshire, p. 86.

91. Harley, B. and J. (1992) *A Gardener at Chatsworth;*

three years in the life of Robert Aughtie, 1848–1850, Bakewell, pp. 153–5.

92. Tinniswood, *Country House Visiting*, p. 144.

93. Chatsworth archives, gardens file, 'nineteenth century', no catalogue number.

94. Colquhoun, *Thing in Disguise, passim*.

Chapter 6: The Park in the Nineteenth Century

1. Chatsworth archives, C14.

2. Chatsworth archives, Building Accounts box: 'Mr Pickford's account for building Edensor Inn', no catalogue number.

3. Three maps entitled *Edensor* (1836), Chatsworth archives, uncalendared; Campbell, E. (1855) *Plan of the lands in Edensor, Pilsley, Birchill and Bakewell belonging to His Grace the Duke of Devonshire*, Chatsworth archives, map 2520.

4. Untitled and unfinished map of Edensor, Pilsley and Beeley (*c.* 1780–85), Chatsworth archives, map 2558 (20).

5. Chatsworth archives, estate accounts, 1798–1810, *passim*.

6. Chatsworth archives, estate accounts 1798, p. 22.

7. Chatsworth archives, estate accounts 1800, p. 26.

8. Hopkinson, G. G. (1957) 'The Development of the South Yorkshire and North Derbyshire Coalfield, 1500–1775, *Transactions of the Hunter Archaeological Society* **7.6**, pp. 295–319.

9. Chatsworth archives, AS/948.

10. Farey, J. (1811) *General View of the Agriculture and Minerals of Derbyshire*, Vol. 1, London.

11. Untitled map of the southern half of Baslow Colliery and Chatsworth Old Park Colliery, dated 1832, Coal Authority Archives, plan EM 817.

12. Chatsworth archives, AS/1064.

13. Chatsworth archives, AS/1064.

14. Chatsworth archives, L91/1/4; L94/56.

15. Untitled 1832 coal mines map.

16. Farey, *General View*, p. 193.

17. There are references in the estate accounts (C14) to 'pareing the north end of the park', but this may have been to improve the grass sward.

18. Chatsworth archives, C16.

19. Chatsworth archives, estate accounts 1798–9, pp. 10, 22.

20. Chatsworth archives, estate accounts 1800–01, pp. 77, 105.

21. Chatsworth archives, estate accounts 1800–01, pp. 15, 72, 79–82, 85; 1804, p. 13.

22. Chatsworth archives, estate accounts 1800–01, pp. 4, 17, 61; 1803–4, p. 30.

23. Unwin, map of Devonshire holdings.

24. See Elliott, *Victorian Gardens*.

25. Map of Edensor Town (1785), Chatsworth archives, uncalendared; Plan of Edensor Village, (1856), Chatsworth archives, map 2514.

26. Chatsworth archives, estate accounts 1799, p. 72.

27. Chatsworth archives, estate accounts 1817, p. 8.

28. Chatsworth archives, estate accounts 1818, p. 18.

29. Chatsworth archives, estate accounts 1820, p. 74.

30. Chatsworth archives, estate accounts, *passim*.

31. Chatsworth archives, estate accounts 1820, p. 54.

32. G. Unwin, map of Devonshire holdings.

33. Adam, W. (1838) *The Gem of the Peak*, London, p. 77.

34. Chatsworth archives, estate accounts 1820, p. 72.

35. Thompson, *History of Chatsworth*, p. 239; Chatsworth archives, L/76/40.

36. Chatsworth archives, estate accounts 1831, pp. 101–102.

37. Chatsworth archives, estate accounts, *passim*.

38. Chatsworth archives, estate accounts 1811, pp. 9, 14–15.

39. Chatsworth archives, estate accounts 1822, pp. 76–7.

40. Chatsworth archives, Green Drawers.

41. Cavendish, *Handbook of Chatsworth and Hardwick*, p. 186.

42. Cavendish, *Handbook of Chatsworth and Hardwick*, p. 186; Chatsworth archives, estate accounts 1833, pp. 93–98; 1834, pp. 94–97; 1835, pp. 92–97.

43. Chadwick, G. F. (1961) *The Works of Joseph Paxton, 1803–1865*, London, pp. 22–42; Donner, P. F. (1944) 'Edensor, or Brown Comes True', *Architectural Review* **95**, pp. 39–43; Read, H. (1995) *Edensor 1760–1860: a Century of Change*, unpublished typescript, Chatsworth archives; Barnatt and Bannister, *Vestiges of a Rich and Varied Past*, pp. 98–103.

44. Barnatt and Bannister, *Vestiges of a Rich and Varied Past*; Bannister and Bannister, *Chatsworth Buildings Survey 1996–1997*.

45. Thompson, *History of Chatsworth*, p. 238.

46. *Edensor and Pilsley* (1867), Chatsworth archives, uncalendared map; Ordnance Survey six inch sheet, 1879.

47. Darley, G. (1975) *Villages of Vision*, London.

48. Jewitt, L. (1872) *Chatsworth*, Buxton, p. 79.

49. Untitled survey of Edensor and Pilsley.

95. Chatsworth archives, estate accounts 1853, pp. 45–46; 1854, pp. 31–2; 1855, pp. 31–2.

96. Campbell, E. *Plan Shewing the Covered Streams, Pipes and Drains in Chatsworth Grounds*, corrected 1858, Chatsworth archives, map 2603 (11).

50. Chatsworth archives, estate accounts 1839, pp. 72–75, 78–80; 1842, p. 77.
51. Chatsworth archives, estate accounts 1855, p. 47; 1856, p. 32.
52. Chatsworth archives, estate accounts 1836, *passim*.
53. Ordnance Survey, first edition one inch sheet, 1839; E. Campbell, *Plan of the lands in Edensor*.
54. Chatsworth archives, estate accounts 1860, p. 68.
55. Chatsworth archives, estate accounts 1847, p. 53.
56. Chatsworth archives, estate accounts 1818, pp. 11, 16.
57. Chatsworth archives, estate accounts 1819, pp. 44, 47.
58. Chatsworth archives, estate accounts 1826, p. 66.
59. Barker, *A plan of Chatsworth Park*.
60. Barker, *A plan of Chatsworth Park*.
61. Barker, *A plan of Chatsworth Park*.
62. Barker, *A plan of Chatsworth Park*.
63. Unwin, untitled map.
64. Chatsworth archives, estate accounts 1826, p. 65.
65. Chatsworth archives, estate accounts 1826, p. 65.
66. Chatsworth archives, estate accounts 1836, pp. 77–79.
67. Chatsworth archives, estate accounts, 1837–44, *passim*.
68. Chatsworth archives, estate accounts 1838, pp. 45–50.
69. Chatsworth archives, estate accounts 1842–3, *passim*.
70. Chatsworth archives, estate accounts 1843, pp. 49–51.
71. Chatsworth archives, estate accounts 1851, pp. 41–42; 1852–7, *passim*.
72. Campbell, *Plan of the lands in Edensor*; Campbell *Plan of the Extra Parochial Place or Liberty of Chatsworth and parts of the Townships of Baslow and Brampton in the County of Derby*.
73. Unwin, untitled map.
74. Campbell (1857) *Plan of the Extra Parochial Place or Liberty of Chatsworth and parts of the Townships of Baslow and Brampton in the County of Derby*.
75. *Chatsworth* (1867), Chatsworth archives, uncalendared map.
76. Campbell, *Plan of the Extra Parochial Place or Liberty of Chatsworth and parts of the Townships of Baslow and Brampton in the County of Derby*.
77. Barnatt, *Chatsworth Inbye Land*; Barnatt, *Chatsworth Moorlands*; Barnatt, 'To Each Their Own', pp. 1–86.
78. Barnatt and Bannister, *Vestiges of a Rich and Varied Past*, p. 98.
79. Chatsworth archives, estate accounts 1847, p. 60.
80. Chatsworth archives, estate accounts 1849, p. 88.
81. Chatsworth archives, estate accounts 1861, p. 20.
82. Chatsworth archives, 'Notes on Forestry', no date or author, garden file.
83. Chatsworth archives, estate accounts 1811, p. 6; 1818, pp. 12, 16, 181; 1819, p. 35.
84. Chatsworth archives, estate accounts 1817, pp. 5, 9; 1819, pp. 18, 41.
85. Chatsworth archives, estate accounts 1820, p. 58.
86. Barker, *A plan of Chatsworth Park*; Untitled survey of Edensor and Pilsley.
87. Chatsworth archives, Green Drawers, Wyatville Folder.
88. Unwin, untitled map.
89. Chatsworth archives, estate accounts 1827, p. 70.
90. Chatsworth archives, estate accounts 1860, p. 68.

Chapter 7: The Recent Past

1. Cannadine, 'The Landowner as Millionaire' pp. 77–97; Bickley, *Cavendish Family*, pp. 274–289; Pearson, *Stags and Serpents*, pp. 210–14.
2. Pearson, *Stags and Serpents*, pp. 223–244; Bickley, *Cavendish Family*, pp. 290–312; B. Holland (1911) *The Life of Spencer Compton, Eighth Duke of Devonshire*, 2 volumes, London.
3. Holland, *Life of Spencer Compton*, pp. 236–241.
4. Note, undated (c. 1952?) on 'Admissions to Chatsworth House and Gardens', Chatsworth archives, gardens box file, 'Twentieth Century', no catalogue number.
5. Holland, *Life of Spencer Compton*, p. 228.
6. The Duchess of Devonshire, *The Garden at Chatsworth*, p. 29.
7. Chatsworth estate office, no catalogue number.
8. Pearson, *Stags and Serpents*, pp. 240–1.
9. J. Brown (1987) *Gardens of a Golden Afternoon*, Harmondsworth.
10. Thompson, *History of Chatsworth*, p. 226.
11. Chatsworth archives, letter from the 10th Duke (when Marquess of Hartington) to the 9th Duke (in Canada), Chatsworth, 27 May 1920: transcript in gardens box file, 'Twentieth Century', no catalogue number.
12. *Gardeners Chronicle* (1933), **2**, p. 8.
13. *Gardeners Chronicle* (1933), **2**, p. 8.
14. *Gardeners Chronicle* (1933), **2**, p. 8.
15. Pearson, *Stags and Serpents*, pp. 277–8.
16. Chatsworth archives, typescript by the Duchess of Devonshire, 'The Gardens Since 1950', gardens box file, 'Twentieth century'.
17. Pearson, *Stags and Serpents*, pp. 285–6.
18. For the following account, see the Duchess of Devonshire's own descriptions in *The House: a portrait of Chatsworth*, and *The Garden at Chatsworth*. See also Chatsworth archives, typescript by the Duchess of Devonshire, 'The Gardens Since 1950', gardens box file, 'Twentieth century'; and typescript by Mr Bert Link, 'Notes of work done at Chatsworth since 1950', gardens box file, 'Twentieth century'.

Chapter 8: Chatsworth Today: A Tour Through History

1. Brailsford, *Plan of the house.*
2. Senior, *The Mannor of Chatsworth.*
3. Senior, *The Mannor of Chatsworth.*
4. Barker, *A plan of Chatsworth Park.*
5. Senior, *The Mannor of Chatsworth.*
6. Untitled and unfinished map of Edensor, c. 1780–85.
7. Senior, *The Mannor of Chatsworth.*
8. *The Liberty of Baslow, Derby.*
9. Barker, *A Plan of Chatsworth Park*; Untitled and unfinished map of Edensor.
10. Untitled and unfinished map of Edensor.
11. Untitled and unfinished map of Edensor.
12. Senior, *Lees and Edensore.*
13. Senior, *Lees and Edensore.*
14. Senior, *Lees and Edensore.*
15. Barker, *A plan of Chatsworth Park.*
16. Untitled survey of Edensor and Pilsey.
17. Senior, *Lees and Edensore.*
18. Barker, *A plan of Chatsworth Park.*
19. Untitled survey of Edensor and Pilsey.
20. Untitled survey of Edensor and Pilsey.
21. Untitled survey of Edensor and Pilsey.

Index

....

Numbers in bold refer to the Figures